Preface

Hike Distribution

Section 1: East Bay – 25 Hikes

Section 2: North Bay – 11 Hikes

Section 3: San Francisco Peninsula and South Bay – 24 Hikes

Preface

Despite I grew up in countryside and was surrounded by mountains, I did not start hiking until February, 2010 when I was in my late 40s. At the time I was having free time on weekends and did not know what to do. So on a sunny day, I climbed up Shell Ridge in Walnut Creek Open Space whose entrance is only a few blocks away from my home. It immediately drew my attention by its beauty: green rolling hills dotted with bright California puppies, mule's ears and other wild flowers. For the next few weekends, I explored the area thoroughly because of my nature curiosity. Just when I thought I ran out of places to go, someone I met in the hills told me to drive to Regency Drive in Clayton and hike from there. I am very glad I followed his advice. Once I arrived there and walked on Donner Creek Road, I was deeply impressed by the great meadows and rush Donner Creek! I spent a few weekends there to explore there too. Before that I had no idea all those trails are connected. I was afraid of getting lost so I routely remembered the trails I went and followed them back. Then I learned that not only I could get maps for many of the trails at trailheads, but I could also find trail information from library! Since then I have hiked almost 10 years on weekends and visited all the parks, open spaces and preserves in San Francisco Bay Area. I used to use books from local libraries and AllTrails software to look for new trails. They are vey helpful for beginners. But I find that they no longer satisfies my need. As a avid hiker, I like hiking at least 10 miles each time and prefer loops over point-to-point route. I also don't like to hike the same route week after week. Sometimes, I go through a few books without finding a single hike I like. There are too many short trails and too much scenery description in those books. That is the reason why I write this booklet.

You will find 60 great hikes in this book. These hikes scatter all over the whole bay area. Their lengths range from 10 miles to 30 plus miles. They have very little overlap. You can hike one route per week for 60 weeks without repetition! For each hike, I provide trail map, length (distance), elevation, shade and parking information to help you plan your trip. Once you arrive there, you can follow the hike easily by reading my turn by turn Direction. There is very little scenery description. So you don't need to spend valuable time to search for hike Direction.

I have the honor to hike with many serious hikers over the years. I also led East Bay Mountaineer hiking group for a couple of years. We have great funs. Thank you! In particular, I want thank my buddy Andy Sui. We hiked together many of the trails described here. Some of the hikes are based on Andy's suggestions. Thank you, Andy. I also want to thank my wife, Audrey. Without her help and understanding, I won't be able to go out to hike so many trails.

Approximate Locations of the 60 Hikes

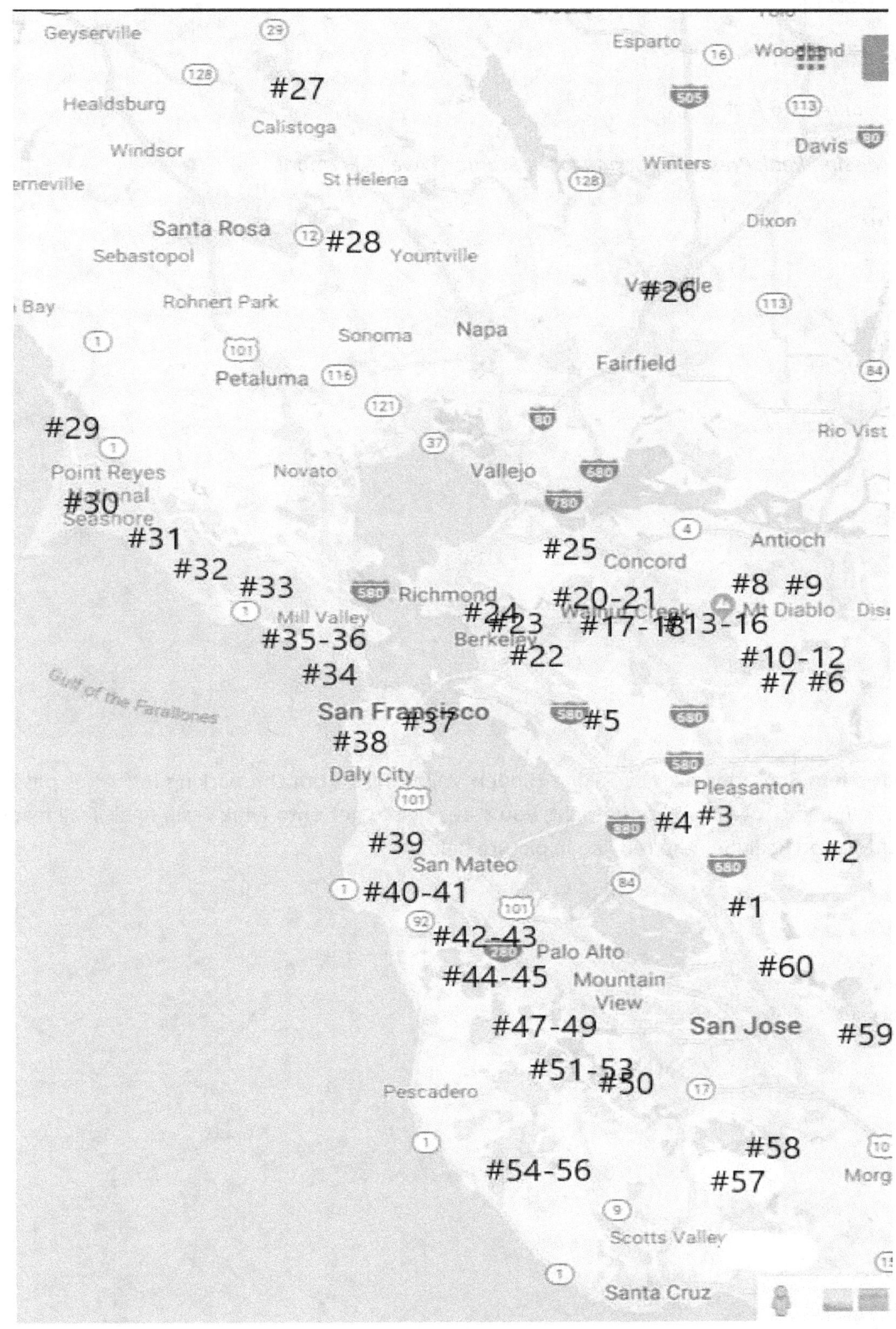

Hike Overview

Distance= 17 miles

Elevation Gain=4626 feet

Parking: Mission Peak Preserve parking lot or Stanford Ave in Fremont

Shaded: No

Trail Map:

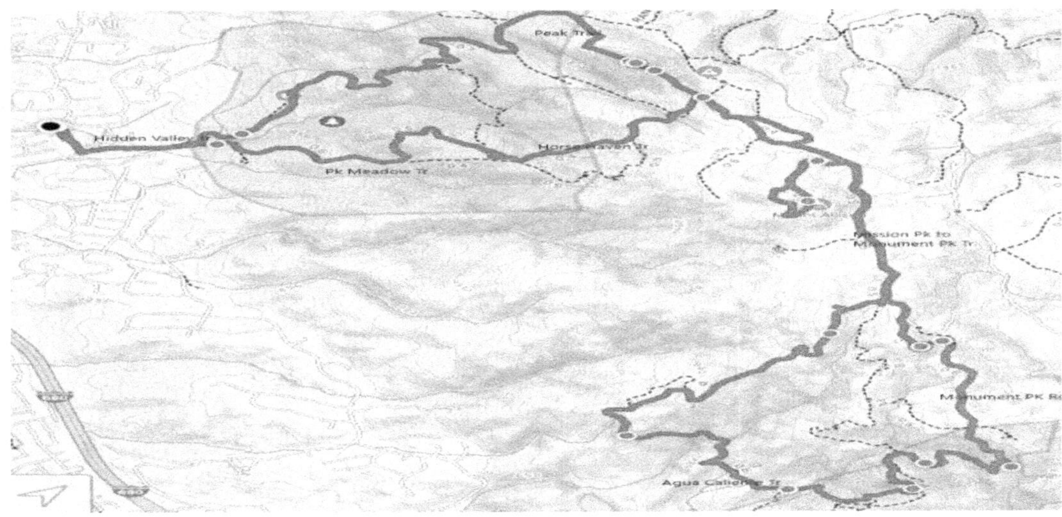

Detail Direction: Start this hike by taking Hidden Valley Trail from the parking lot. After passing Peak Meadow Trail and Grove Trail on the right, you stay right to get onto Peak Trail. Peak Trail leads you to the top of Mission Peak(See the red line in picture below).

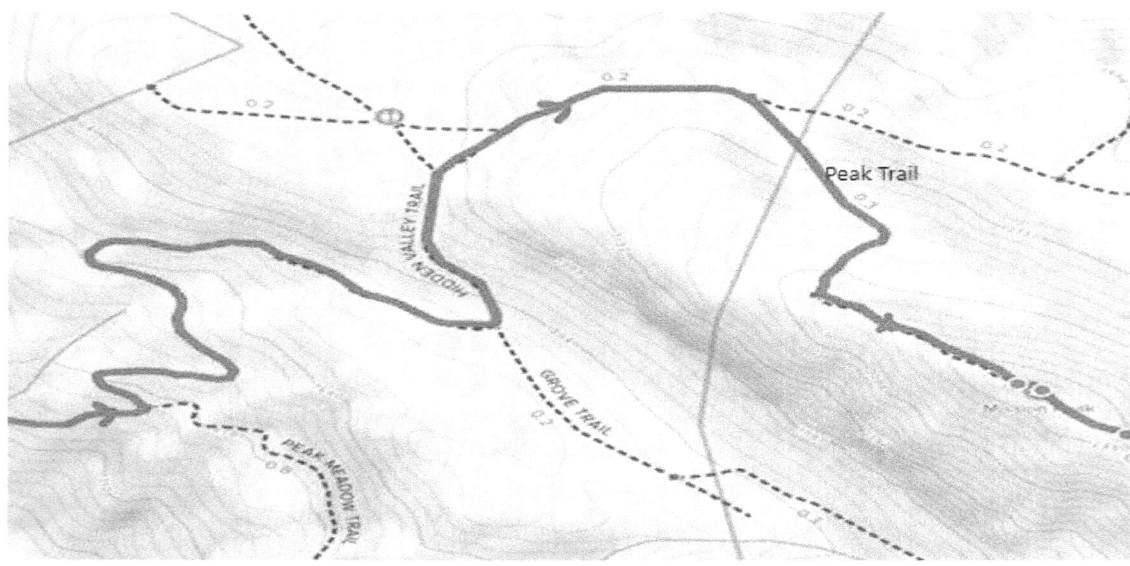

Descend Mission Peak from the opposite side to get on Mission Peak to Monument Peak Trail(It is also known as Bay Area Ridge Trail). At the junction with Weller Road, you keep right. It climbs a little before descends toward Ed Levin County Park.

At bottom of the trail, you will see sign for Agua Caliente Trail. Stay on this trail until the junction with Monument Peak Road. Turn left on Monument Peak road for 0.1 miles. Then turn left again onto Monument Peak Trail for 1.4 miles.

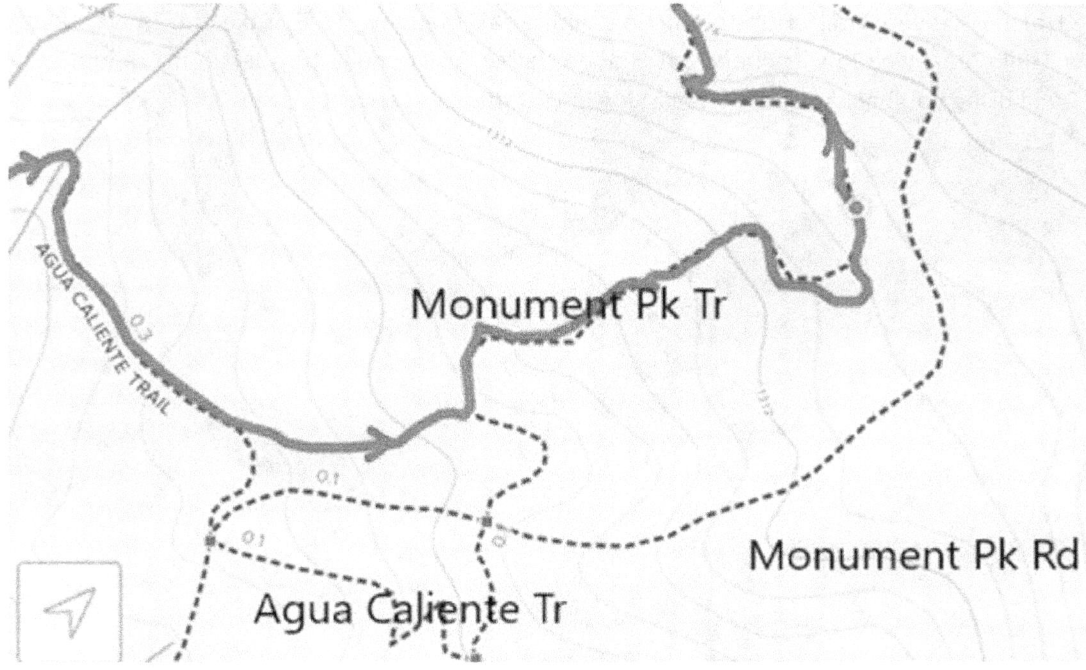

Then you get on Monument Peak Road, which is on your right side, to continue uphill. Continue on Monument Peak Road for 2.3 miles. There is an access trail on your left to summit Monument Peak. Take this unnamed trail to the summit(pictured below).

Then descend the summit from the other side and get on Weller Road. Stay left on Weller and stay right on the junction with previously mentioned Mission Peak to Monument Peak Trail. Follow the trail back to Mission Peak Preserve. But before you actually arrive the peak, you turn left onto Horses Heaven Trail. Stay on Horses Heaven Trail until its junction with Peak Meadow Trail. Take the left branch of Peak Meadow Trail. Peak Meadow Trail ends at Hidden Valley Trail. Finally turn left onto Hidden Valley Trail and HVT will bring you back to trailhead parking and Stanford Avenve.

Hike Overview

Distance=19.5 miles

Elevation gain=4997 feet

Parking: Sailor Camp Parking at South Shore of Lake Del Valle

Shaded: No

Trail Map:

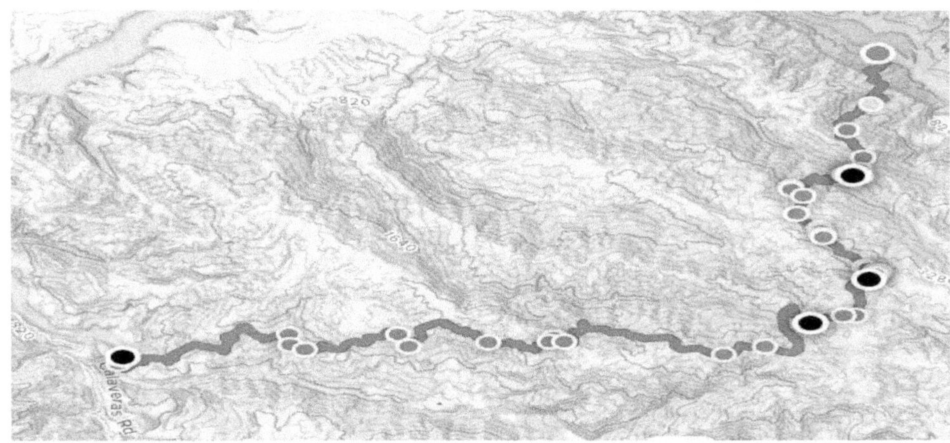

Detail Direction

For this hike, you need arrange car shuttle. When we did this hike, we divided into two groups. One group drove to Sunol Visitor Center and hiked from Sunol to Lake Del Valle. Another group drove to Lake Del Valle and hiked from there. We met at Rose Peak and exchanged car keys. I belonged to the group that started the hike from Lake Del Valle. We parked our car at Rocky Ridge Visitor Center parking lot at Lake Del Valle Regional Park and started the Ohlone traverse by taking Sailor Camp Trail uphill.

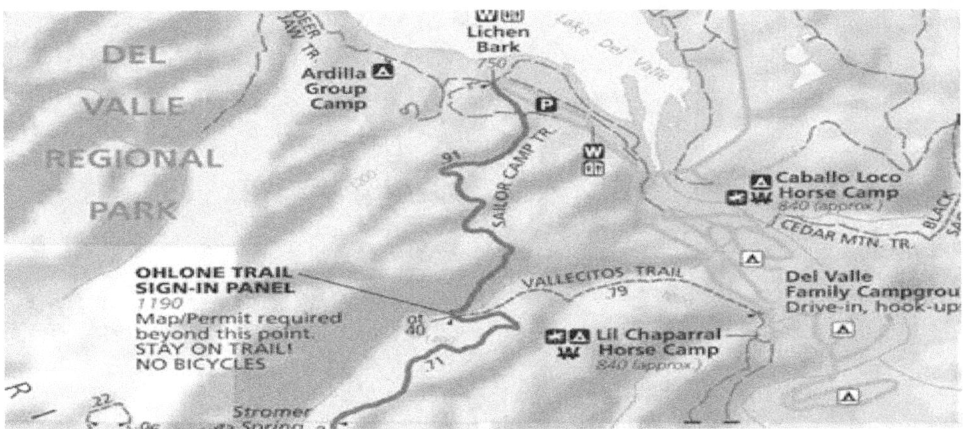

0.9 miles late, we came to a junction with Vallecitos Trail and Ohlone Trail. We chose Ohlone Trail. There is a sign-in panel. Permit is required beyond this point. Stay on Ohlone Trail for about 18 miles by following Ohlone Trail posts marked as ot40, ot39, etc. There are a few places you may want to be more careful: the trail turns right at ot34 and ot32, and turns sharp left at ot31(see picture below). If you miss the signs and go straight, you may get lost.

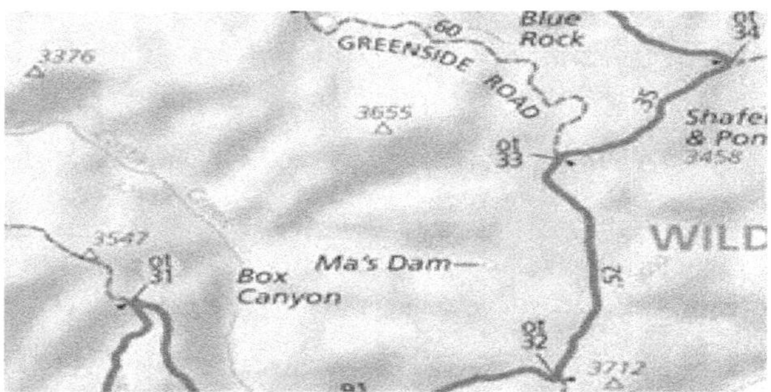

Between posts ot28 and ot29, you can take a little detour to the highest point of the hike to the summit of 3817 foot Rose Peak.

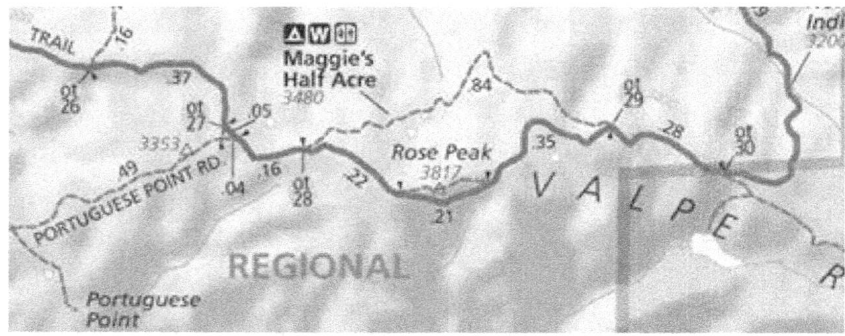

After ot19, the trail is marked as McCorkle Trail. Stay on McCorkle Trail for about 2.5 miles. Finally turn right on Camp Ohlone Road for 0.2 miles to the parking lot at Sunol Visit Center.

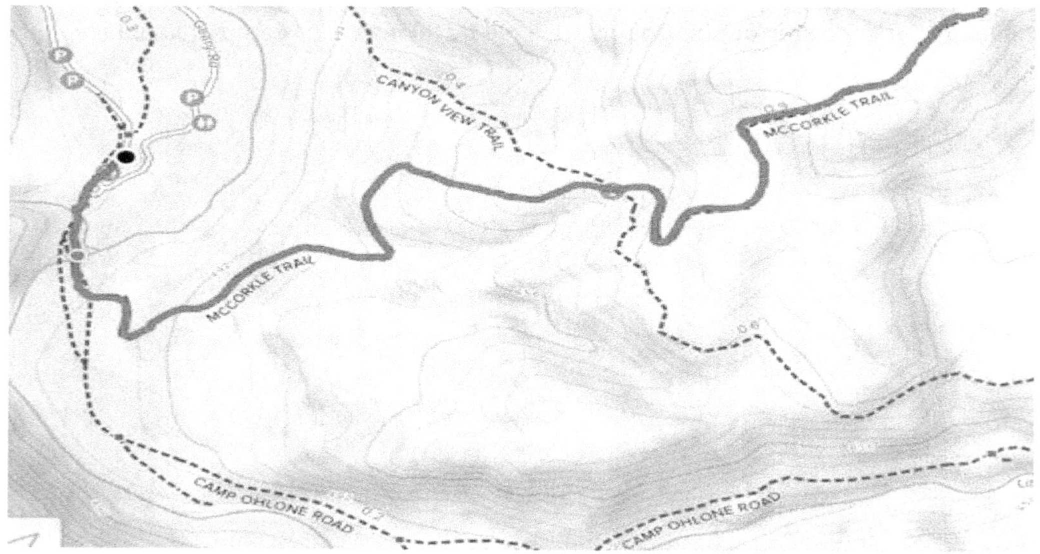

Hike Overview

Distance=13.3 miles

Elevation gain=2546 feet

Parking: Pleasanton Ridge Regional Park parking lot

Shaded: 10%

Trail Map:

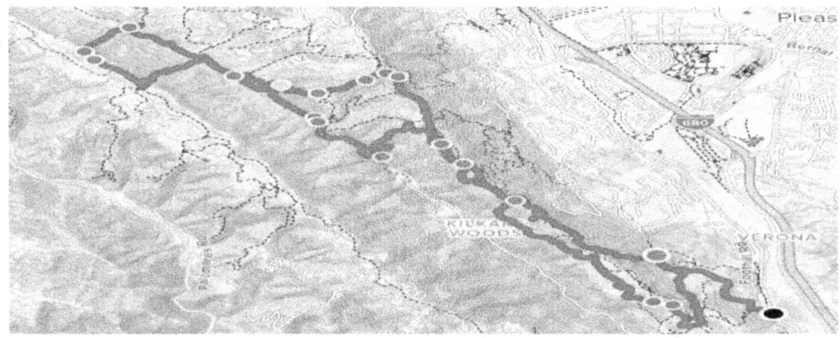

Detail Direction

Start your hike from the parking lot by taking Oak Tree Trail. Next stay left to climb up the steep Woodland Trail. When Woodland Trail meets again with Oak Tree Trail, you turn left onto Oak Tree Trail.

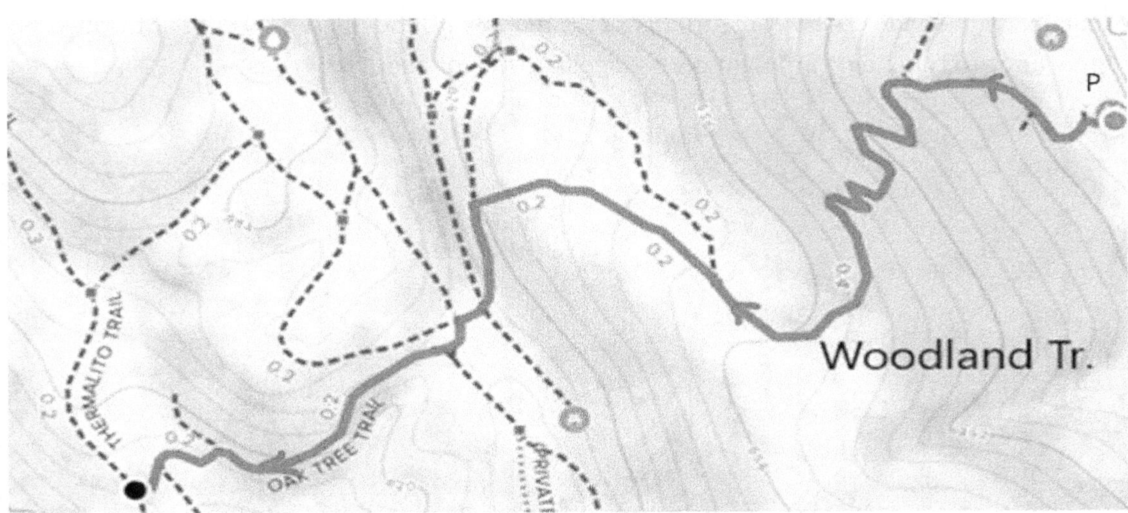

Next you turn right onto Thermalito Trail. Stay on Thermalito Trail umtil it ends at Ridgeline Trail. Turn left onto Ridgeline Trail.

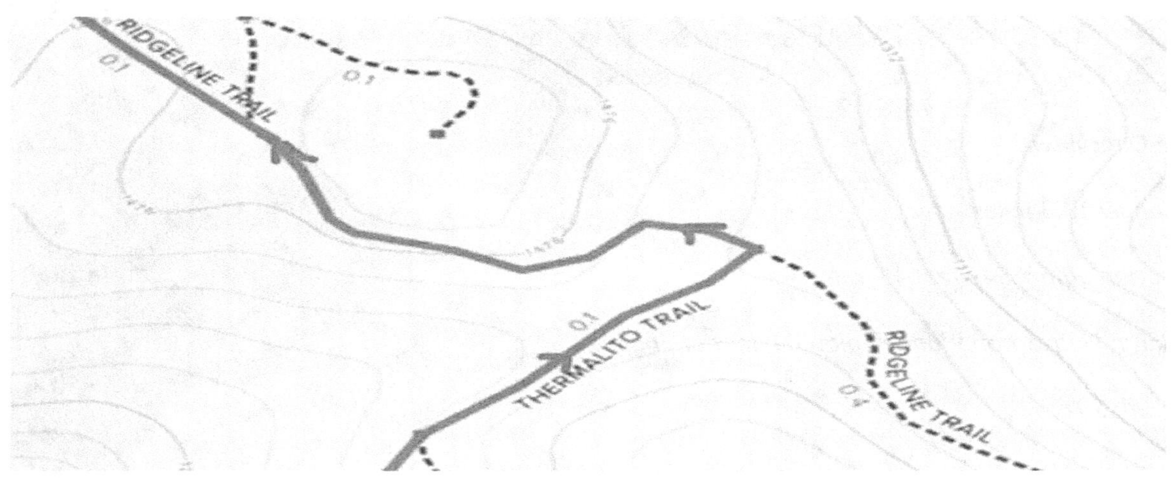

Stay on Ridgeline all the way to the junction with Sinbad Creek Trail. Turn left onto Sinbad Creek Trail for 0.7 miles to hike down to canyon. Cross the seasonal creek and turn right on Sinbad Creek Trail.

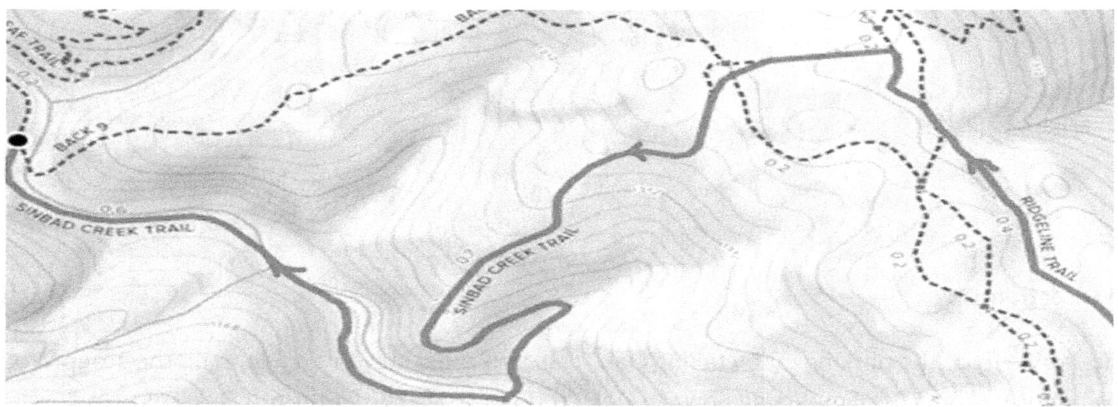

At the junction with Shady Creek Trail, turn right to climb toward the ridge. Stay right at the next junction to continue upward climbing. Turn right onto Ridgeline Trail for about 0.6 miles.

Next you turn left to Front 9 for 0.7 miles. At the junction with Toyon Trail, turn right on Toyon. When Toyon merge into Ridgeline, you turn left on Ridgeline and stay on it until its junction with Upper Christmas Trail. Turn left onto Upper Christmas Trail for 0.4 miles. Next get on Sycamore Grove Trail and stay on it until its ends at Oak Tree Trail. Turn left on Oak Tree Trail to get back to the parking lot.

Hike Overview

Distance=16.4 miles

Elevation gain=2858 feet

Parking: Cal State University East Bay Hayward Campus parking Lot C1

Shaded: 10%

Trail Map:

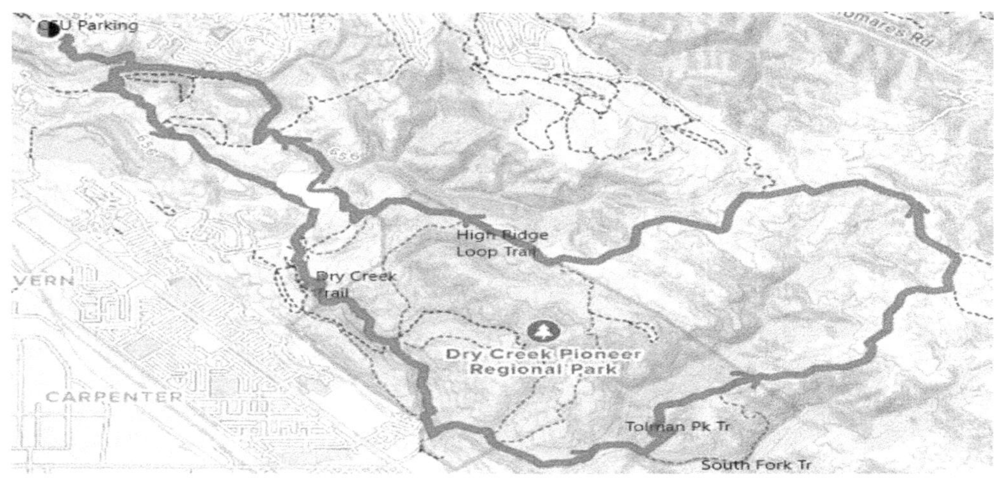

You can park your car on Parking Lot C1 for free on weekends. Take the fire road that leaves the parking and heads for the hills. There is a small trail on your left after you walk on the fire road for about half miles. At the junction with Ziele Creek Trail, you turn right to go down a creek and then go up on the other side of the Creek. At the junction with Vista Peak Loop, turn left to continue uphill. At the next two junctions, always stay right.

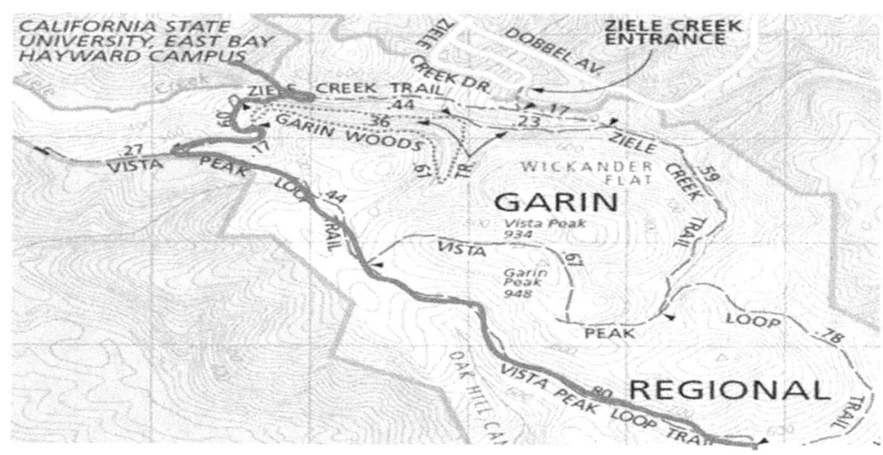

After about 1.5 miles on Vista Peak Trail, you come to the junction with Old Homestead Trail. Turn right on Homestead Trail and follow it to the red barn. Continue ahead to get on Dry Creek Trail.

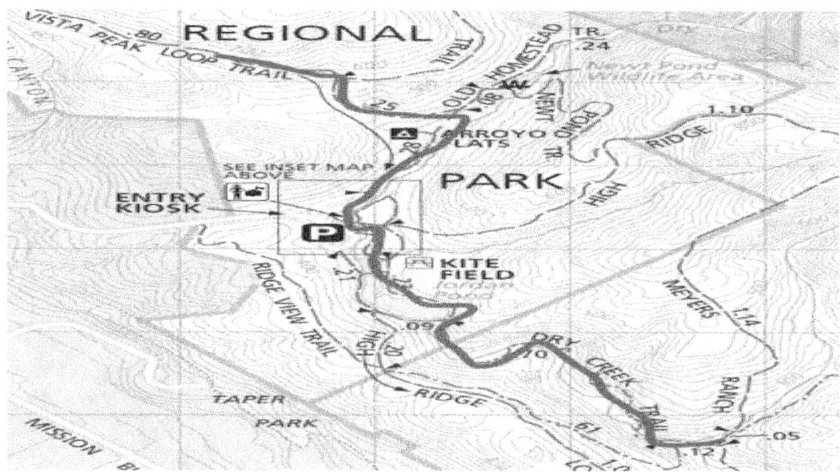

At the junction with Meyers Ranch Trail, turn right onto Meyers Ranch Trail. At the junction with High Ridge Loop Trail, you turn left onto HGLT. But only for 0.5 miles. Next you stay right to get onboard of Tolman Peak Trail to climb up Tolman Peak.

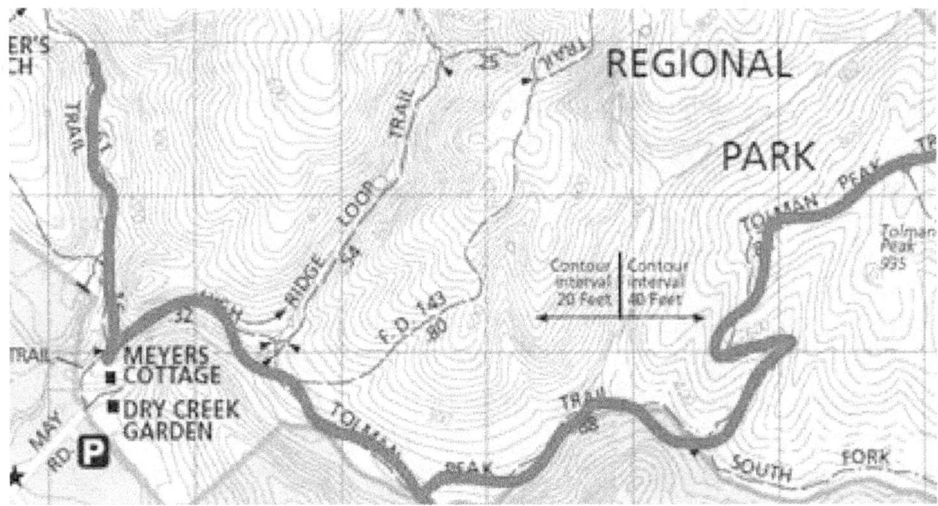

The regional park's boundary is junction a few hundred yards away. I climbed over the locked gate and continued hike along the main ridge for 2.5 miles. At the junction with a trail that leads to TPC Stonebrae, don't take that trail. Instead, you turn left for 1.2 miles to get back to the regional park. Once inside the park, you turn right onto High Ridge Loop Trail for 1.1 miles. Watch for a small trail on your right. Its name is Newt Pond Trail.

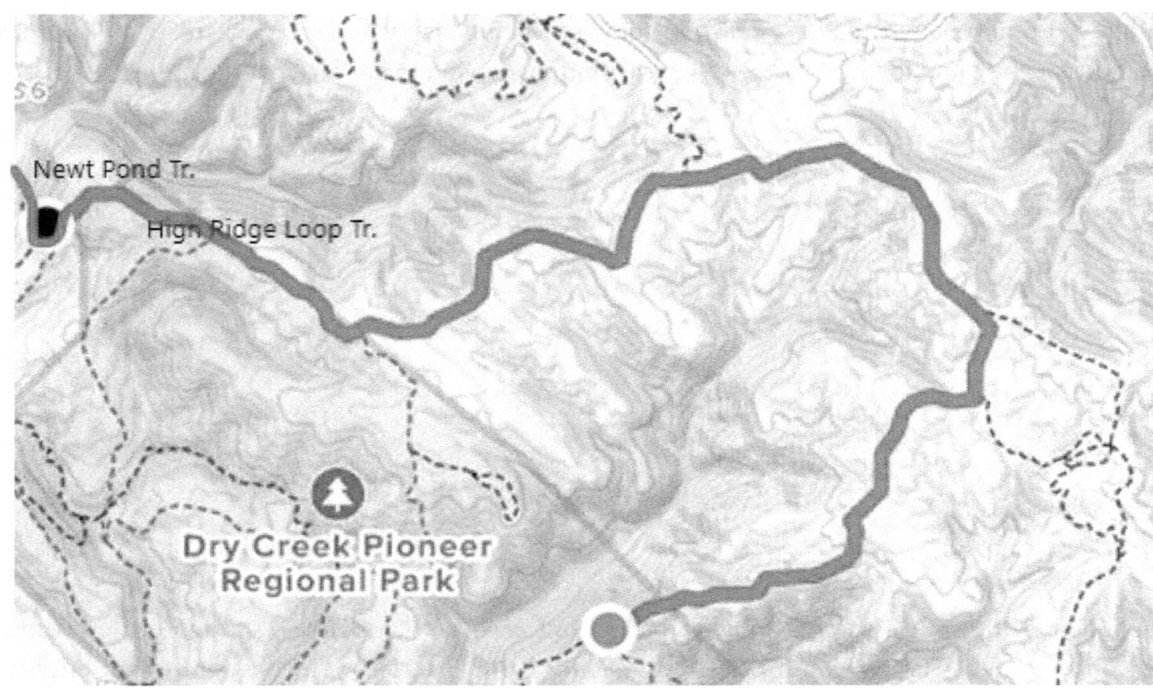

Turn right onto Newt Pond Trail which leads you down steeply to Old Homestead Trail. Turn left on Old Homestead Trail. Watch an unmarked Trail on you right side. Take this trail uphill to get onto Vista Peak Loop Trail. Turn right onto VPLT and stay on it until the junction with Ziele Creek Trail. Turn right on ZCT and stay right to exit the park and back to the fire road which leads you back to CSU campus.

Hike Overview

Distance=23.8 miles

Elevation gain = 2890 feet

Parking: Lake Chabot Marina parking lot or Lake Chabot Road roadside parking

Shaded: 25%

Trail Map:

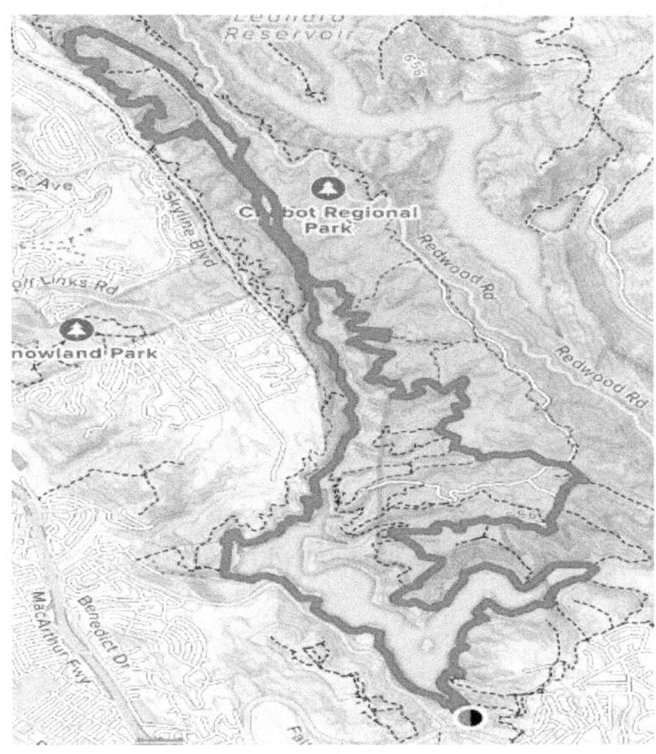

Detail Direction

Drive to Lake Chabot Marina. Start your hike from the East Shore Trail. At the junction with Honker Bay Trail and Live Oak Trail, turn left onto Honker Bay Trail to stay close to the lake. Stay with Honker Bay Trail to its end at Towhee Trail. Continue your uphill hike on Towhee Trail until its junction with Brandon Trail. Then turn left onto Brandon Trail. At the junction with Escondido Trail, turn left onto Escondido Trail for 1.3 miles. Turn left again onto Brandon Trail for 0.9 miles. Then Brandon Trail continues on the other side of a stone bridge. But you don't cross the bridge. Instead, you continue your hike on Grass Valley Trail for 2 more miles. Then the trail turns left and becomes Ranch Trail. Ranch Trail ends at Goldenrod Trail in 0.4 miles. Turn Left onto Goldenrod Trail for 1.3 miles.

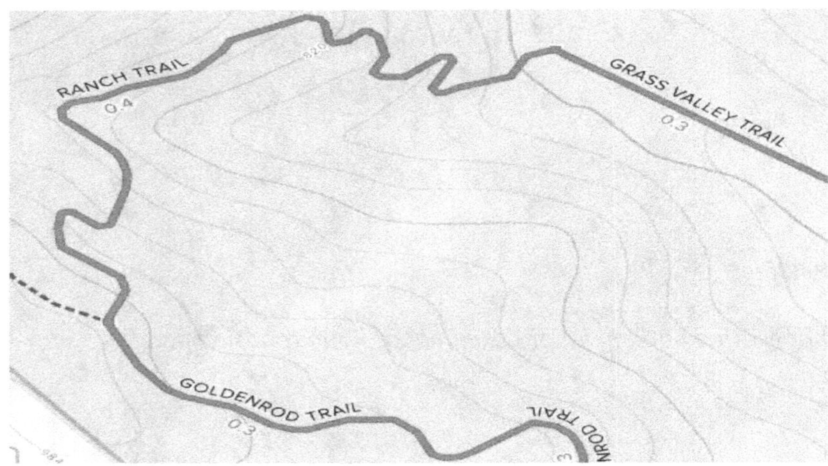

Next you turn left on Horseshoe Trail for 0.3 miles. At the end of Horseshoe Trail, you turn right onto Brandon Trail for 1.2 miles.

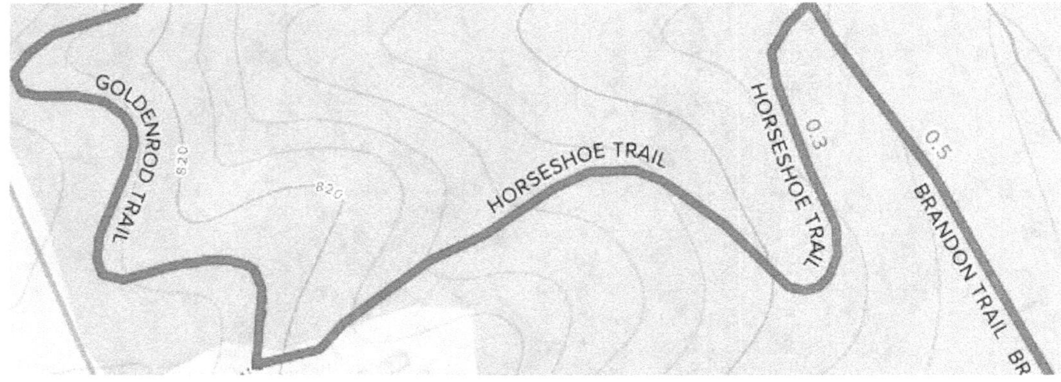

You are back to the stone bridge. Again, don't cross the bridge. Continue hike on Cascade Trail for 1 mile. Turn left to get onto Columbine Trail. At the junction with Bass Cove Trail, stay right to continue your journey on Bass Cove Trail.

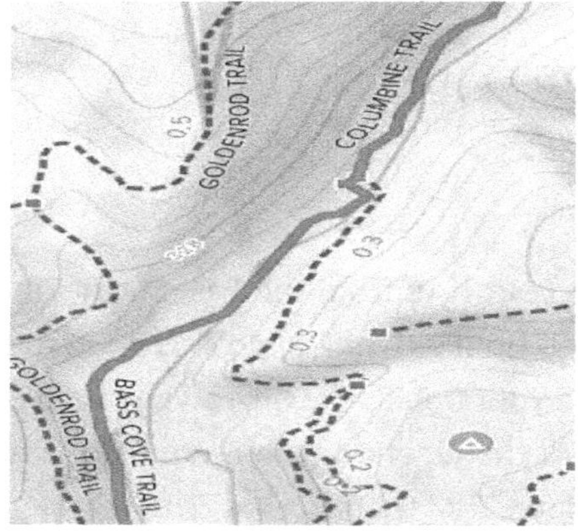

BCT ends at West Shore Trail. Turn left onto West Shore Trail and stay on it all the way to back to Lake Chabot Marina.

Hike Overview

Distance=15.1 miles

Elevation gain=3264 feet

Parking: Morgan Territory Preserve parking lot

Shaded: No

Trail Map:

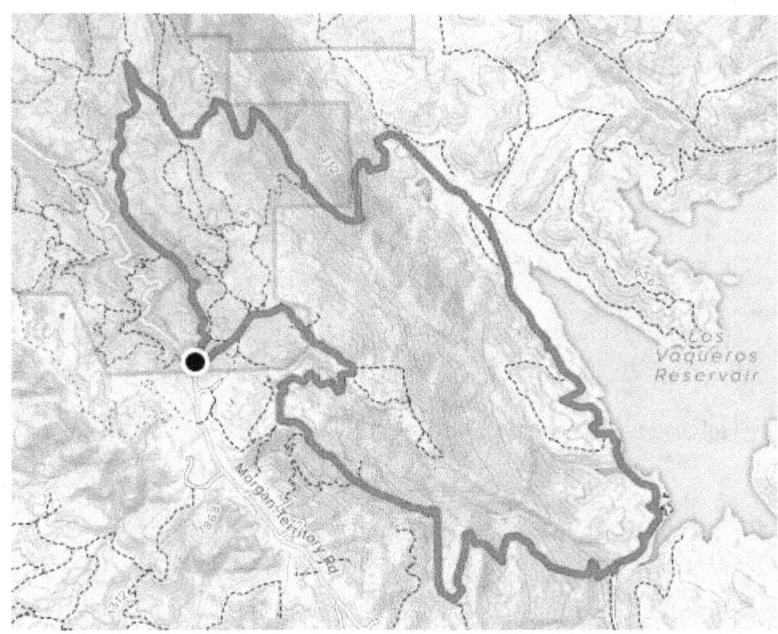

Detail Direction

Start your hiking from Condor Trail on the northeast side of the Morgan Territory main parking lot. Turn right on a connector trail for 0.1 miles. Then turn left on Volvon Trail:

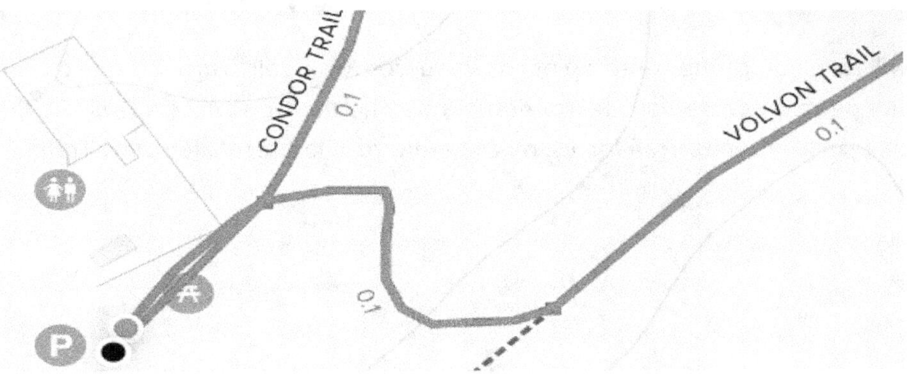

At the junction with Whipsnake Trail, stay slightly right to take Whipsnake Trail.

Take right on Black Hills Trail for about 2.7 miles:

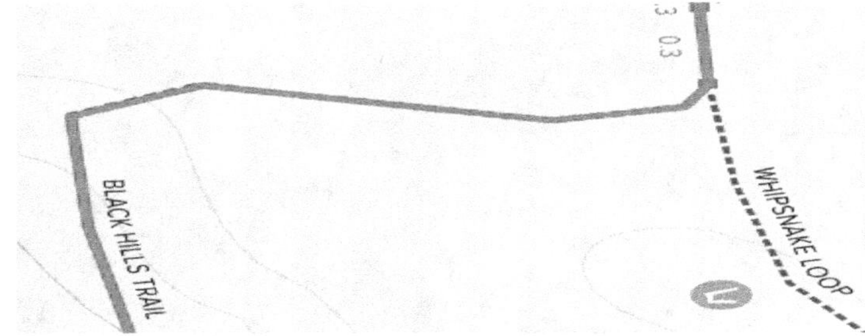

Then leave Black Hills Trail and turn left on Canada Trail:

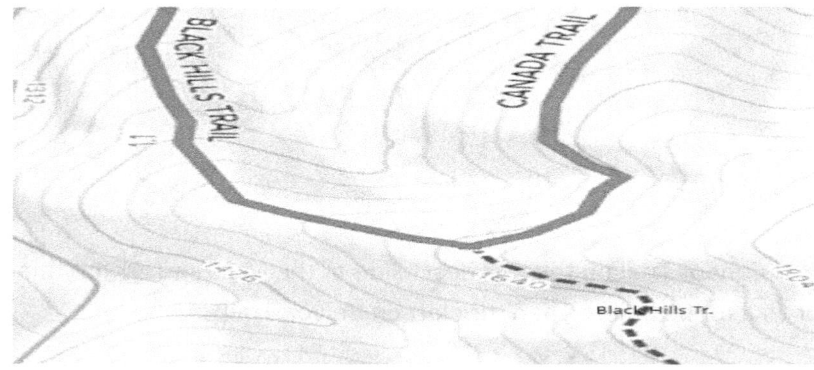

 Canada Trail will take you to the south tip of Los Vaqueros Reservoir. Turn left on Los Vaqueros Trail. At the north west side of the reservoir, take Adobe Trail. Then left on Miwok Trail. At the junction with Manzanita Trail, take Manzanita Trail for 1.2 miles before turn left for Valley View Trail.

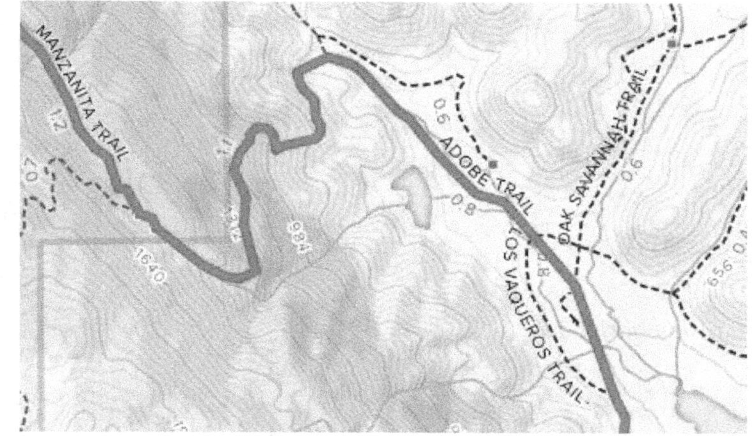

At the next junction, turn right onto Volvon Trail. Make a left turn on Stone Corral Trail.

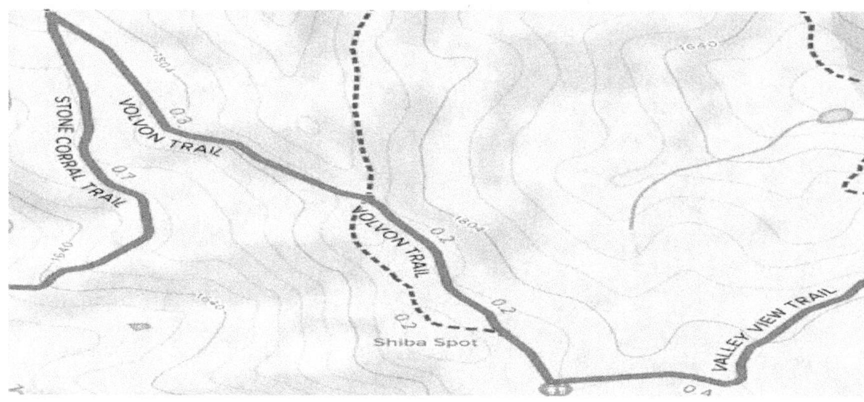

Finally make a left turn on Coyote Trail and Coyote Trail connects Condor Trail which leads to the parking lot.

Hike Overview

Distance=15.7 miles

Elevation gain=3295 feet

Parking: Finley Road roadside parking

Shaded: 50%

Trail Map:

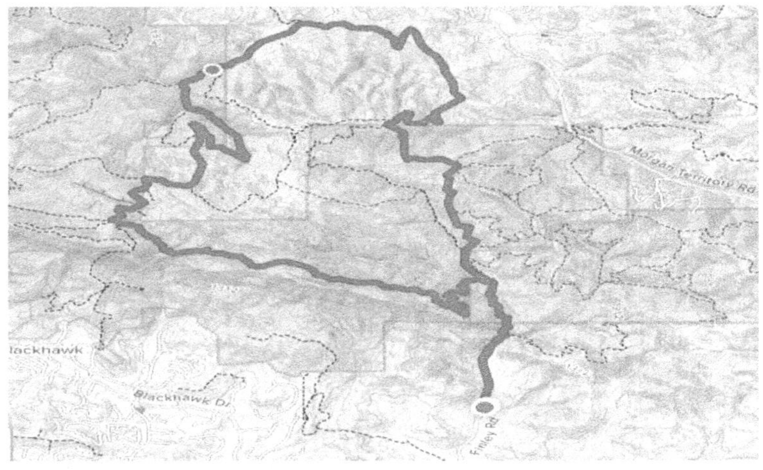

Detail Direction

This hike starts from Finley Road in San Ramon. You park your car on the right side of Finley Road and walk 0.75 miles on the should toward the mountains. Then you arrive at the gate which is the start of Old Finley Road. After 0.6 miles, Oyster Point Trail is on your left. Take OPT for 3.5 miles.

At the end of Oyster Point Trail, it's a 5-way junction.

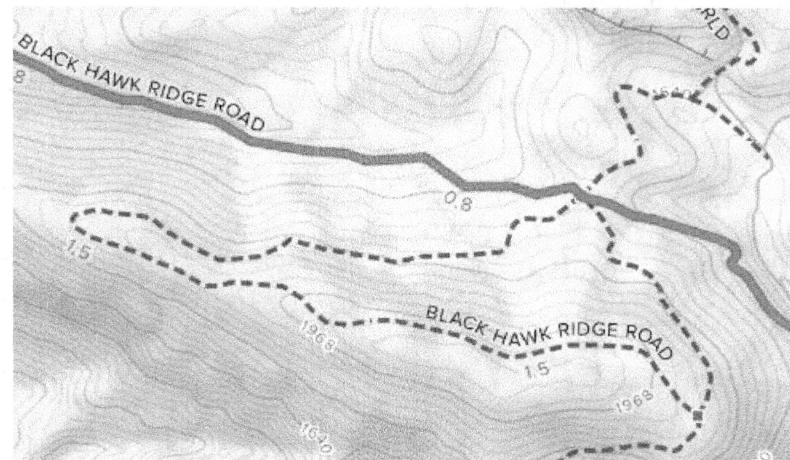

Take the second trail on your right. Black Hawk Ridge ends at Knobcone Point Road. Turn left on Knobcone Point Road. Stay on the trail until you come to the junction with Curry Canyon Road. Then turn right on Curry Canyon Road.

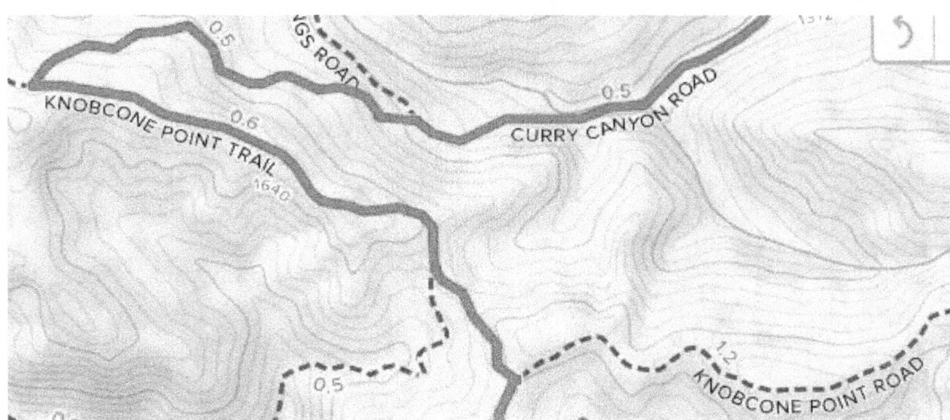

Stay on Curry Canyon Road for about 2.3 miles and then turn right on an unnamed fire road just0.2 miles before Curry Canyon Road becomes paved road:

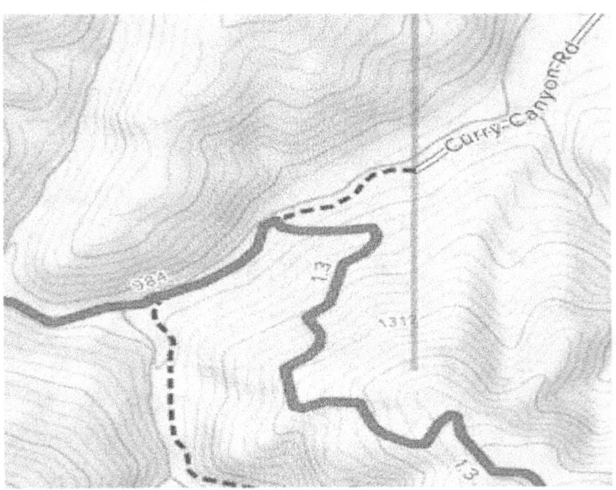

Climb steadily for 1.3 miles before you see the junctions with Windy Point Trail. Turn left on Windy Point. Then turn right and turn right on Tassajara Creek Trail.

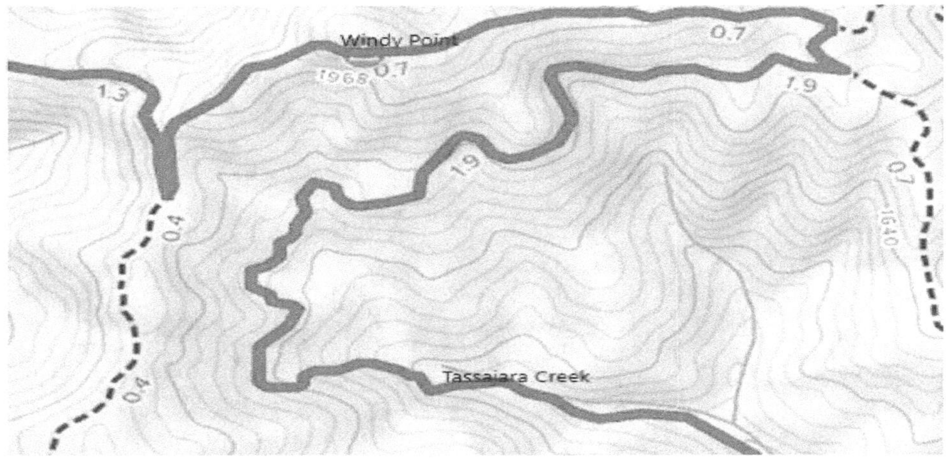

Tassajara Creek will end at Old Finley Road. You turn right onto Old Finley Road. OFR leads you all the way back to the trail head.

Hike Overview

Distance = 12.3 miles

Elevation gain=2703 feet

Parking: Black Diamonds to Mt Diablo Regional Trail parking in Clayton (GPS: 37.94105,-121.92818)

Shaded: 10%

Trail Map:

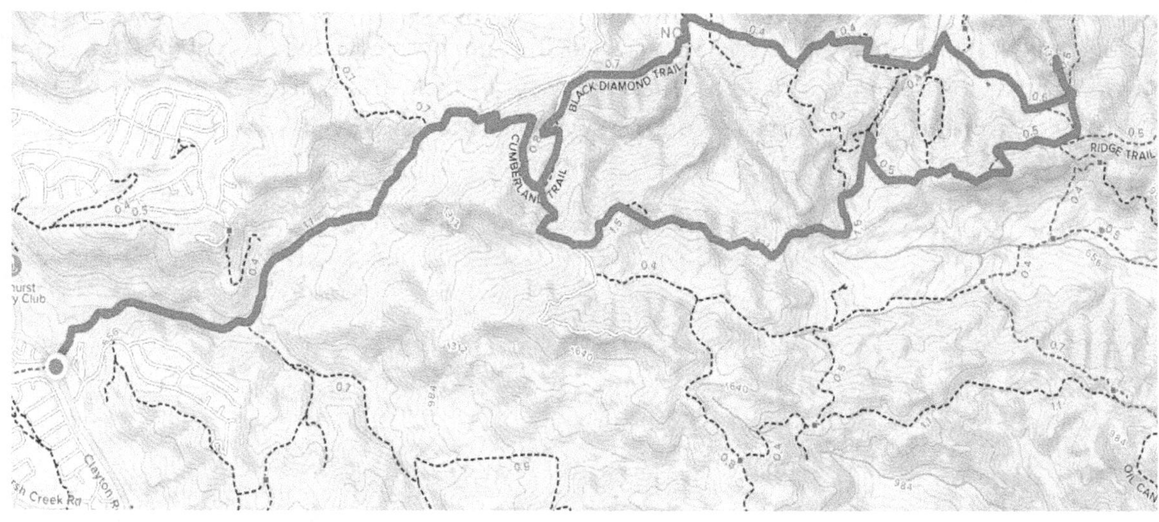

Detail Direction

Follow the Black Diamonds to Mt Diablo Regional Trail for 1.5 miles. At the junction with a paved road, stay right to get on Cumberland Trail. Stay on Cumberland Trail for about half mile before turn right for paved road again. At the start of Black Diamond Trail, Take the trail by turning right.

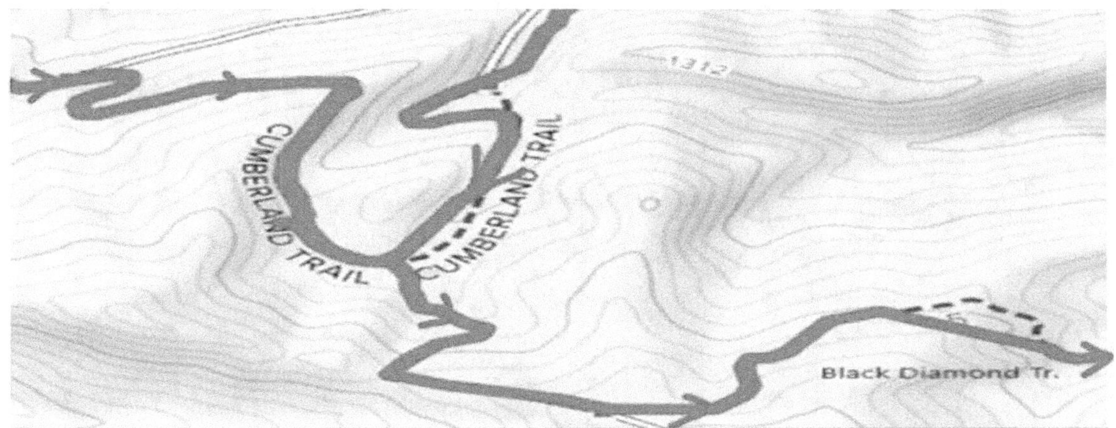

Stay on BDT for 1.5 miles. Then turn onto Manhattan Canyon Trail for 0.3 miles. Next you turn right onto Chaparral Loop Trail for 0.5 miles. Then go straight to get on Ridge Trail.

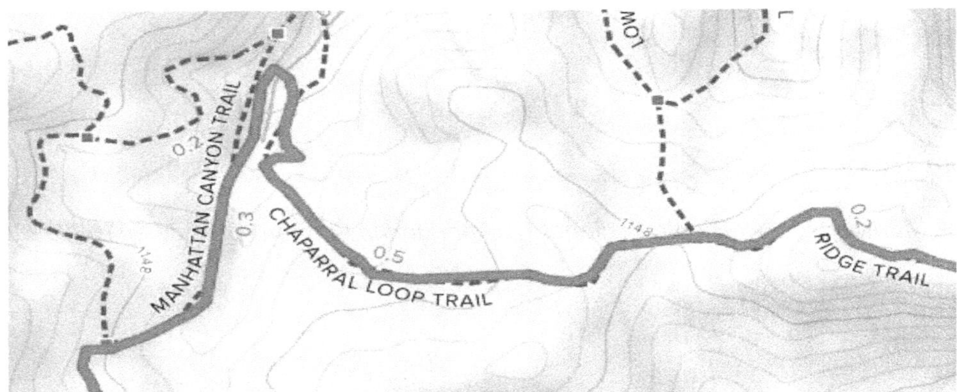

At the junction with Carbondale Trail and Stewartville Trail, get onto Carbondale Trail for 0.5 miles. Then slightly left to get the summit to have a panoramic view of the park. Retrace your steps back to the junction of Stewartville Trail and turn right onto Stewartville Trail for 0.6 miles.

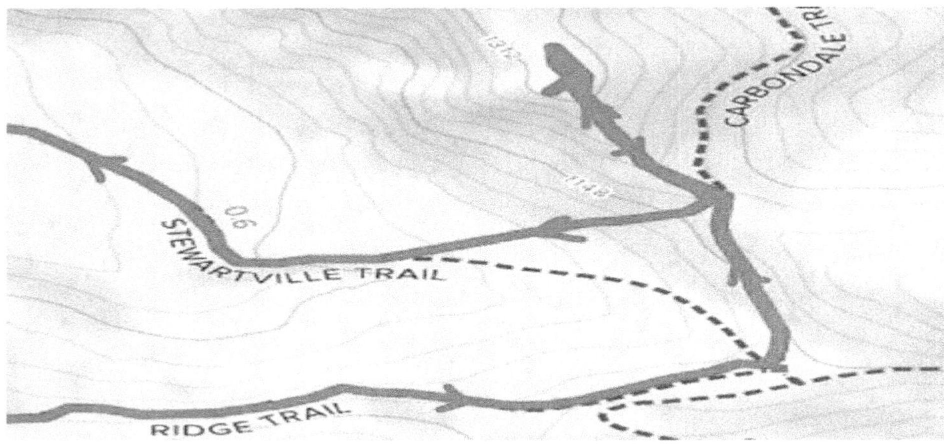

Then turn left onto Somersville Road for 0.1 miles. At the junction of Chaparral Loop Trail and Nortonville Trail, stay right to get onto Nortonville Trail(you come from right side on the map below).

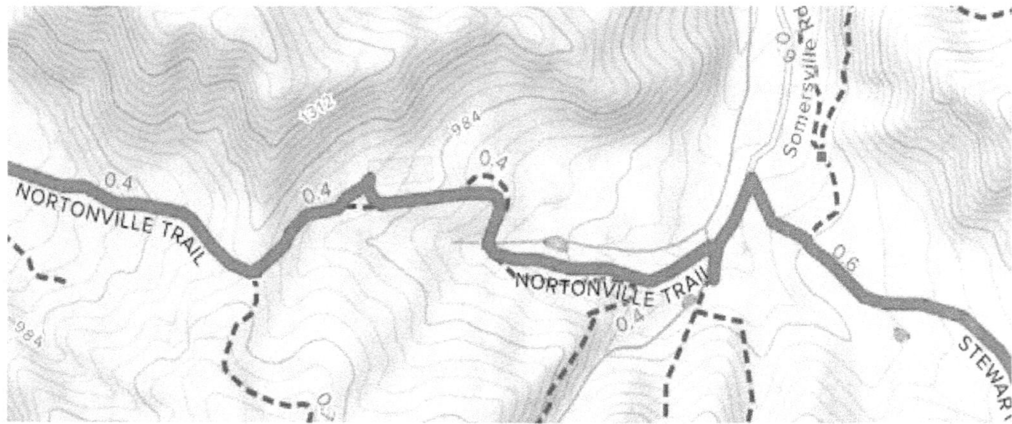

Stay on Nortonville Trail until it meets Black Diamond Trail for the second time, turn left onto Black Diamond Trail. Continue on Cumberland Trail. Finally follow Black Diamonds to Mt Diablo Regional Trail to get back to your car.

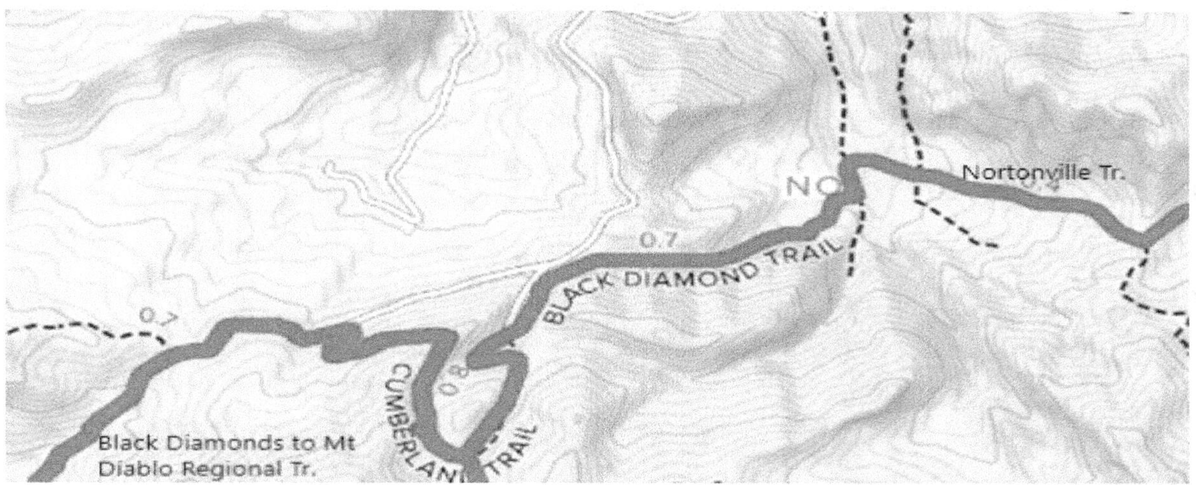

Hike Overview

Distance=11.4 miles

Elevation gain=2014 feet

Parking: Black Diamond Mine Regional Park Visitor Center

Shaded: No

Trail Map:

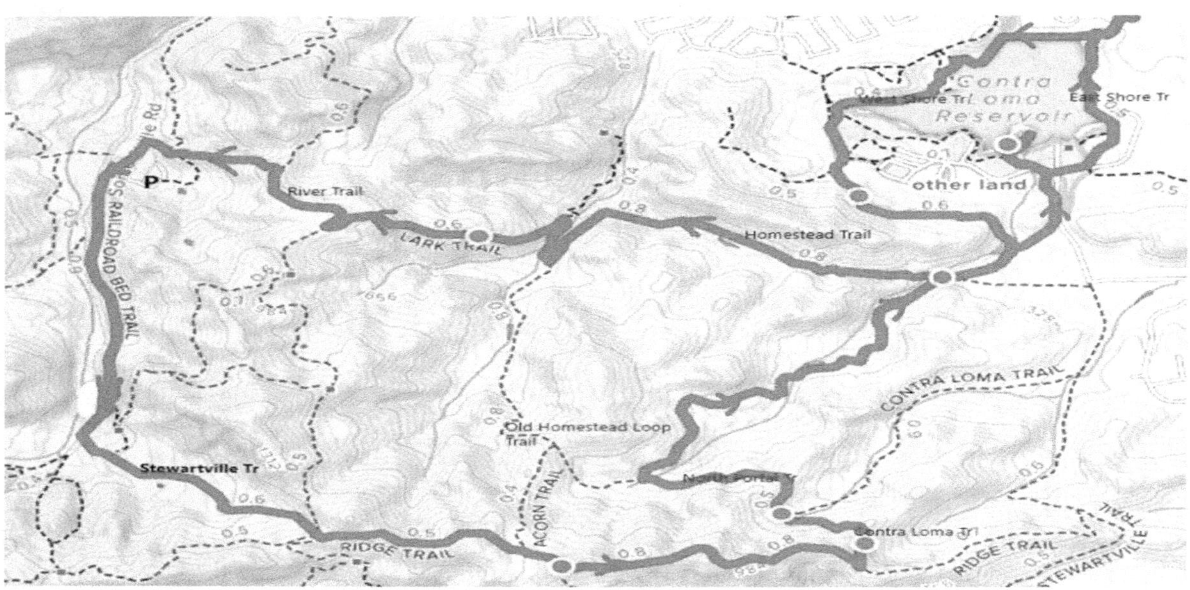

Detail Direction

I parked my car at the Visitor Center parking lot on the left side of Somersville Road and start the hike on Railroad Bed Trail in the same direction as I came in. Then stay slightly left to get on Stewartville Trail to climb up. On top of the ridge, there is the 5-way junction (from left to right): Carbondale Trail, Ridge Trail, Stewart Trail, Ridge Trail, and Stewart Trail (the one you come from). I chose the 2nd from the left, Ridge Trail. Next I turned left onto Contra Loma Trail. Then I stayed left to get on North Portal Trail. North Portal Trail ends at Old Homestead Loop Trail. Turned right on Old Homestead Loop Trail for 1.2 miles. Crossed Homestead Trail and turn left on Contra Loma Blvd. Contra Loma Blvd ends at Contra Loma Reservoir south shore. Turn right on East Shore Trail. As you hike around the reservoir, cross the dam, the trail becomes West Shore Trail. Before you arrive the swimming lagoon, turn right onto Ride Trail and very soon turn left onto Lake View Trail. At the junction of Homestead Trail and Old Homestead Loop Trail, turn right on Homestead Trail for 1 mile. There is a short connector trail that connects Homestead Trail and Lark Trail. Turn right on this trail and turn left onto Lark Trail. Next turn right on River View Trail. Stay left on River View Trail at the next junction with Loop Trail. Only 0.2 miles later, leave River View Trail and take the trail on your left to get back to your car at the Visitor Center.

Hike Overview

Distance=14.7 miles

Elevation gain=4557 feet

Parking: End of Regency Driver in Clayton

Shaded: 20%

Trail Map:

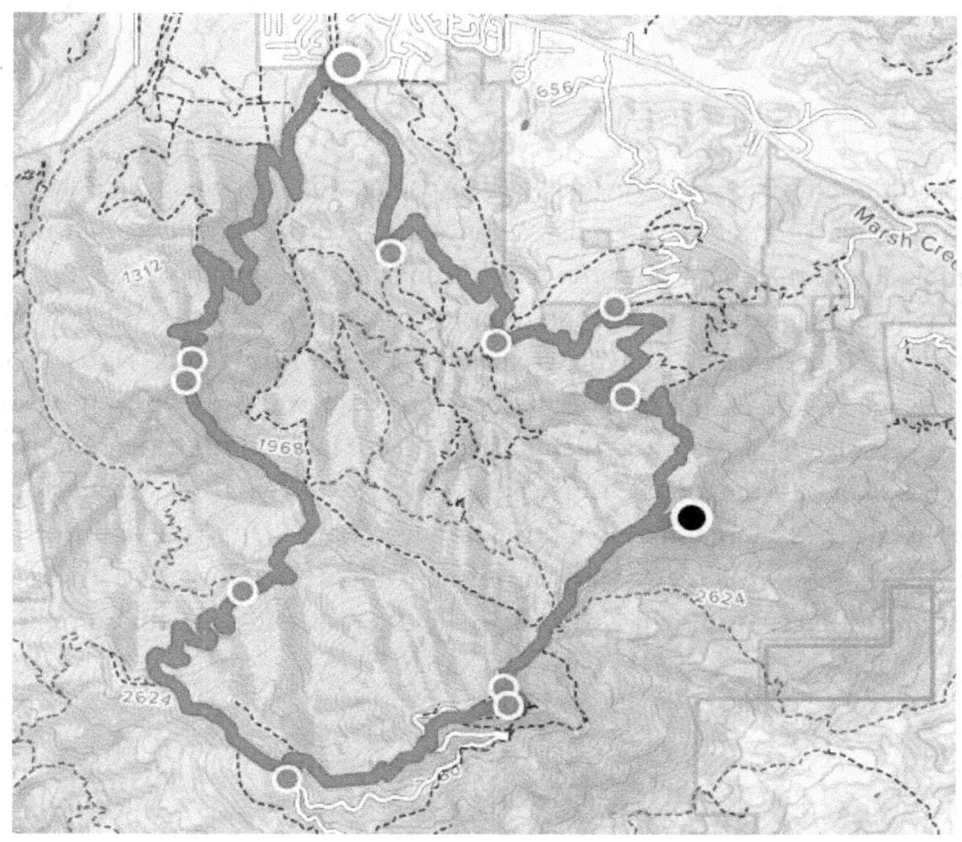

Detail Direction

This hike starts from the end of Regency Driver in Clayton. You walk down the slope from Regency Driver toward the Donner Canyon Road, turn left on Donner Canyon Road. Walk one mile and turn left on Bruce Lee Spring Trail. When you reach the junction of Wasserman and Lower Donner Trails, keep left to follow Wasserman trail. This trail will end at Cardinet Oaks Road.

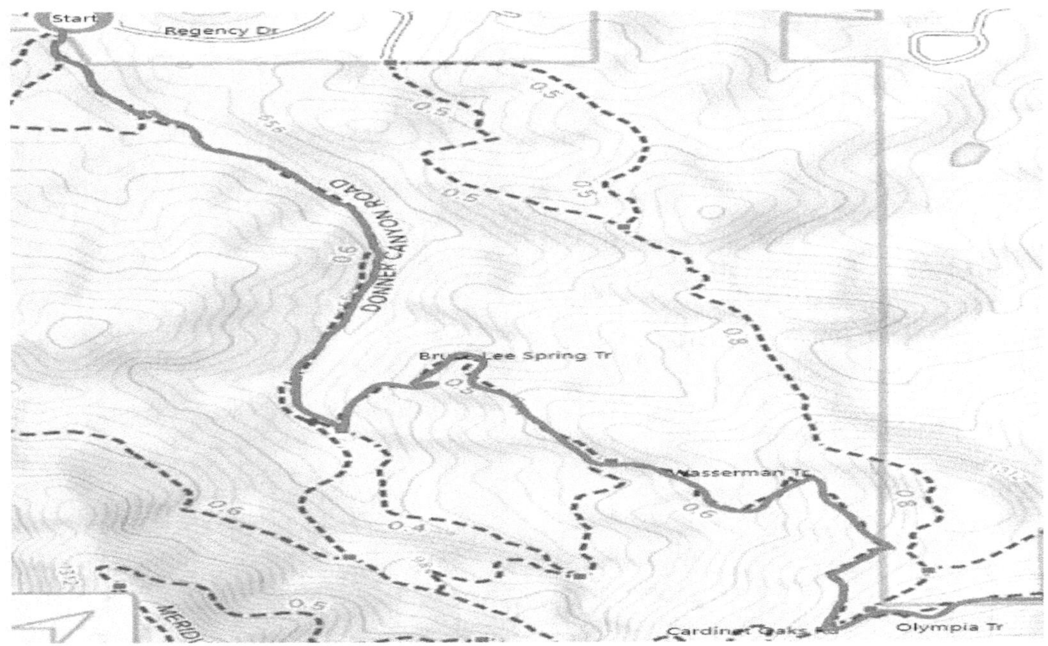

Turning left and climbing 0.1 miles, you will face a closed gate. Then you turn right onto Olympia Trail and walk uphill for another 1.3 mils. When you reach the junction of Olympia Trail and Mount Olympia Road, turn right onto the later. It ends at the summit of the 2945 feet Mount Olympia. In a clear winter day, you can see the snowcapped Sierra. From the summit of Mount Olympia, there is a trail that will lead you to North Peak Road. Turn left on North Peak Road and walk .23 miles, you will reach the summit of our 2nd peak-North Peak. North Peak's elevation is 3565 feet, the 2nd highest peak in the Diablo range. Trace back North Peak Road all the way to the 6-way junction of Bald Ridge Trail, North Peak Road, North Peak Trail, Prospector's Gap road. You choose the steepest unmarked uphill trail between Bald Ridge Trail and North Peak Trail. After about 0.5 miles, you will reach Mary Bowerman Trail. Turn left onto Mary Bowerman Trail and walk a short distance. Turn right when you see a use trail leading to the summit museum.

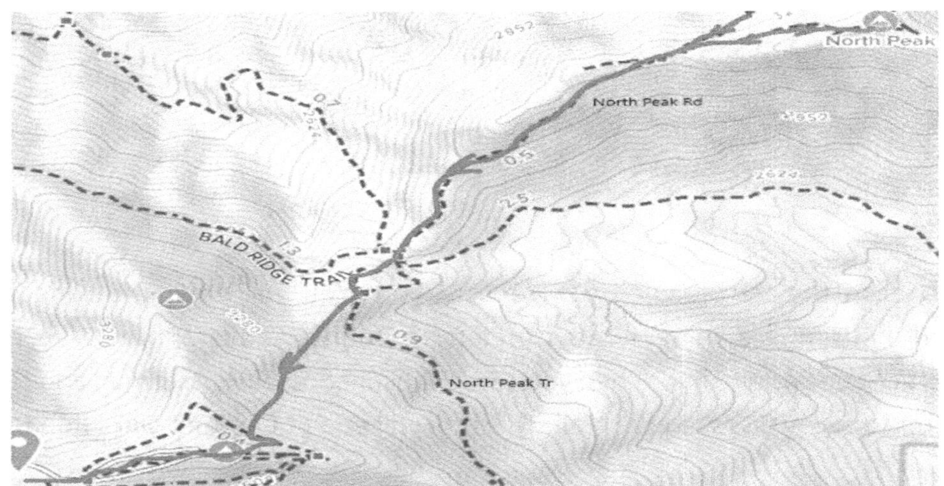

This highest peak is Diablo peak. Its elevation is 3849 feet. To get our 4th peak – Eagle Peak, you walk toward the lower summit park. On the far west end of the park area, you will see the start of Juniper Trail. Follow Juniper trail to Juniper Camping ground, and Turn right on Deer Flat Road. At the junction of Deer Flat, Burma and Meridian Ridge, keep right to stay on Meridian Ridge.

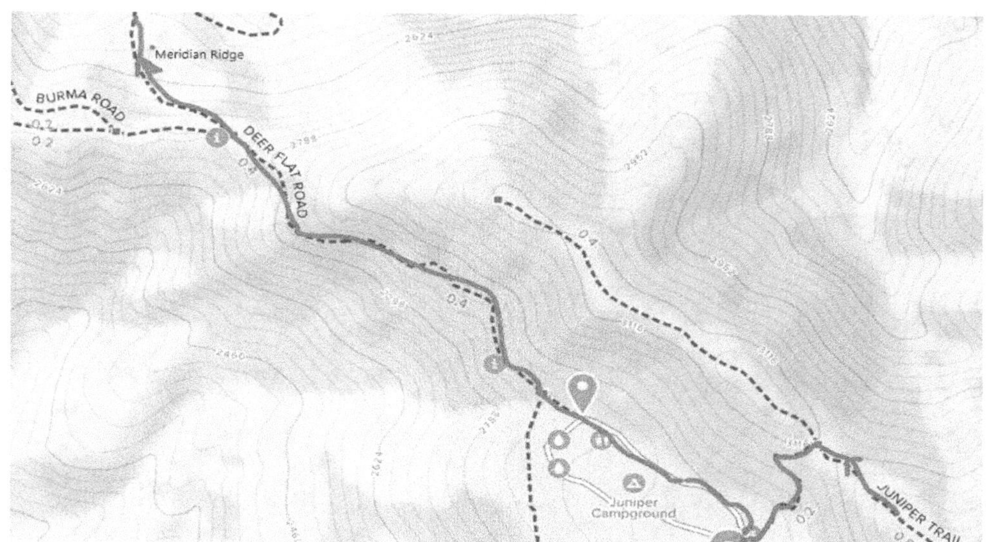

When you reach a 5-way junction, turn left on Eagle Peak Trail which leads you to the 2369 feet Eagle Peak:

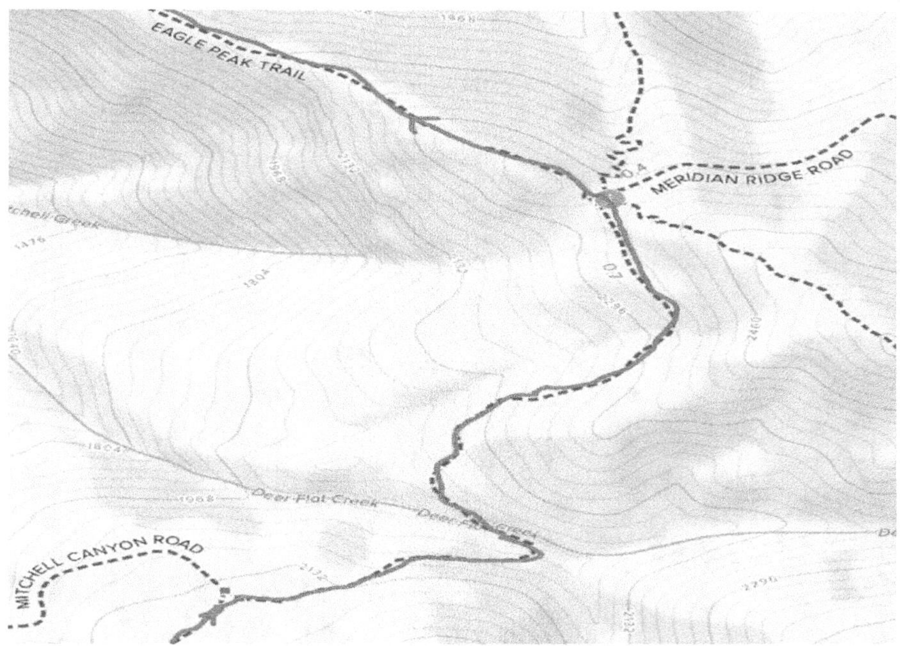

Continue on Eagle Peak trail. Turn right on Bruce Lee Road at the foot of Eagle Peak, turn left on Back Creek Trail, and Back Creek Trail ends at Donner Canyon Road.

Walk up the slope toward Regency Driver and you just finish the magnificent Diablo 4-Peak loop. Congratulations!

Hike Overview

Distance=12.6 Miles

Elevation gain=4400 feet

Parking: End of Regency Driver in Clayton

Shaded: 10%

Trail Map:

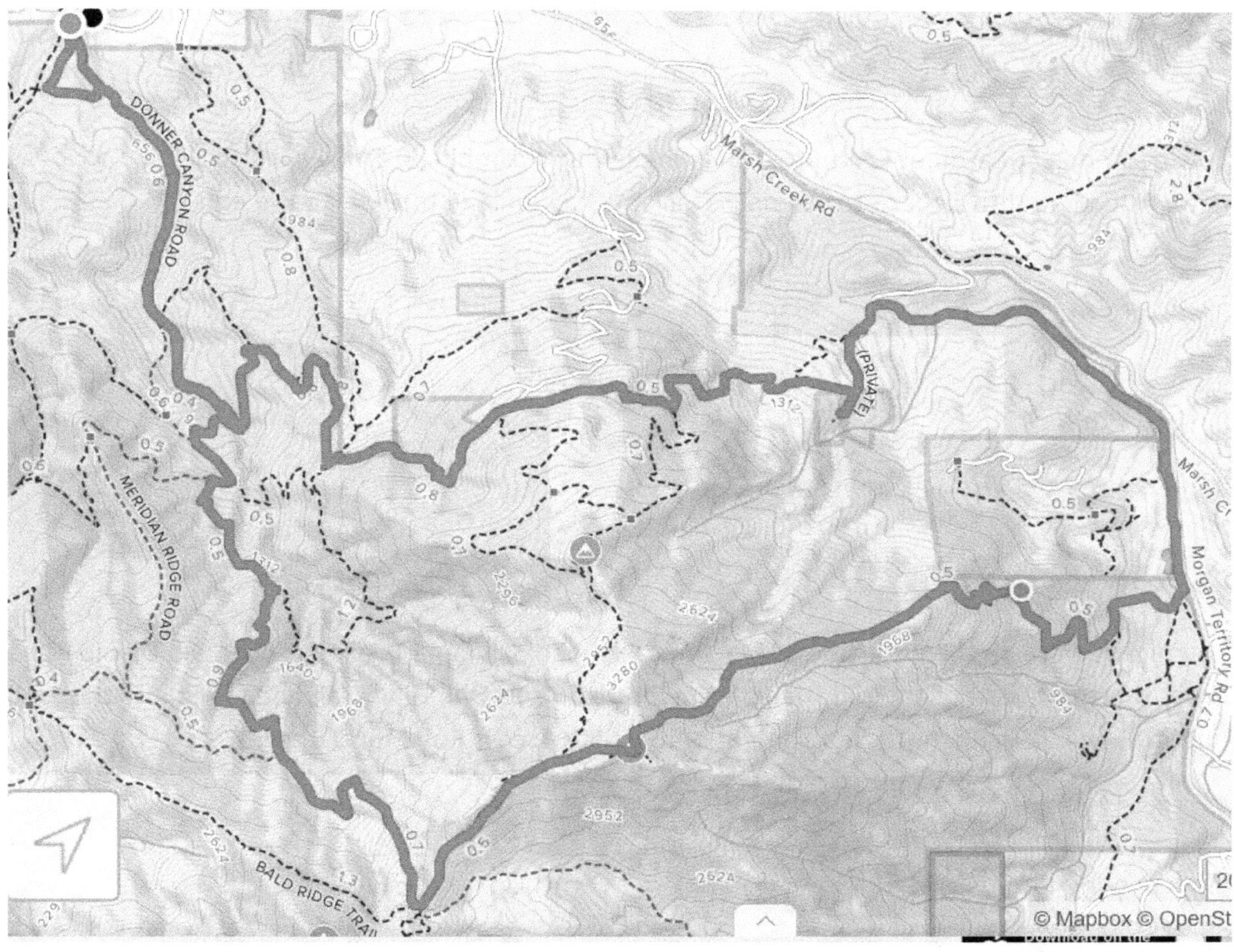

Detail Direction

This hike starts from the end of Regency Driver in Clayton. You walk down the slope from Regency Driver toward the Donner Canyon Road, turn left on Donner Canyon Road. Walk 1.2 miles and then turn slightly left onto Hetherington Loop Trail. When you reach the junction of Hetherington

Loop Trail and Lower Donner Trail, turn sharply left onto Lower Donner Trail. Next turn right to the Wasserman trail.

This trail ends at Cardinet Oaks Road. Turning left and climbing 0.1 miles, you will face a closed gate. Then you turn right onto Olympia Trail and stay on it all the way to the end.

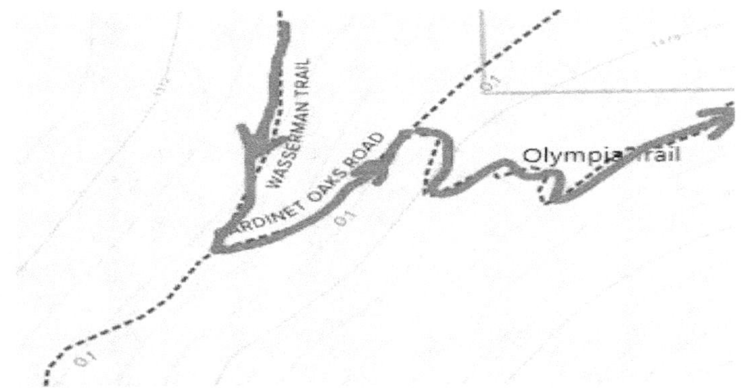

You find you are on the west side of Marsh Creek Road. Olympia Trial ends near Old Diablo Mine Cross the front yard of the old Diablo Mine and you see Oak Hills Trail ahead. Follow this trail until Utility Access Road. Then turn right onto Utility Access Road for 0.8 miles.

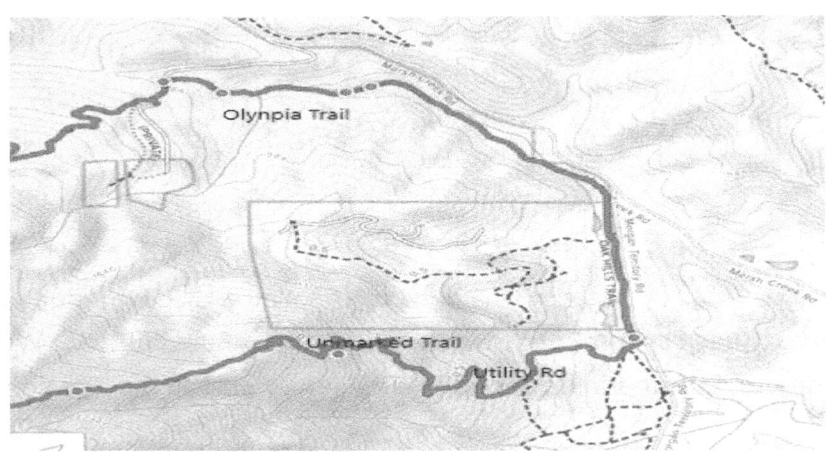

When Utility Road begins to dip, you turn left onto a unmarked trail which leads all the way to the east side of North Peak. Go down North Peak Road to Prospector's Gap and turn right onto Prospector's Gap Road.

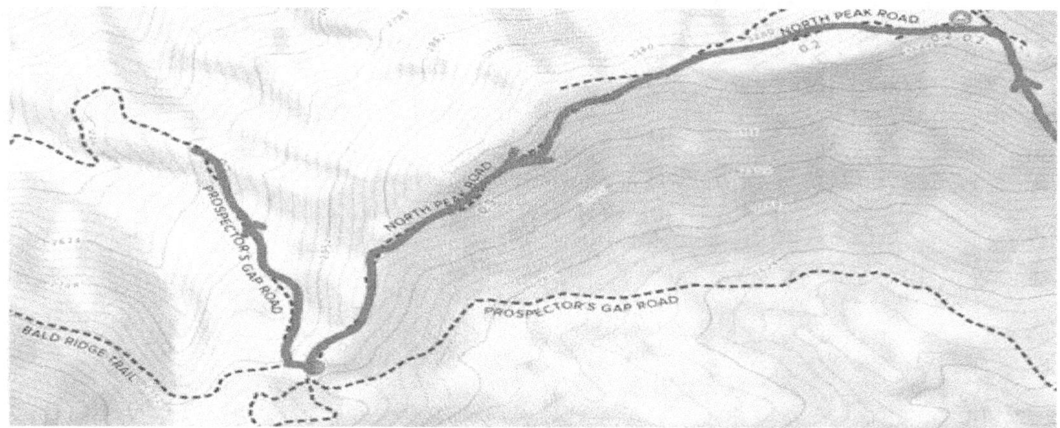

After 0.8 miles, turn right on Middle Trail. Then turn right on Meridian for 0.1 miles. Then turn left on Donner Canyon Road which brings you back to the Regency Driver.

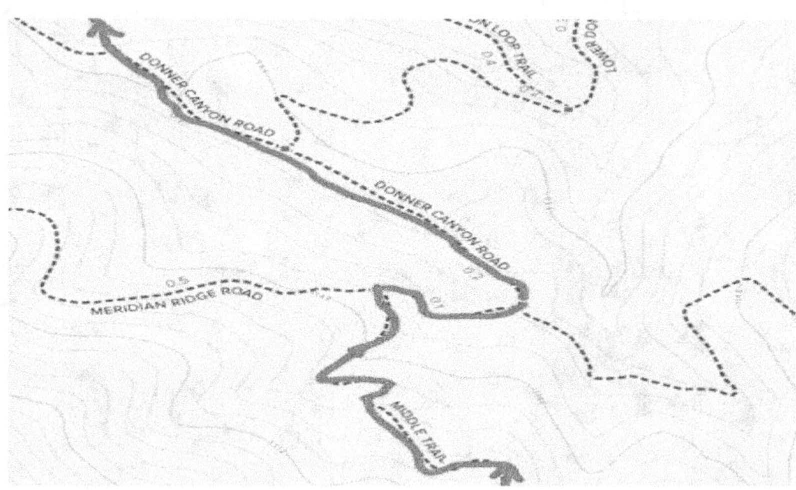

Hike Overview

Distance=14.7 miles

Elevation gain =3921 feet

Parking: Mitchell Canyon Visitor Center in Clayton

Shaded: 20%

Trail Map:

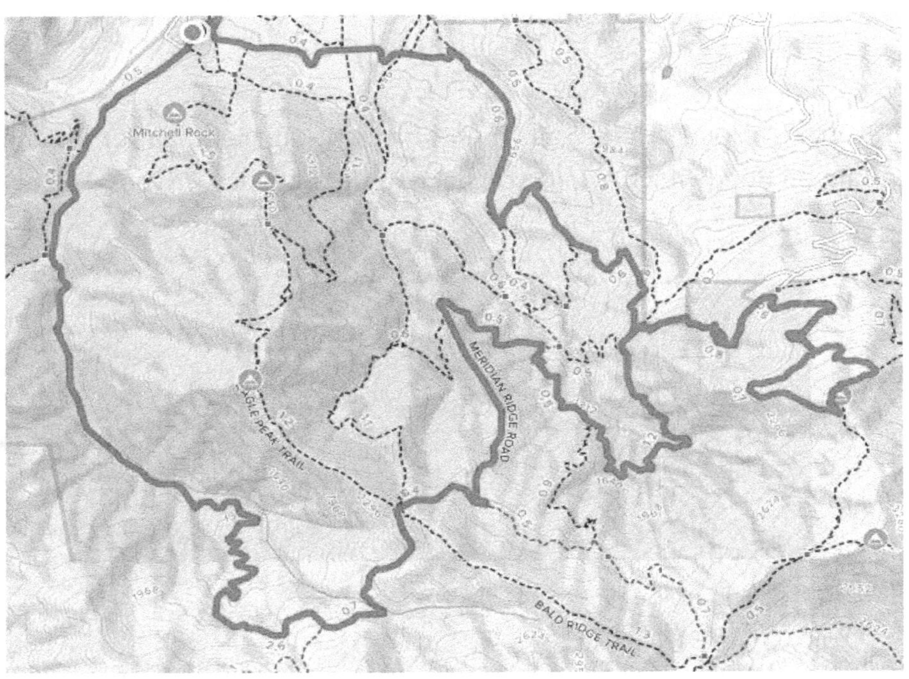

Detail Direction

You start this loop at the Mitchell Canyon Visitor Center parking lot and follow Mitchell Canyon Road for 3 miles. After you reach the junction at Deer Flat, you turn left onto Meridian Ridge Road. Stay on MeridianRidge for about 1.1 miles until you reach the junction with Prospector's Gap.

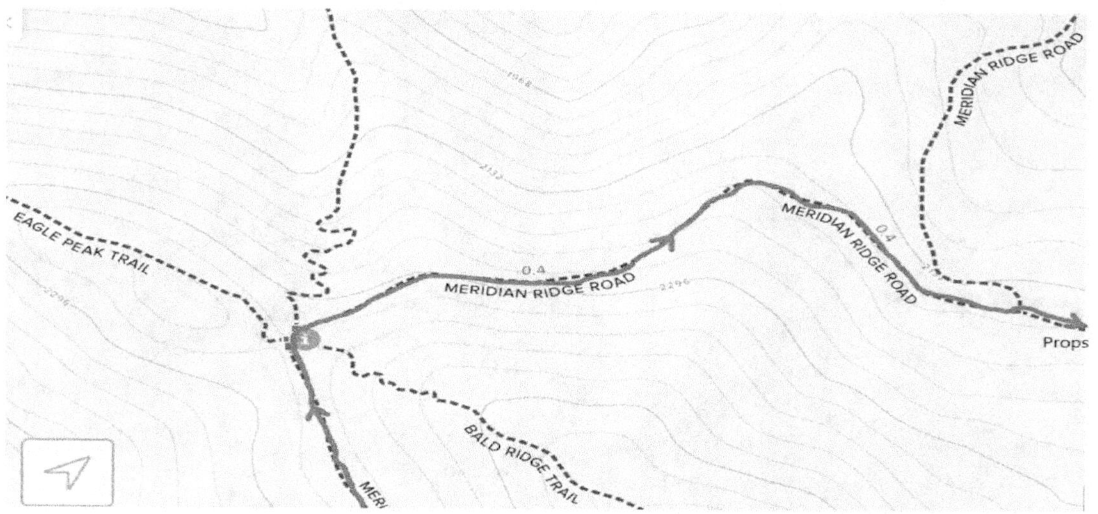

Continue On Prospector's Gap for 0.5 miles. Then turn left on Middle Trail. Half miles later, turn right on Falls Trail. The Falls Trail is 1.2 miles long. You can see at least 5 waterfalls during winter and spring seasons. The Falls Trail ends at Cardinet Oaks Road. Turn right on Cardinet Oaks Road. After walking up the fire road for 0.1 miles, you will see Wasserman Trail on the left. If you are exhausted, you can go back by turning left. Otherwise, continuing uphill for another 0.1 miles, you will see Olympia Trail on your right. Turn right onto it and walk for 0.8 miles.

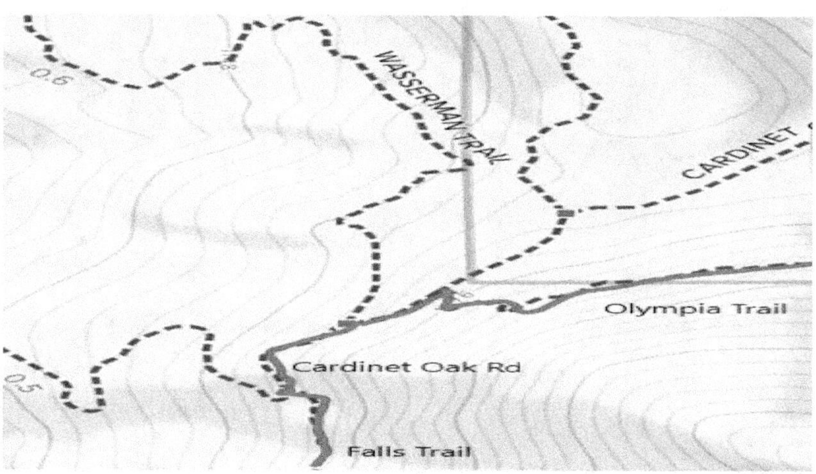

Turn right onto Mount Olympia Road. 0.6 miles later, you turn left on Zippee Trail. 0.3 miles later, turn right on East Trail. Climbing up the East Trail for 0.2 miles, you reach the summit of Mount Olympia. You come down the summit by taking Mount Olympia Road on the other side of the East Trail since East Trail is steep and not safe to travel downhill.

Stay on Mount Olympia Road until you reach the junction with Olympia Trail. Turn left on Olympia Trail and turn left on Cardinet Oaks Road. Turn right onto before mentioned Wasserman Trail. Wasserman Trail will become Brice Lee Spring Trail. Turn right on Hetherington Trail and turn right on Donner Canyon Road. After you reach bottom of the hills, watch for Murchio Road on the left. Turn left when you see it. After crossing a few huge meadows, you finally see the Water Tower. Turn left on Tower Trail, then right on Oak Road and right on Mitchell Canyon Road. And you are back to the parking lot. Total distance: 14.7 miles with 3921 feet elevation gain.

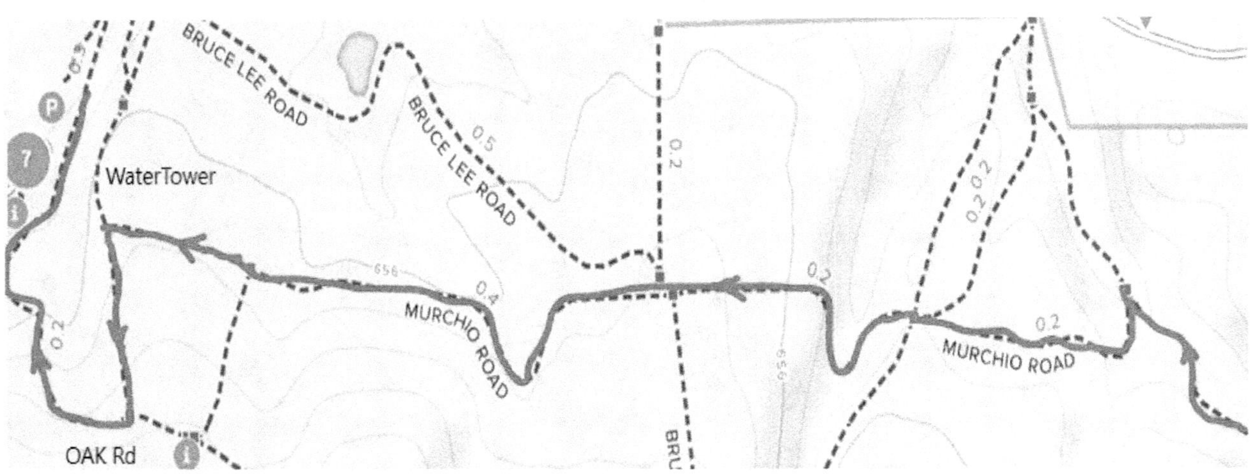

Hike Overview

Distance=16 miles

Elevation gain=3839 feet

Parking: Castle Rock Regional Park parking lot in Walut Creek

Shaded: 25%

Trail Map:

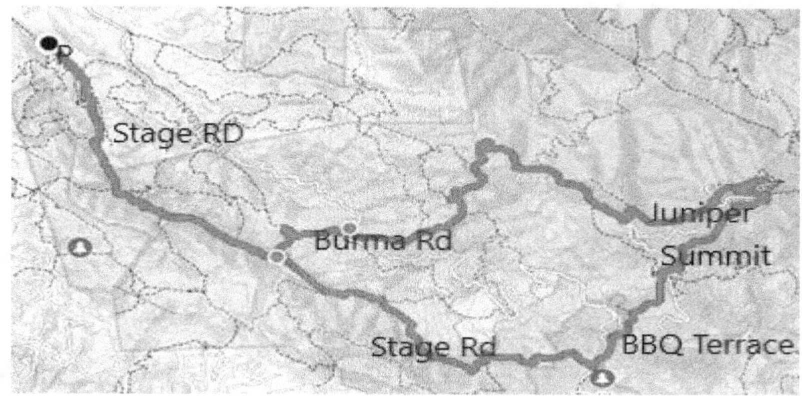

This loop starts at Stage Road at the far end of the Castle Rock Regional Park parking lot. Hike on Stage Road for 1.5 miles and you arrive at the gate that separates the regional park and Diablo State Park. At 2.4 miles, you reach the junction with Burma Road. Turn left onto Burma Road. After climbing 0.9 miles on Burma Road, you come across North Gate Road. Burma Road continues on the other side of North Gate Road. After climbing two steep slopes and then it dips slightly. At the saddle, Burma Road wears left slightly and you go straight onto Angel Kerley Road for 0.3 miles before you turn left onto Mother's Trail.

The Mother's Trail is 0.6 mile long. It ends at Burma Road. You turn right on Burma which leads you to the Junction with Meridian and Deer Flat. Keep right to hike on Deer Flat until it meets Juniper Trail on your left. Turn left onto Juniper Trail and follow the trail all the way to the lower summit parking.

Cross the parking lot and follow Summit Trail to the top of Mt. Diablo. To get back, hike summit trail down to BBQ Terrace.

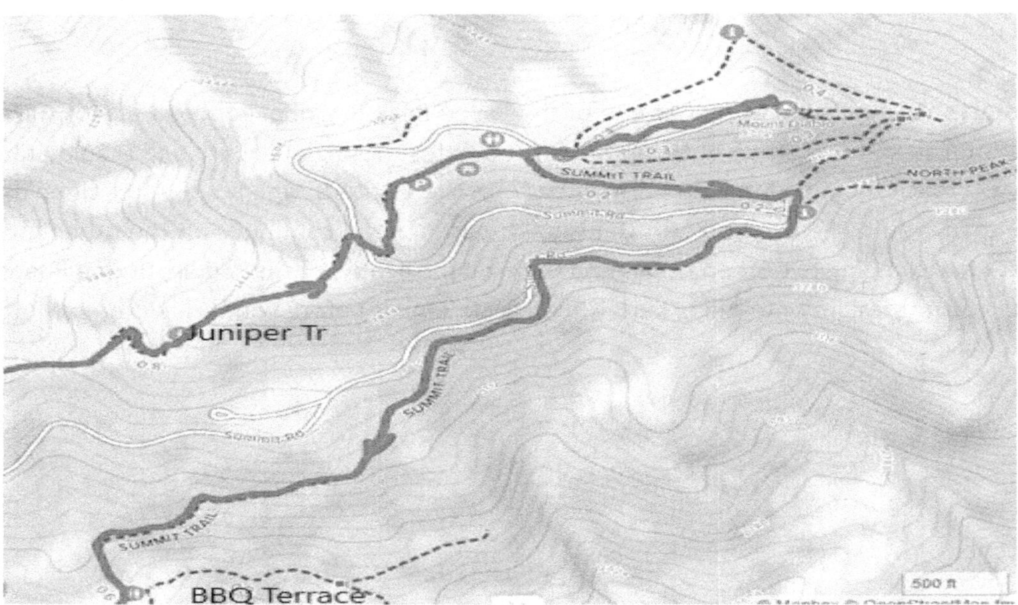

Then turn right onto BBQ Terrace Road and hike to the bottom of the canyon where you meet with Stage Road.

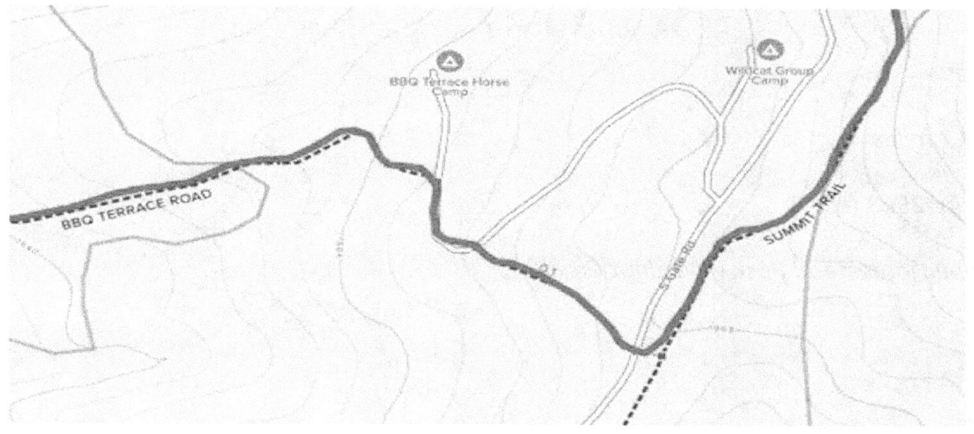

Straight ahead and hike all the way to the end of Stage road.

Hike Overview

Distance=13.7 miles

Elevation gain=2963 feet

Parking: Howe Homestead Park in Walnut Creek

Shaded: No

Trail Map:

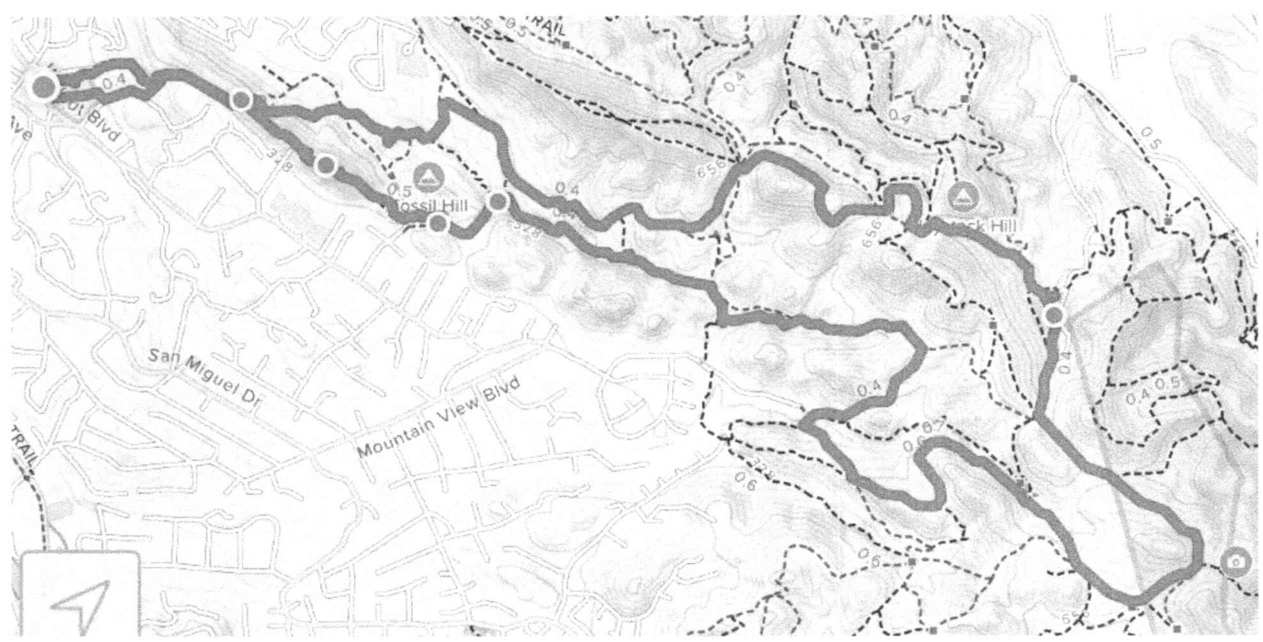

Detail Direction

Kovar Trail leaves the parking lot for the rolling hills. Follow it to the junction with Summit Ridge Trail. Keep left to stay on Kovar Trail to downhill. Save Summit Ridge Trail for your return. At its junction with Fossil Hill Trail, keep left to get on Fossil Hill Trail. At the junction with Briones to Mt Diablo Regional Trail, don't turn left (which brings you to Indian Valley Elementary School) or right (which bring you toward Mt Diablo). Instead, you go straight for 0.2 miles. Now you are at the junction with Corral Spring Trail and Ridge Top Trail. Take the first one on your right, and continue on Ridge Top Trail until you are at the junction with Costanoan Trail.

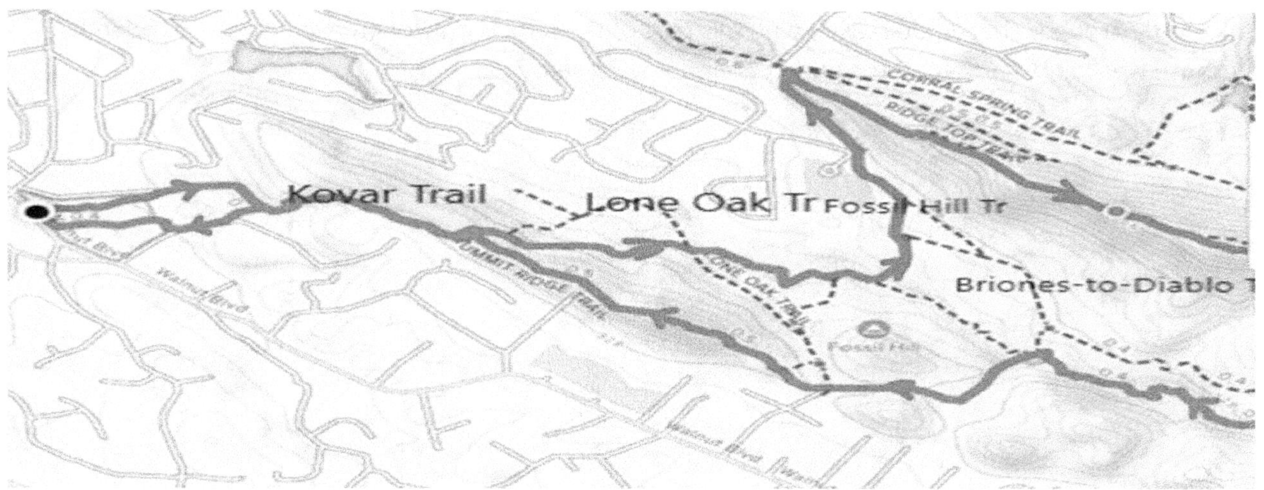

Turn right on Costanoan Trail. At the junction with Borges Ranch Trail and Hanna Grove Trail, stay left on Hanna Grove Trail and keep Bob Pond on your right. Then the trail continue on the other side of Borges Ranch Road for 0.2 miles. At the junction, turn right onto Shell Ridge Trail to climb uphill.

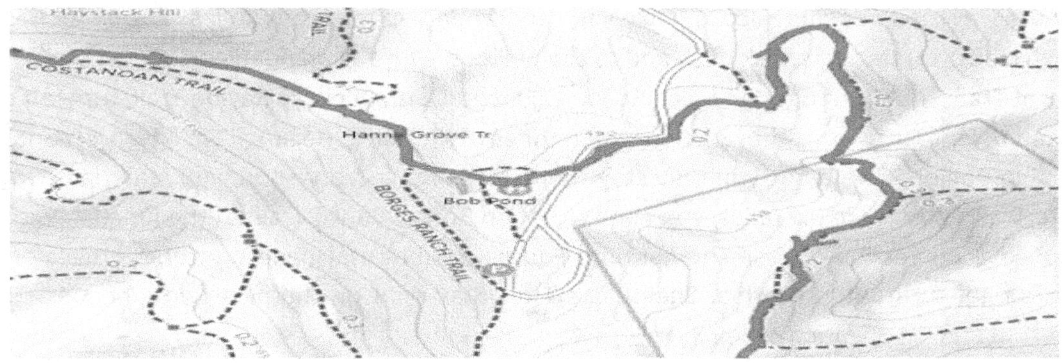

Stay right on the next few junctions. When come to the junction with Fairy Lantern Trail, turn left. At the junction with Stage Road, turn right toward Mt Diablo.

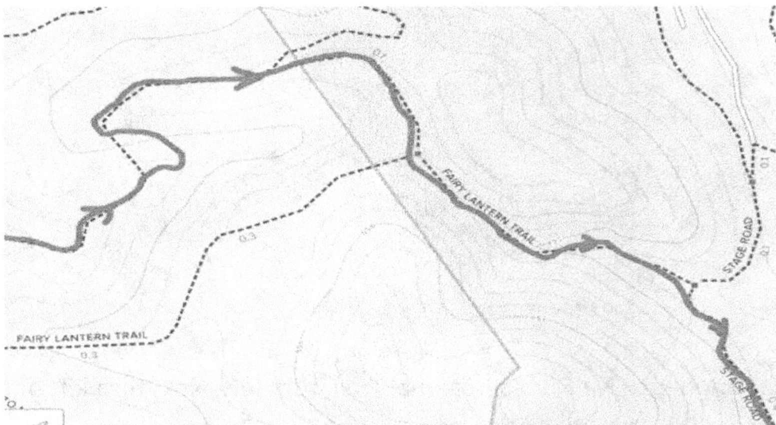

Stay on it for only 0.4 miles. Watch out for a small trail on your left that crosses the creek and climbs up steeply on the other side along with Castle Rock. Once on top of Castle Rock, you may notice that penguin falcons fly around. That is the reason why this part of the park is only open from August 1 to January 31 because we want to protect them during their breeding seasons.

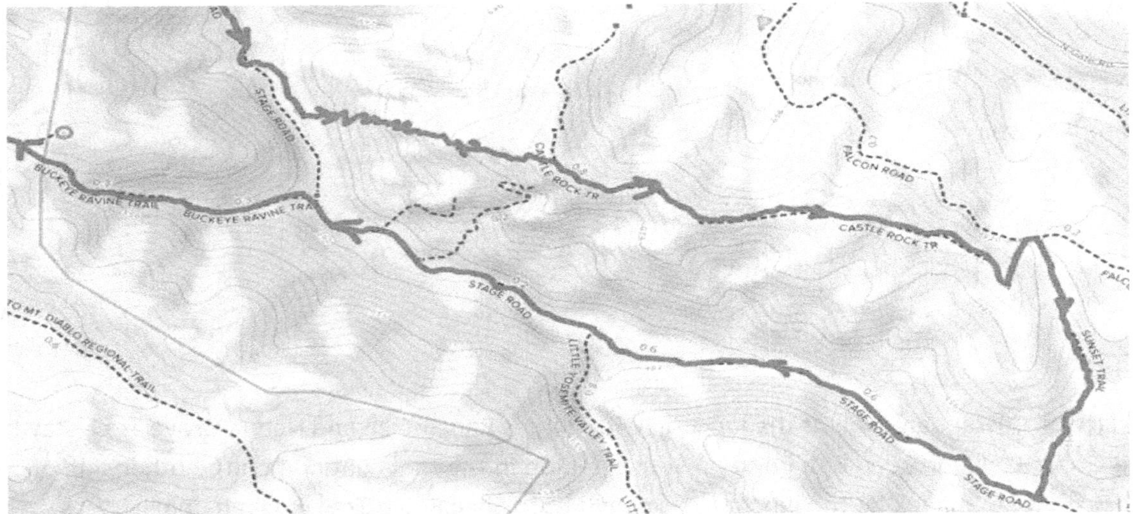

So enjoy the view and penguin falcons while you can. When you are ready to leave, look for Castle Rock Trail which leads you through thick bush and to the junction with Falcon Road and Sunset Trail. Turn right onto Sunset Trail. Then turn right on Stage Road. At junction with Buckeye Ravine Trail, turn left onto BRT to climb out of Pine Canyon. At the junction with Briones to Mt Diablo Regional Trail, turn left onto Briones to Mt Diablo Regional Trail. But you only stay there very briefly. Very soon, you stay right to get onto Stonegate Trail. After mere 0.1 miles, you need to get on Borges Ranch Trail. At the junction with Foothill Trail, you leave Borges Ranch Trail and get onto Foothill Trail by staying left. After 0.3 miles on Foothill Trail, make right turn onto Sugarloaf-Shell Ridge Trail. Stay right on the next two junctions. Then turn sharply left to stay on Sugarloaf-Shell Ridge Trail.

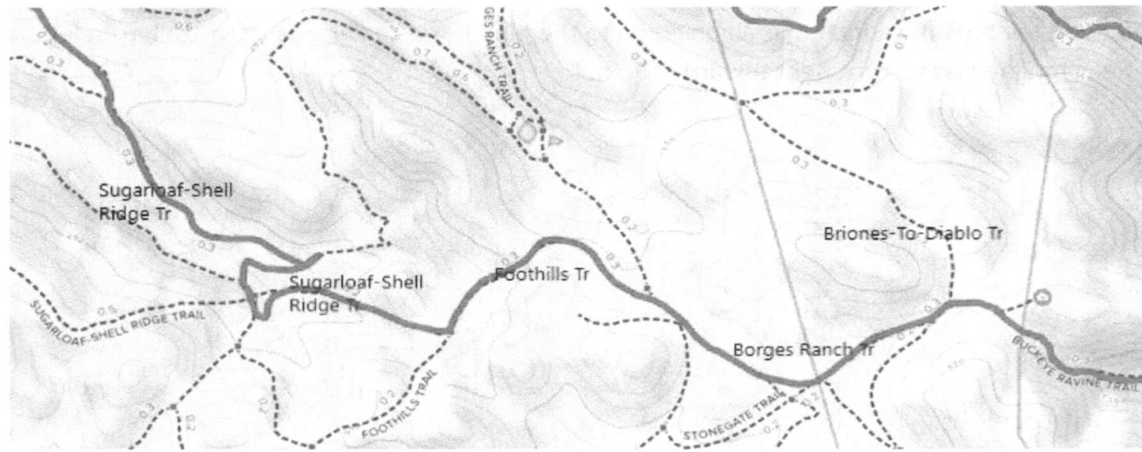

When it finally ends at Briones to Mt Diablo Regional Trail, turn left. Next turn left onto Indian Creek Trail. At the junction with Fossil Hill Trail, you turn left onto Fossil Hill Trail.

Next turn left onto Summit Ridge Trail. Along Summit Ridge Trail, you can easily spot many shell fossils. Summit Ridge Trail ends at Kovar Trail. Turn left on Kovar Trail which brings you back to Homestead Park. Below is the hike overview:

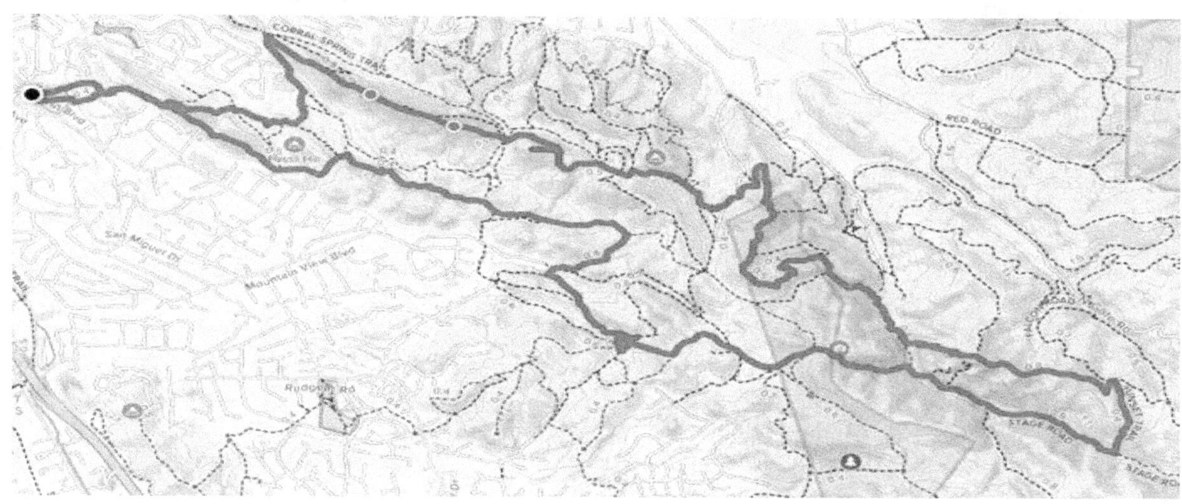

Hike Overview

Distance=29.2 miles

Elevation=6818 feet

Parking: Livorna Staging Area in Alamo

Shaded: No

Trail Map:

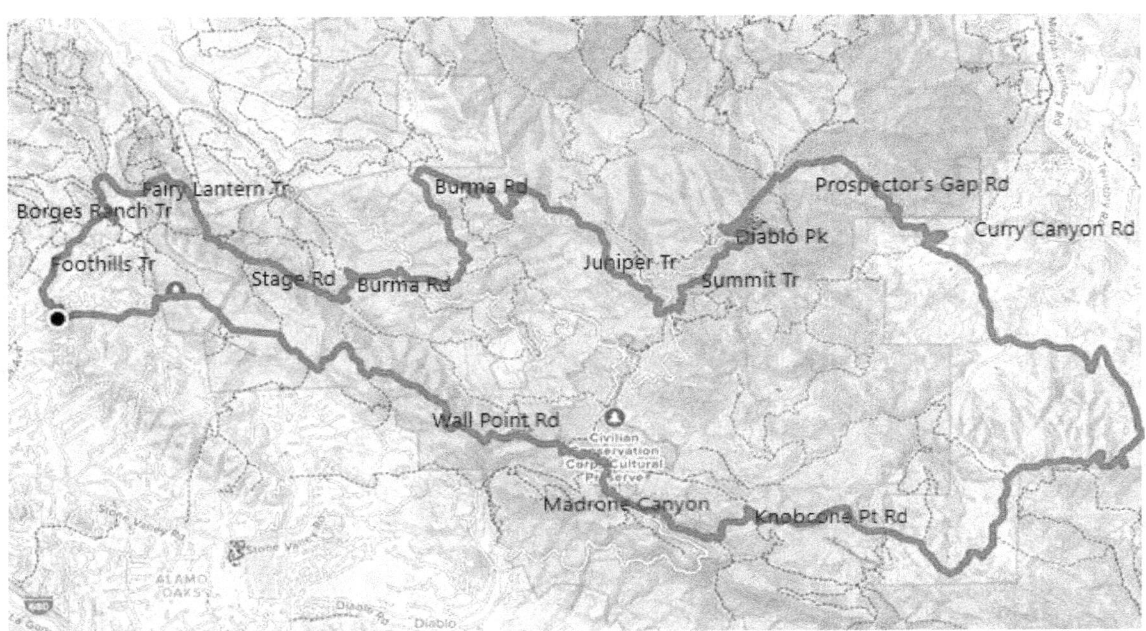

You park your car at the Livorna Stage area parking, and go straight ahead on Alamo Trail. Turn right on Hanging Valley Trail. 0.4 miles later, you turn right on Briones-Mt. Diablo Regional Trail. Briones-Mt. Diablo Regional Trail ends at Wall Point Trail. Turn left on Wall Point Trail and continue to walk on this fire road until you reach Rock City.

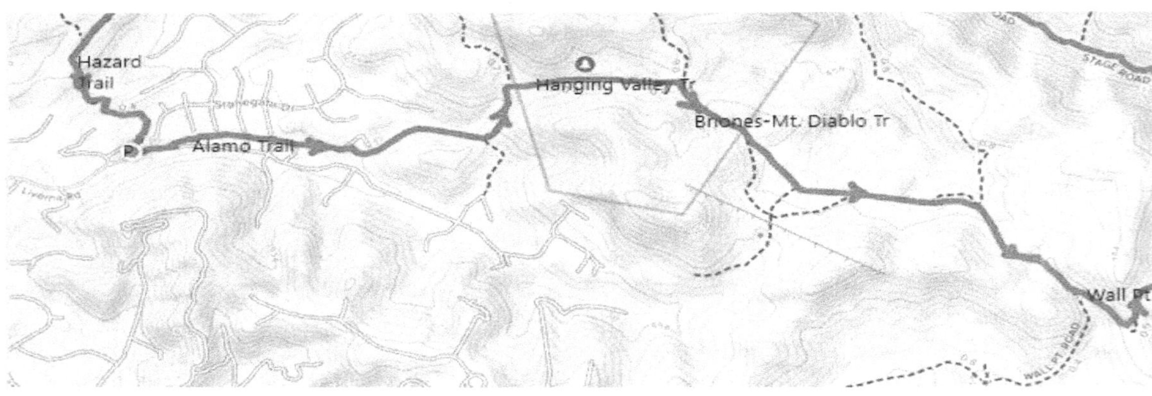

Turn right on Rock City Trail, walk across Rock City camp sites until you reach Trail Through Time (It is also called Madrone Canyon Trail). Then Turn left on Devil's Slide Trail for 0.5 miles.

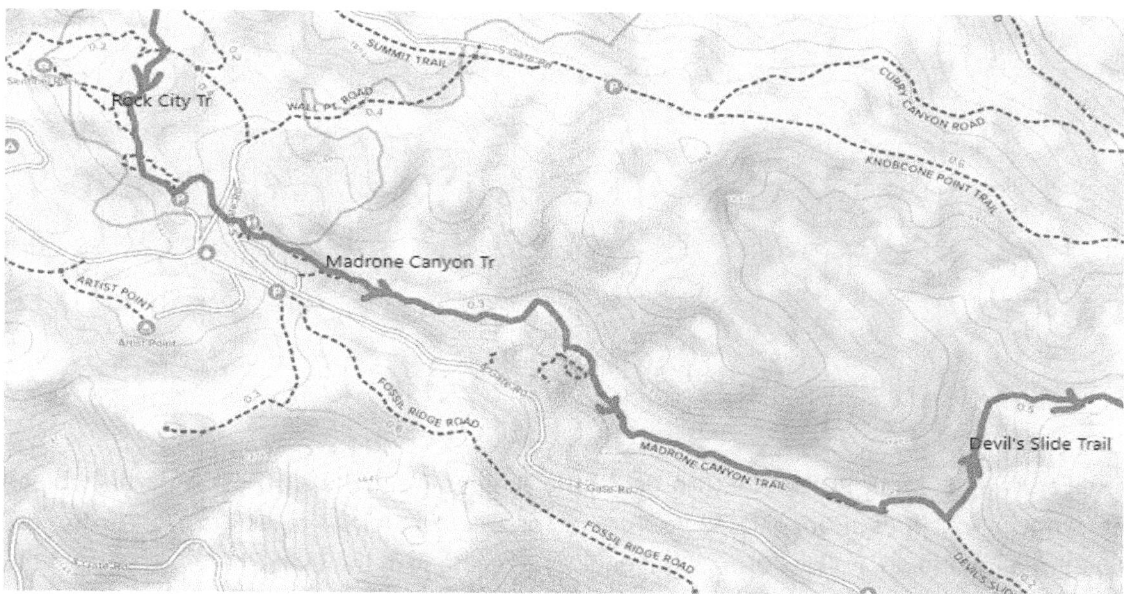

Turn left on Knobcone Point Road. Stay on Knobcone Point Road for 1.2 miles. You reach Save Mount Diablo property boundary. The property is closed by fence and locked gate. This part of the hike is NOT in the state park and there are no trail marks. Please follow the map and stay on indicated trails:

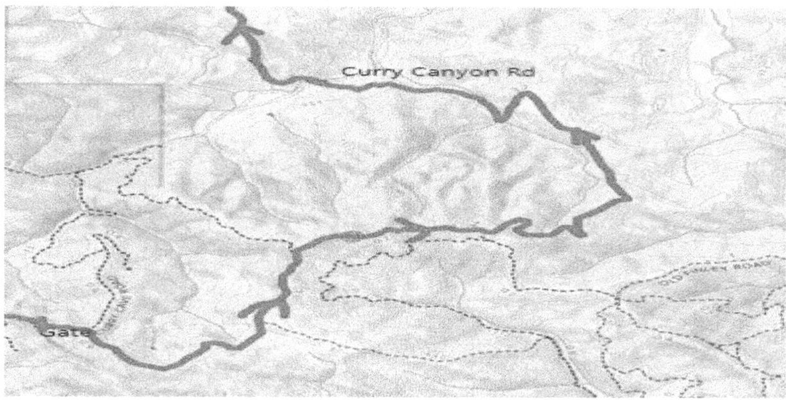

Climb over the fence and continue on the main road until you exit Save Mount Diablo property. When you reach the junction with Curry Canyon Road, you cross Curry Canyon Road and continue on an unmarked trail toward North Peak until you reach the junction with Rhine Canyon Road. Turn right and hike toward Prospector's Gap Road. Turn left on Prospector's Gap Road. 2.5 miles late, you reach Prospector's gap. Here is a six-way junction. Take on the 2nd trail on your left and it ends at Mary Bowerman Loop. Turn left and walk another 0.4 miles, you will see another unmarked trail leading directly to the summit museum.After you take much needed rest at the 3849 feet summit, you go down by taking the Summit Trail.

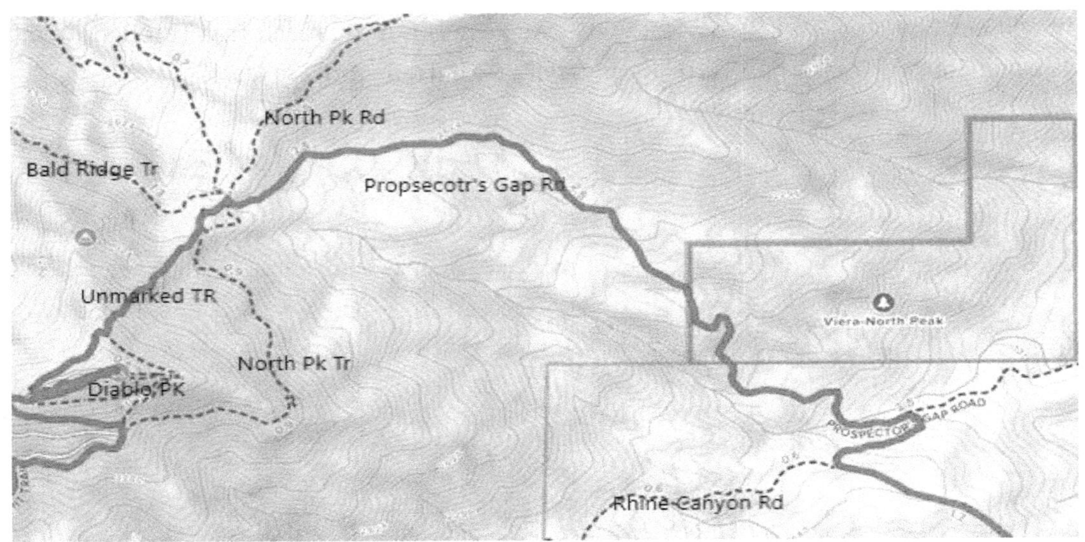

Just after crossing Summit Road, you turn right onto Juniper Trail (The signpost is partially blocked by bushes). Juniper Trail ends at Deer Flat Road. Turn left on Deer Flat for 0.4 miles. Turn left on Burma Road. Stay on Burma for about 6 miles. Burma Road ends at Stage Road in the Pine Canyon. Turn right on Stage Road. Continue on Stage Road. After you exit Mt. Diablo State Park gate, watch for Buckeye Ravine Trail on your left. Turn left when you see it. After you climb up the hill, you are going to turn right on Briones-Mt. Diablo Regional Trail. Walk just 0.3 miles before you turn left onto Borges Ranch Trail. After passing twin ponds 0.2 miles, turn right onto Foothills Trail. Finally turn left on Hazard Trail and walk 0.4 miles. You are back where you start.

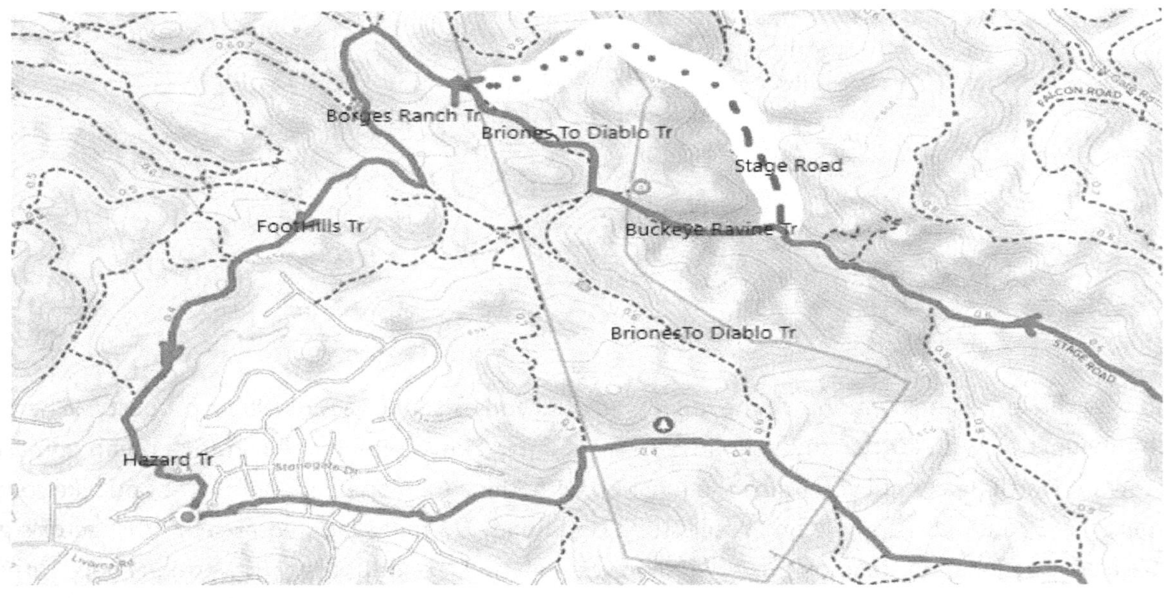

Hike Overview

Distance=24.4 miles

Elevation gain=6713 feet

Parking: roadside of Mt Diablo Scenic Blvd in Danville

Shaded: 10%

Trail Map:

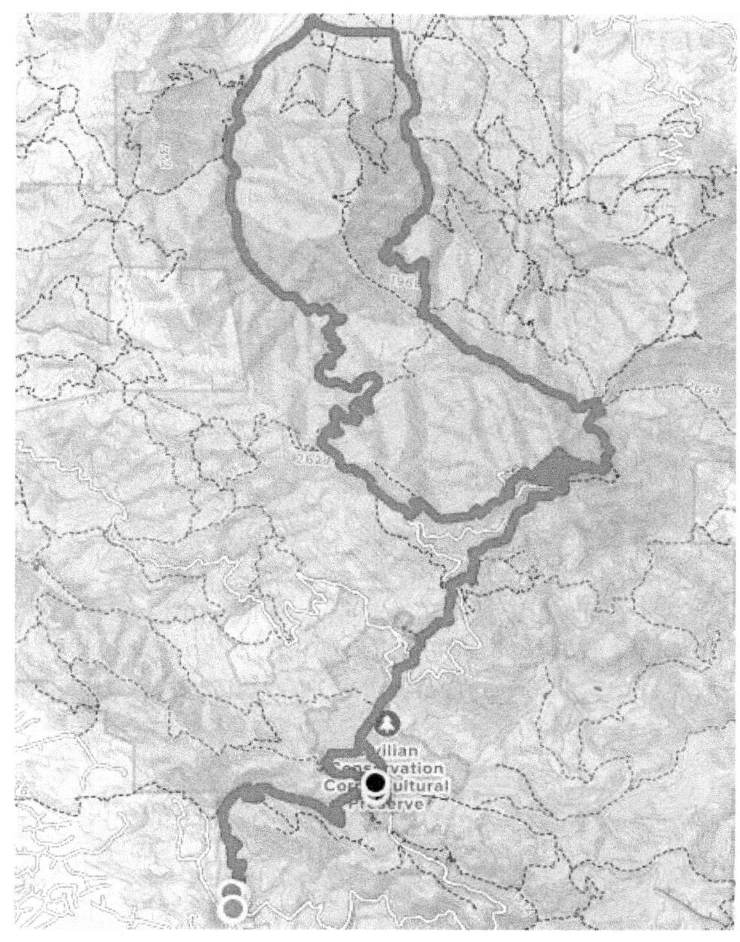

Detail Direction

There are no parking spaces at the trail head. You can park your car at Athenian School on weekends or park wherever you can find on the side of Mt Diablo Scenic Blvd. Start from Mt Diablo Scenic Blvd. The road ends at the start of South Gate Rd. The trail head of Summit Trail is on your left and there is a large sign there. Stay on the trail for 6 miles to get the summit of Diablo. You have the best view of east bay from the peak. After visit the museum at the Summit, access a user trail next to the bathroom and go east.

Next turn left on Mary Bowerman Trail Loop. When the trail crosses the drive way, leave the trail and go to the lower summit parking lot. Juniper Trail starts at the west side of the parking lot. Take Juniper Trail to descend.

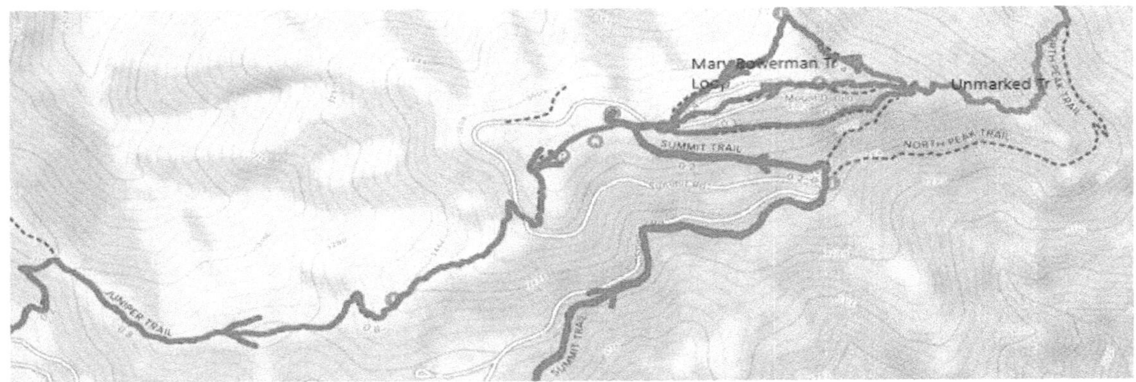

Turn right on Deer Flat Road for 0.4 miles. Turn right again onto Meridian Ridge Road. Turn left onto Mitchell Canyon Road for 3.0 miles.

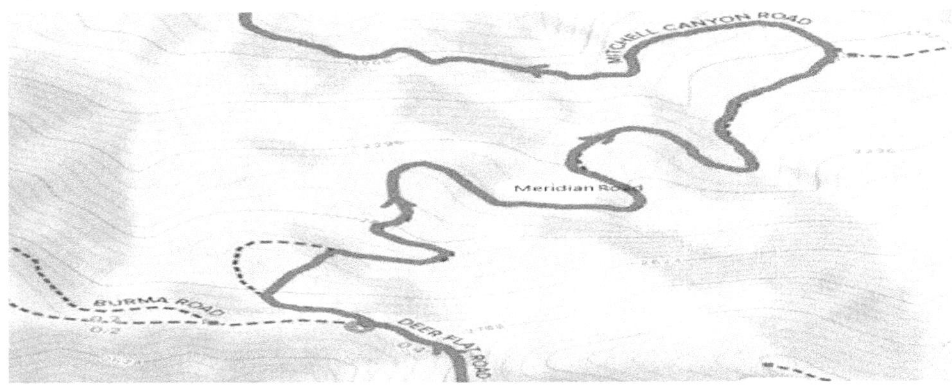

Slightly turn right onto Bruce Lee Trail for 0.1 miles. Then turn right onto Murchio Road. Half mile later we turn right to back on Bruce Lee Trail. Bruce Lee Trail ends at Back Creek Trail. Turn right on Back Creek Trail.

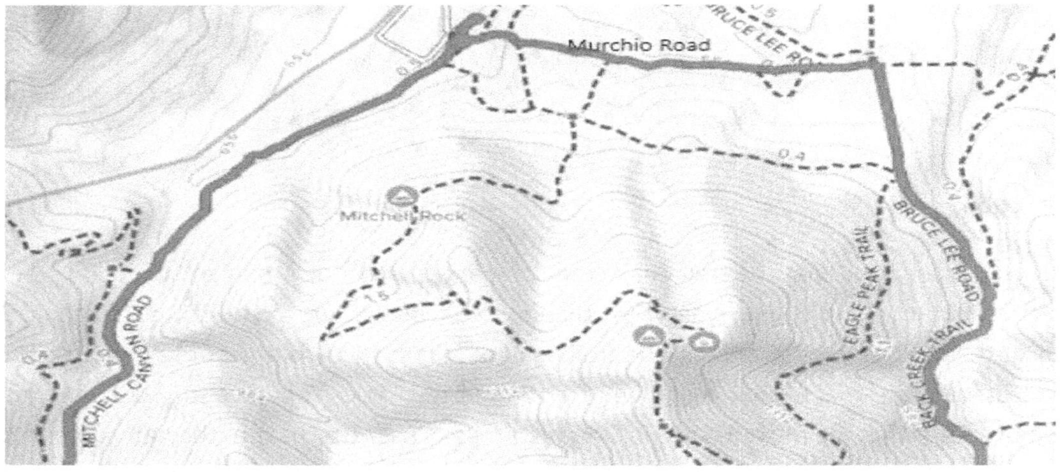

Back Creek Trail ends at Murchio Gap where you have 5-way junction. Take the Bald Ridge Trail all the way to its end at Prospector's Gap. Turn to 2nd right trail-the North Peak Trail. Follow North Peak Trail until you meet a narrow, unmarked trail on the right. Turn right on it and it leads you to a high rock called Devils Pulpit. Continue climbing uphill and then turn left on Mary Bowerman Trail Loop.

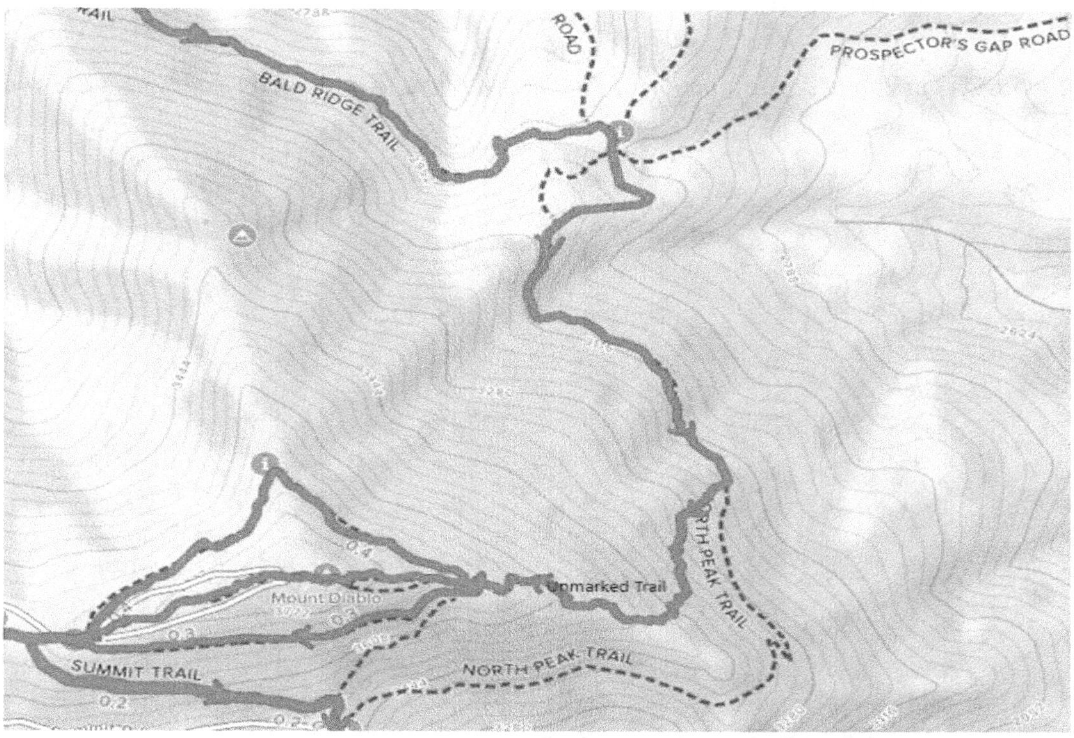

Finally turn left on Summit Trail. Summit Trail goes all the way to its end at the trail head in Danville.

Hike Overview

Distance = 10.9 miles

Elevation = 3406 feet

Parking: roadside parking near the junction of Camille Avenue and Ironwood Place (GPS 37.83446, -122.02584)

Shaded: 20%

Trail Map:

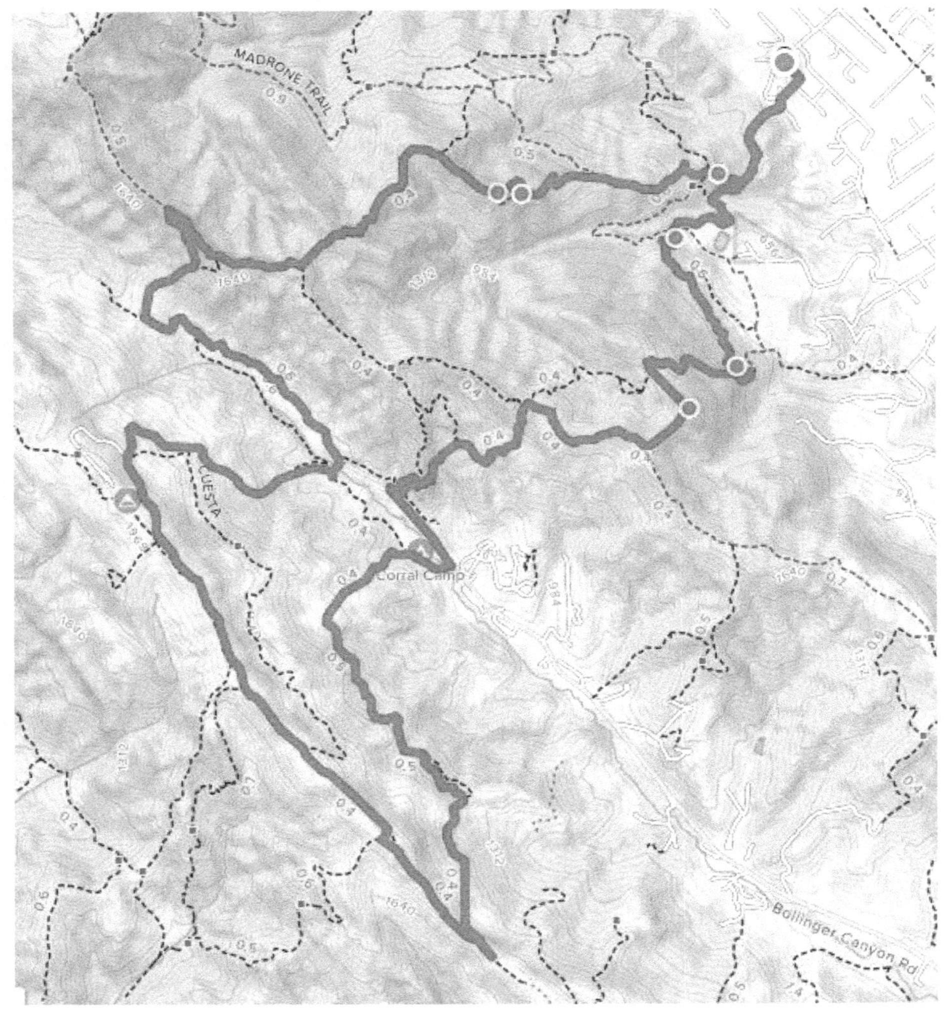

Park your car on the side of Camille Avenue and walk toward the end of the road. Only a few yards away, you will find a trail on your left side. Follow the trail to the hills for 0.3 miles and stay right for 0.1 miles and then turn slightly right onto Madrone Trail for 0.3 miles. Next you stay left to tackle on Corduroy Hills

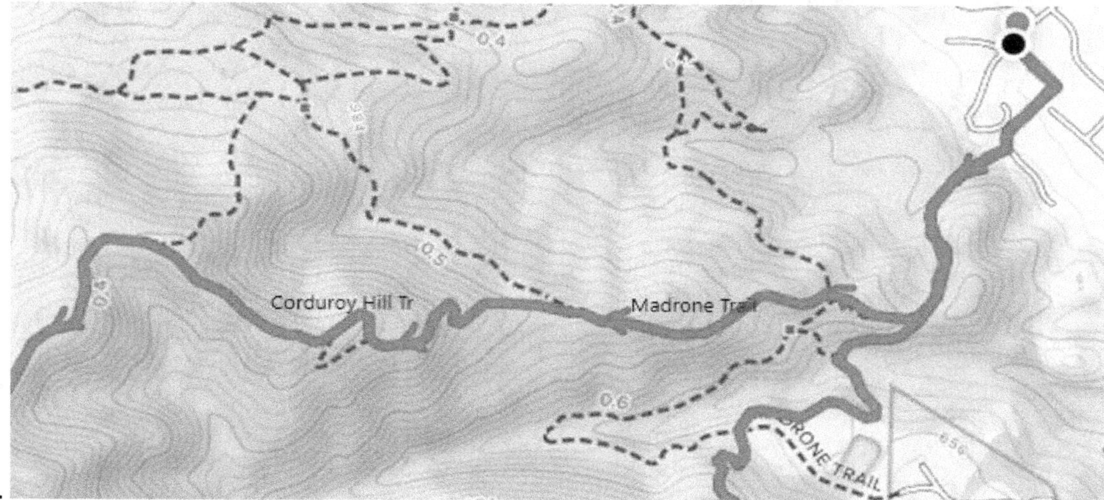

Trail.

At the junction with Las Trampas Ridge Trail, you turn left. Then turn right after 0.3 miles to get on Chamise Trail. At bottom of the other side of the canyon, turn right again onto Bollinger Creek Trail. Next at the Junction with Bollinger Canyon Road, turn left and cross the road. Go up the pave road and take Rocky Ridge Shortcut Trail on your left to climb up Rocky Ridge. Turn left on Rocky Ridge View Trail for 0.7 miles. Stay left at the junction with Ridge View Trail.

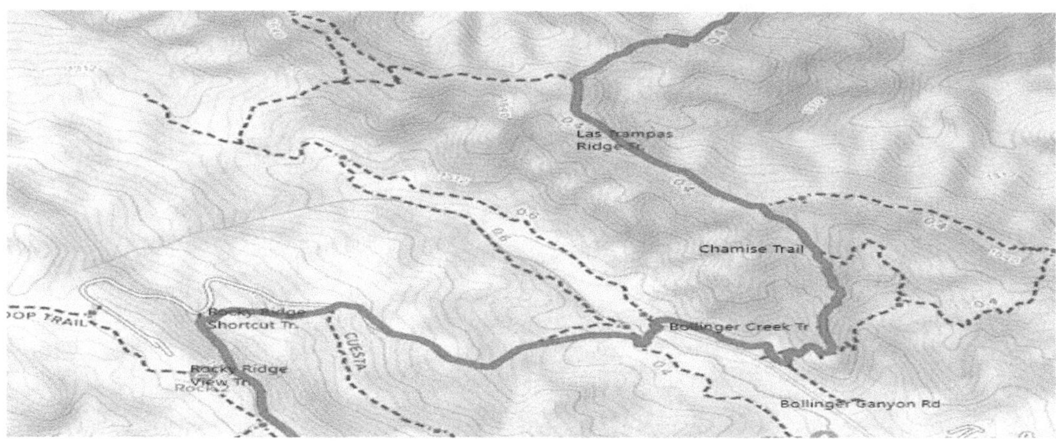

Next turn left onto Elderberry Trail. Stay on Elderberry Trail all the way and cross Corral Camp and turn right onto Bollinger Canyon Road. Look for Water Tank Trail on your left. Next you make two left turns.

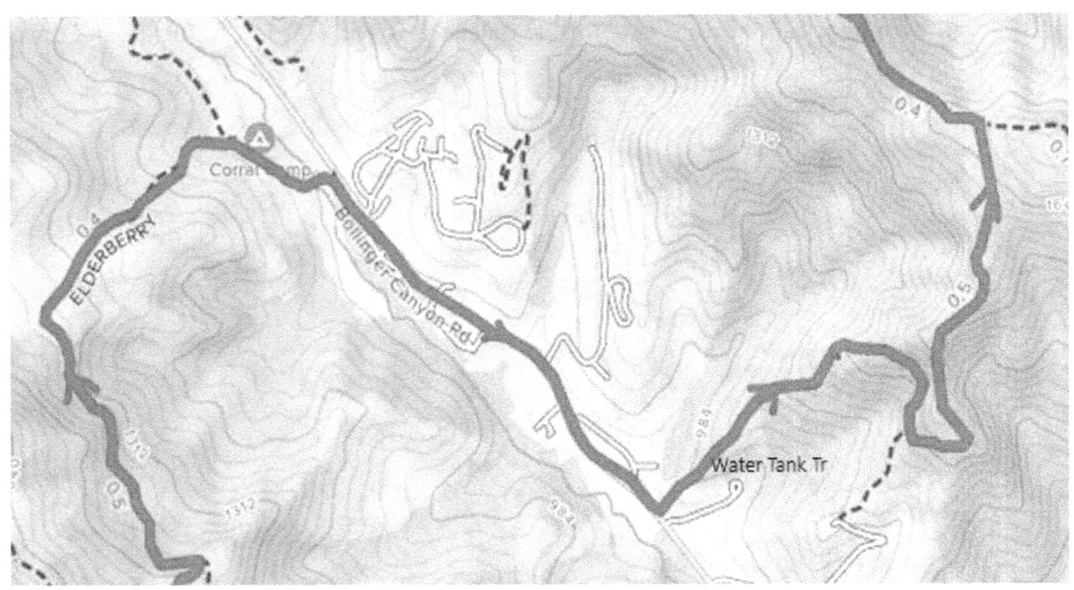

At the junction with Las Trampas Ridge Trail, turn left onto LTRT for 0.4 miles. At the junction with Del Amigo, turn right onto Del Amigo. Follow Del Amigo Trail downhill until the junction with Virgil Williams Trail. Turn left onto VWT. Stay on VWT until it ends at the main fire road near the gate when you turn right for Madrone Trail earlier. Turn right on the fire road and follow it to Camille Ave and get back to your car.

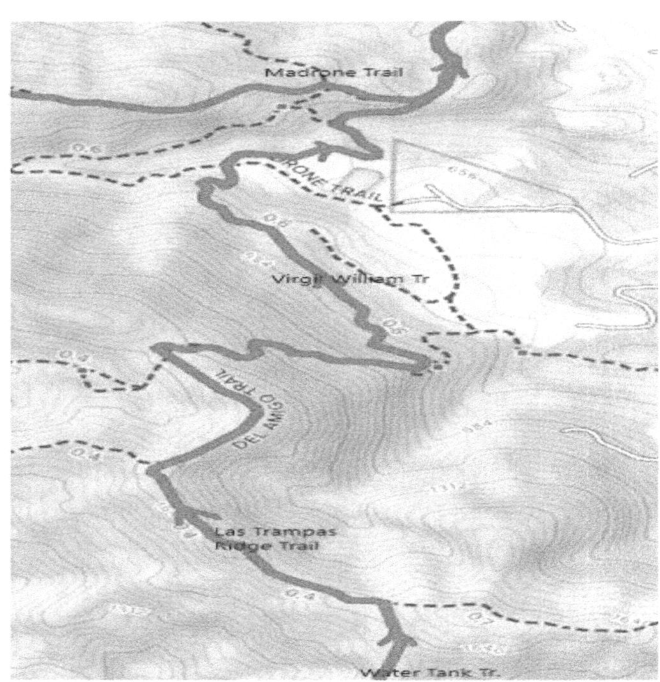

Hike Overview

Distance=20.7 miles

Elevation gain=4275 feet

Parking: Rancho Laguna Park in Moraga

Shaded: No

Trail Map

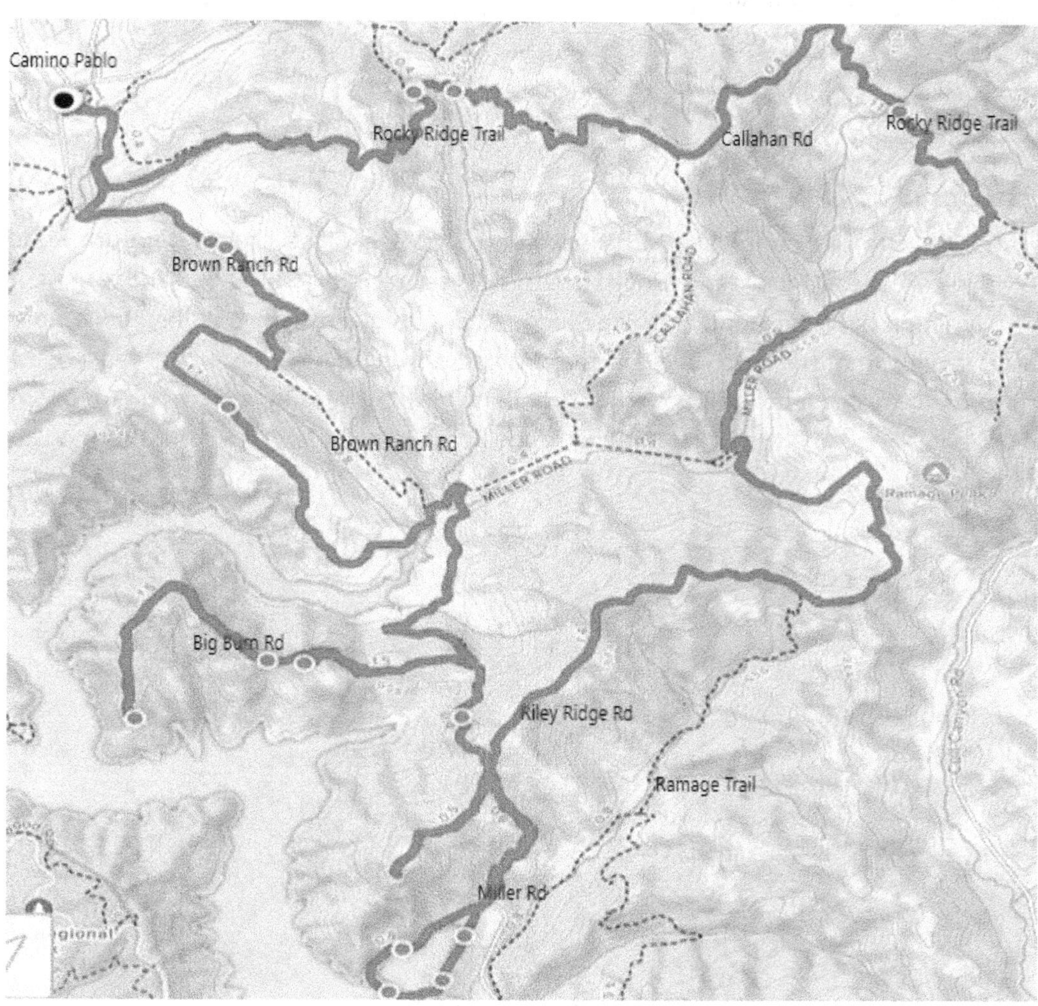

Detail Direction

The loop starts from Rancho Laguna Park in Moraga, CA 94556. Take Rancho Laguna Footpath for 0.2 miles. Then keep right on Rancho Laguna Hiking Trail for 0.3 miles. At the junction with Rocky Ridge Trail, keep right to stay on Rancho Laguna Hiking Trail for another 0.1 miles. Turn left on Brown Ranch Road.

Stay on Brown Ranch Road for 1.1 miles before you turn right onto an unnamed road for 1.7 miles. Then you rejoin Brown Ranch Road for 0.2 miles. Turn right on Miller Road.

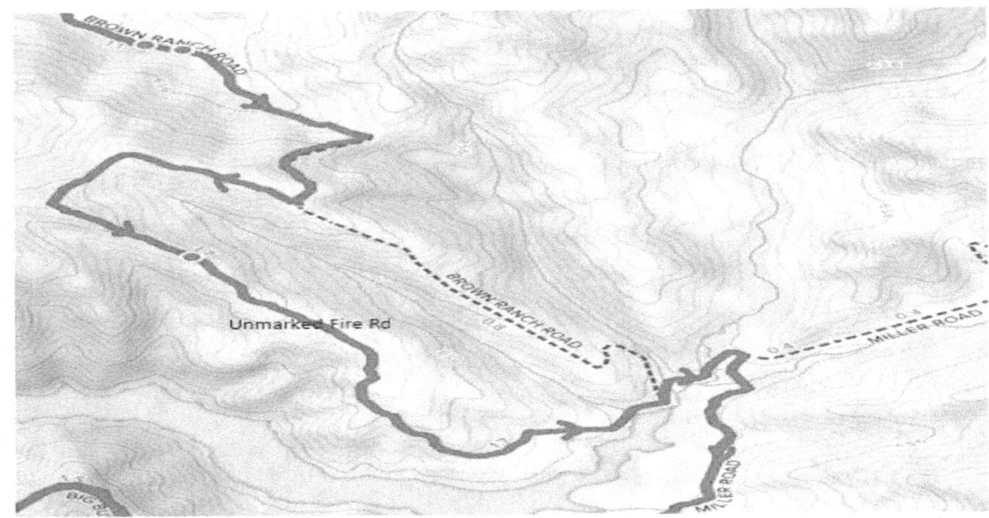

One mile late you turn right onto Big Burn Road for 1.5 miles. At the end of Big Burn Road, you are rewarded with nice view of Upper San Leandro Reservoir. Back track Big Burn Road and turn right on Miller Road. At the junction of Miller Road and Riley Ridge Road, you turn right on Riley Ridge Road to go to another vista at the end of the road. Back track again and turn right on Miller Road. Walk on Miller Road (for 0.4 miles) until you see a beautiful overflow pond. Follow the trail along the pond for 0.9 miles. Then back track on Miller Road and turn right on Riley Ridge Road.

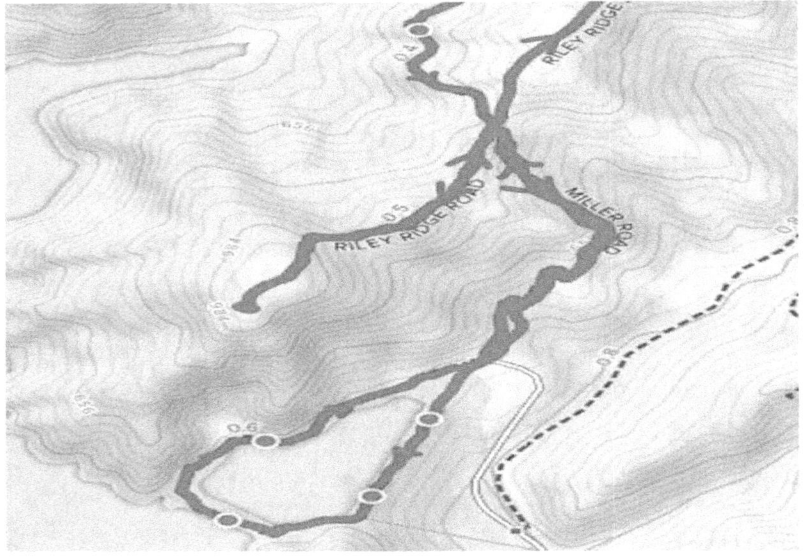

Stay on Riley Ridge Road for 2.5 miles before you turn right on Miller Road. At the junction with Rocky Ridge Trail, you turn left onto Rocky Ridge Trail for 1.1 miles. Then turn left again on Callahan Road. At the next junction, you stay right to back onto Rocky Ridge Trail. Stay on RRT for 2.6 miles. Then turn right on Rancho Laguna Hiking Trail which leads you back to Rancho Laguna Park.

Hike Overview

Distance=11.3 miles

Elevation gain=2283 feet

Parking: Lafayette Ridge Staging Area

Shaded: 10%

Trail Map:

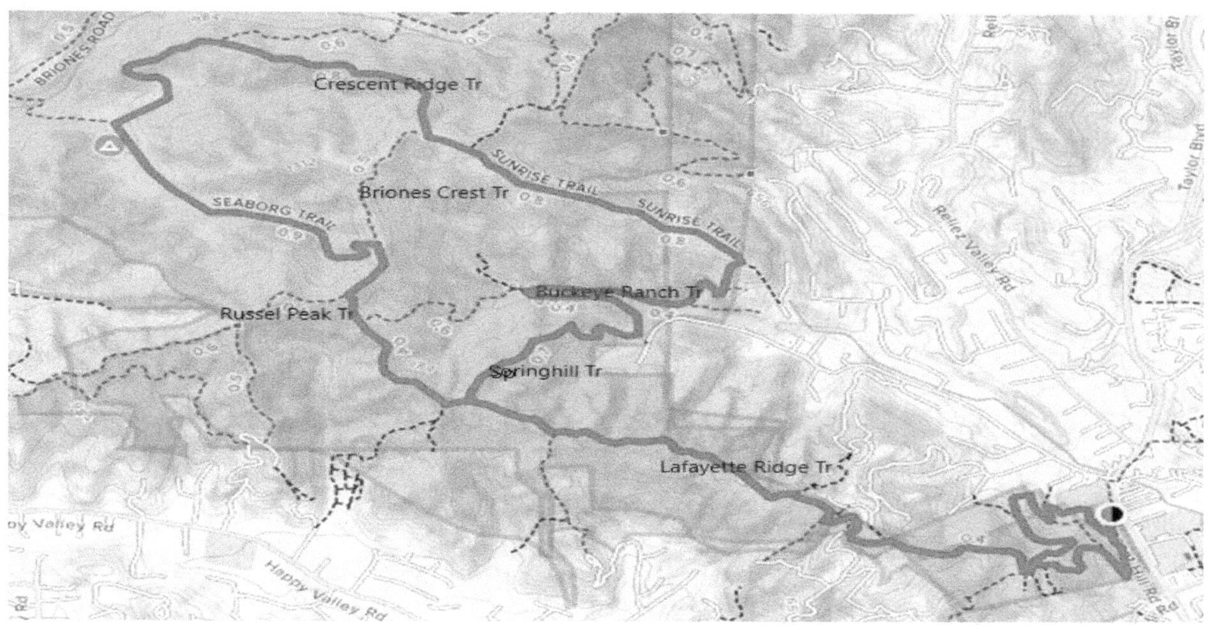

Detail Direction

You expect this is an easy hike. But it is not. Although there is no high peak to climb, there are many ups and downs. First, you climb up Lafayette Ridge Trail for 2.7 miles (sometimes you see multiple trails have the name of Lafayette Ridge Trail. As long as you stay on the main trail, you are OK). Then turn right on Springhill trail at the junction with Springhill Trail to go down the valley floor. At next junction in the bottom of the valley, you turn left on Buckeye Ranch Trail for 0.5 miles. As you approach the junction of Buckeye Ranch Trail with Sunrise Trail, look out the signpost. Make a sharp right at the signpost. Don't use an unmarked trail that turns right because you will see a locked gate at the other end. The first half miles of Sunrise Trail is shaded and flat. Then Sunrise Trail rises steadily all the way to the ridge of Briones. At the junction with Briones Crest Trail, you turn left onto Briones Crest Trail. 0.1 mile late, you turn right on Crescent Ridge Trail. Stay on this trail for 1.4 miles. Then you turn left on Seaborg Trail. Seaborg Trail ends at the junction with Briones Crest Trail. Turn right on Briones Crest Trail. At the next junction, Turn left on Lafayette Ridge Trail. Finally follow LRT all the way to your car.

Hike Overvie

Distance=11.4 miles

Elevation gain=2697 feet

Parking: Reliez Valley Staging Area in Lafayette

Shaded: 40%

Trail Map:

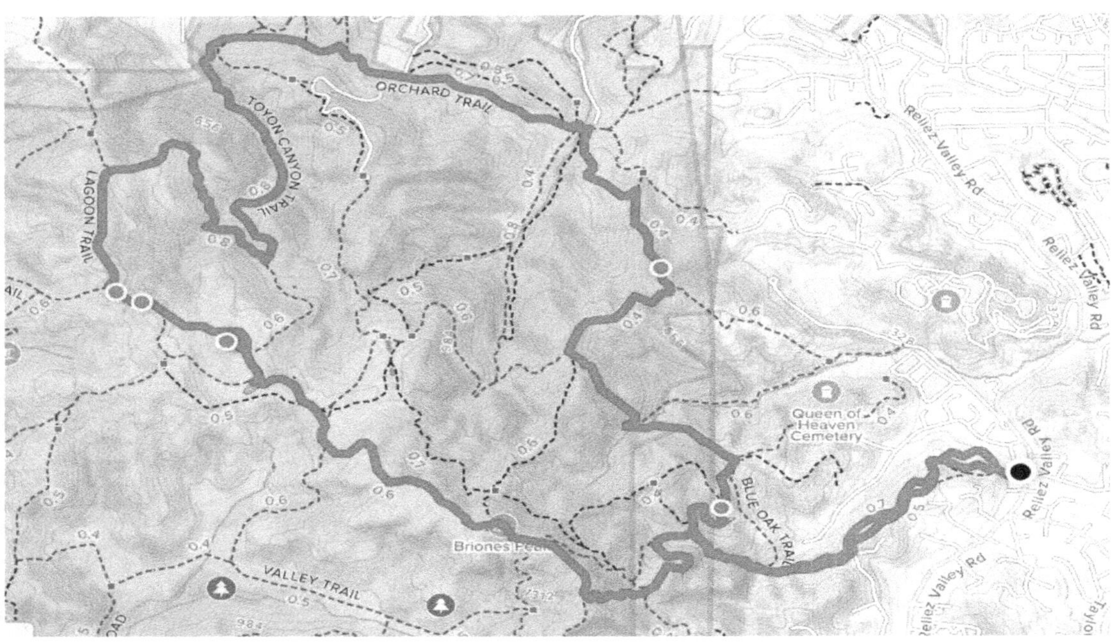

Detail Direction

You start the hike from Blue Oak Trail. One mile late you come a junction: on your right is the Blue Oak Trial, and you go straight by taking Blue Oak Shortcut. 0.2 mile later, you turn right onto Spengler Trail.

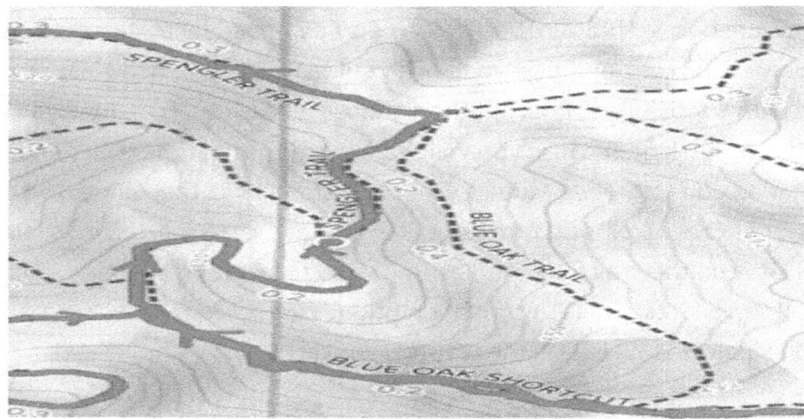

Stay on Spengler Trail on next junction by turning left. On the junction with Diablo View Trail, you turn right on Diablo View Trail. Stay on Diablo View until you reach Alhambra Creek. At this junction, take Orchard Trail for 1.1 miles. At the junction with Pine Tree Trail and Toyon Canyon Trail, you take the later. 0.8 miles late, you turn right on Lagoon Trail. Lagoon Trail ends at Briones Crest Trail.

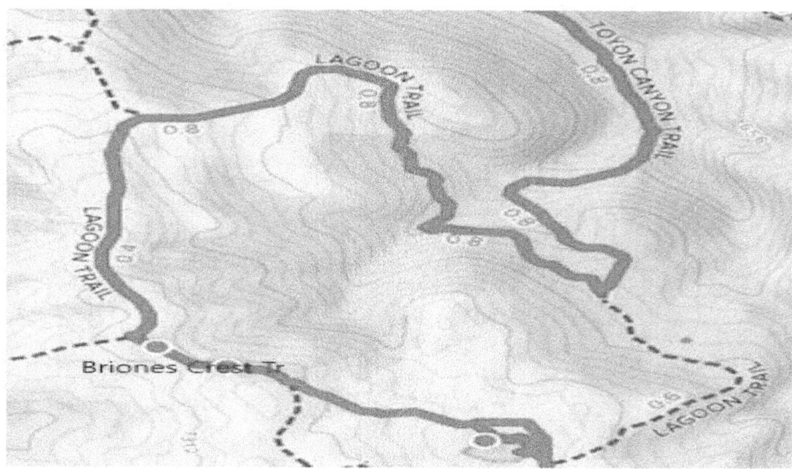

Turn left on Briones Crest Trail for 0.3 miles, you will see an unmarked trail on your left. Take this trail until you see Sindicich Lagoon 1. This beautiful lagoon seems so out of place in summer and autumn since everything else around are so try and brown. Continue the use trail until you hit Lagoon Trail. Turn right on Lagoon Trail. It soon brings you back to Briones Crest Trail. Right in front of you, Sindicich Lagoon 2 appears. After snap a picture or two, continue south on Briones Crest Trail until next junction with Briones Road. Stay on Briones Crest Trail for another 0.6 miles until you see a use trail on your left. This unmarked trail will take you to the Briones Peak.

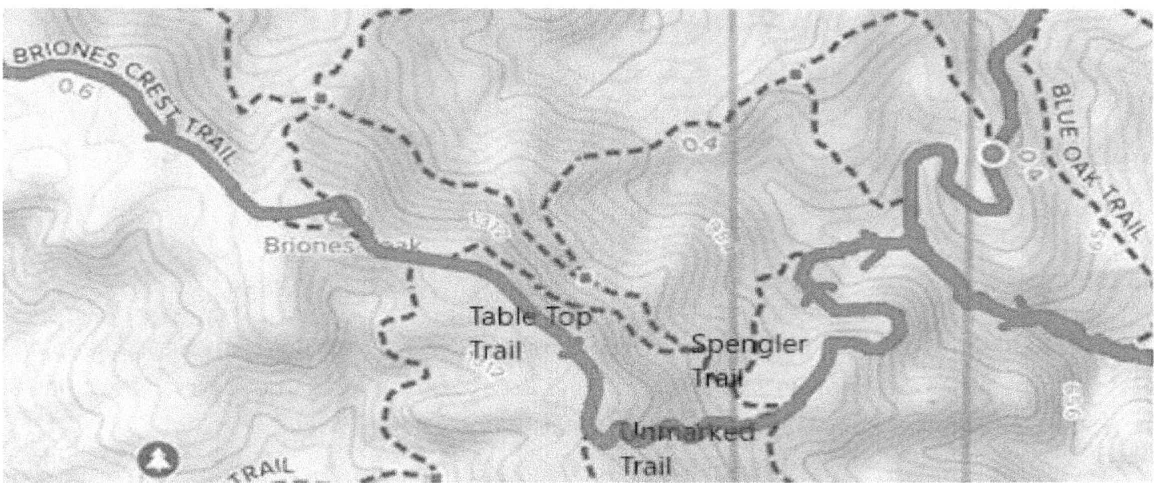

After reaching the peak, you go back Briones Crest Trail and continue onto Table Top Trail. There is a bench on Table Top where you can enjoy the 360 degree views. Continue south on the ridge for another 0.2 miles, you will see a steep use trail on your left. Take this trail downhill until you come across Spengler Trail for the second time. Turn right on Spengler Trail for 0.1 miles before you turn right on Blue Oak Shortcut. Stay right on Blue Oak trail that brings you back to your car.

Hike Overview

Distance=13.5 miles

Elevation gain=2037 feet

Parking: Bear Creek Staging Area

Shaded: No

Trail Map:

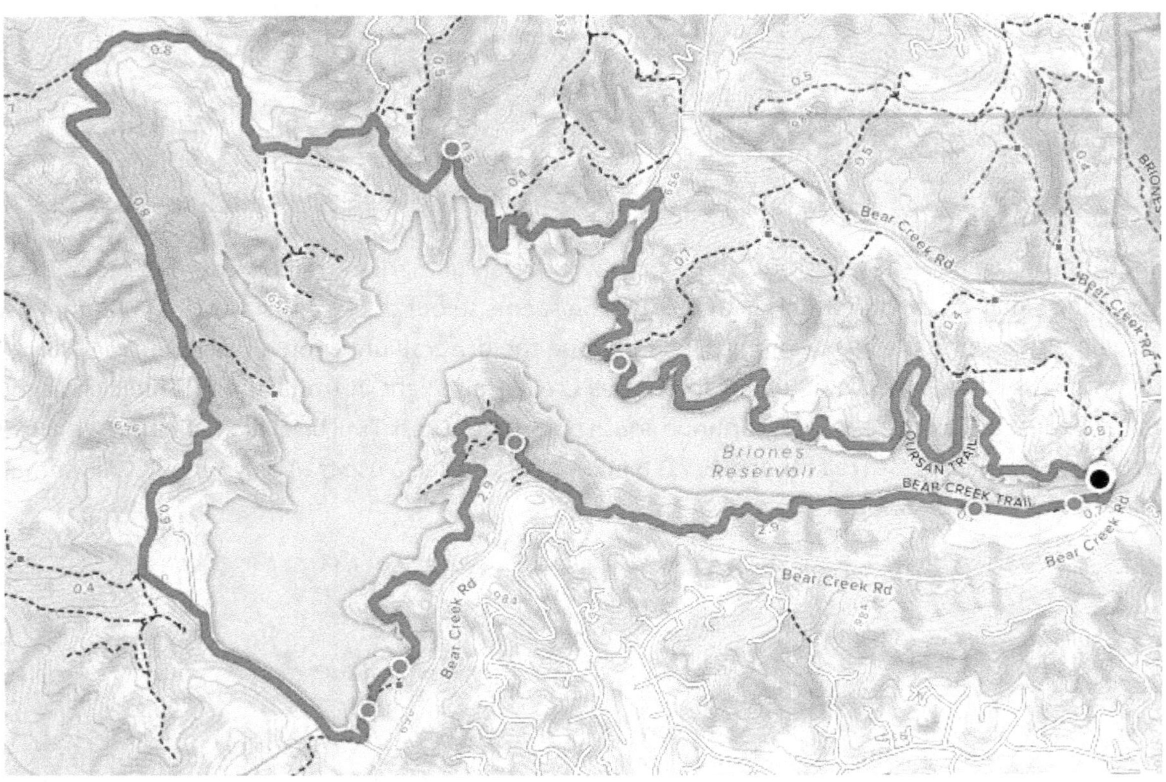

Detail Direction

The route is easy to follow: you basically just need following trails around the reservoir and keeping it on your left. I started the hike from Oursan Trail near Bear Creek Staging Area. Then Oursan becomes Bear Creek Trail which parallels Bear Creek Road. Then follow BCT back to parking.

Hike Overview

Distance=17.4 miles

Elevation gain=3150 feet

Parking: Old Tunnel Staging Area in Orinda

Shaded: 70%

Trail Map:

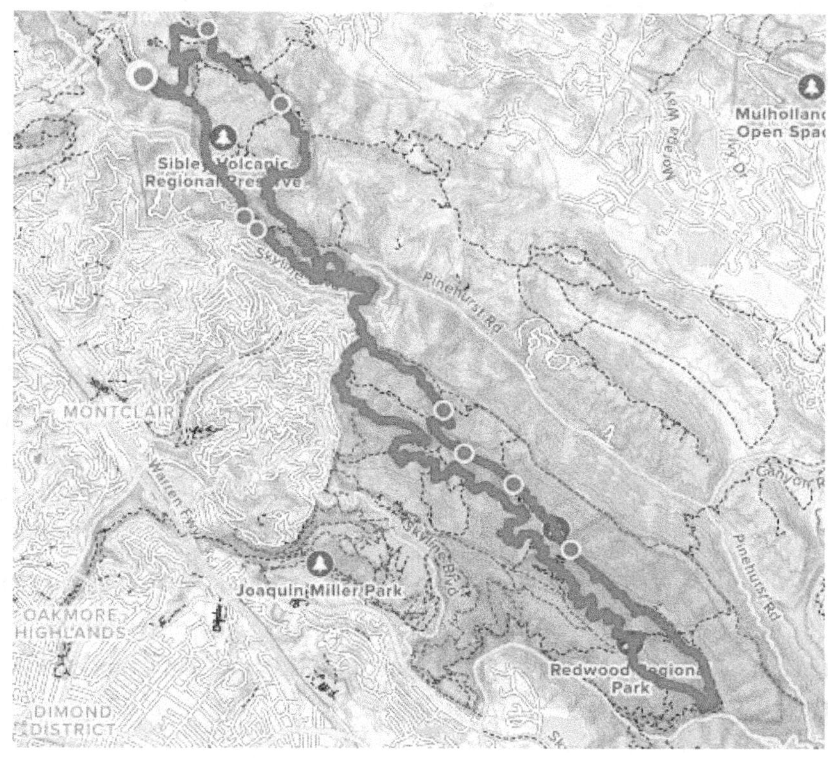

Detail Direction

Start the hike from the parking lot by taking the paved Quarry Road toward Sibley Volcanic Preserve. You turn left on the second bent of the Quarry Road to leave the pavement. There is a signpost that says "To Pond". After about 0.1 miles you will see Pond Trail on your left. But don't turn left here since the bushes are overgrown unless you really want to see the tiny pond. Stay on the trail to go uphills. You need to get onto Volcanic Trail which is 1.1 miles from the trailhead. There are benches and interpete panels along Volcanic Trail. There are multiple ways to get on Volcanic Trail. The way I hiked many times is highlighted below:

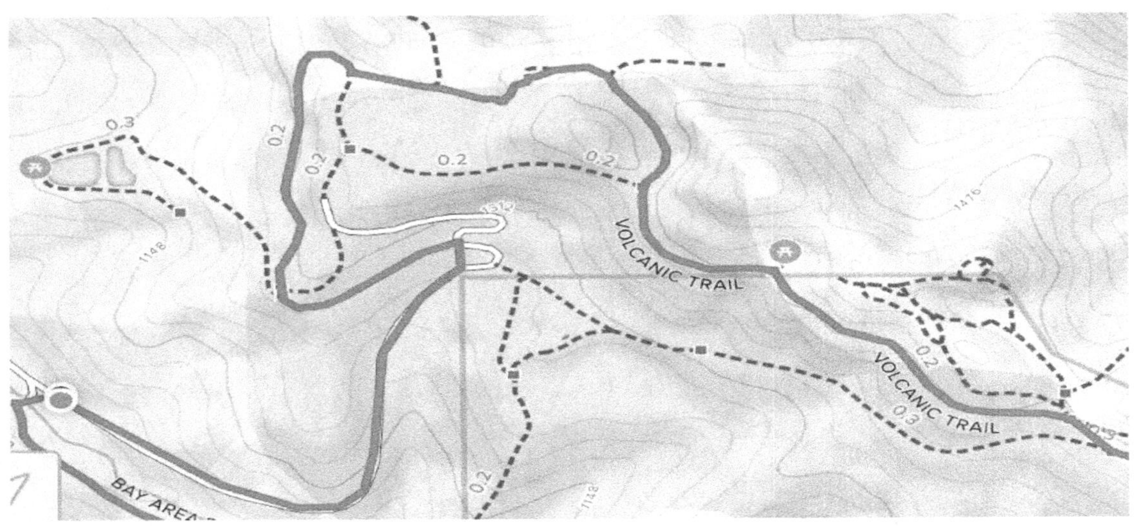

Volcanic Trail ends at Round Top Loop Trail. Turn left onto Round Top Trail:

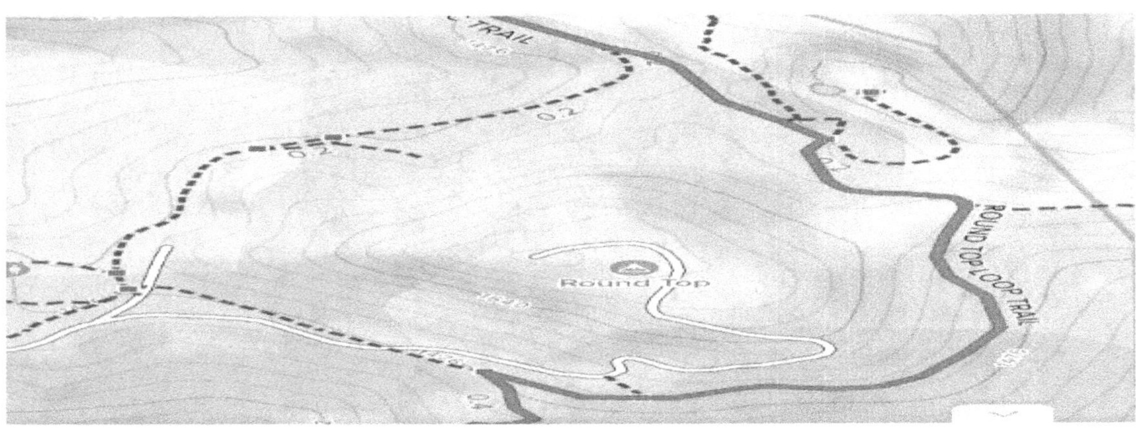

Stay on RTLT for 0.5 miles before taking sharp left onto Bay Area Ridge Trail(BART). BART descends quickly into a valley. Soon after crossing San Leandro Creek, take sharp right to stay on BART. At the next few junctions, keep left to stay on BART. After crossing Pinehurst Rd, and you climb over a hill and turn right at the junction with East Ridge Trail:

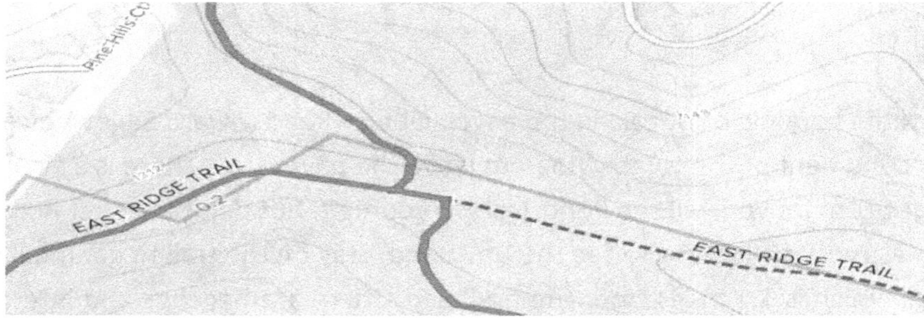

East Ridge Trail ends at Skyline Gate Staging Area. After the Skyline Gate the trail becomes West Ridge Trail. Stay 0.6 miles on West Ridge Trail before turn left on French Trail. Stay on French Trail for 4 miles. At the junction of French Trail with Orchard Trail, turn right onto Orchard Trail for 0.2 miles. Orchard Trail ends at West Ridge Trail. Turn left on West Ridge Trail for one mile. West Ridge Trail ends at Bridle Trail. Turn left on Bridle Trail for 1.2 miles. When Bridle Trail ends, continue on Stream Trail.

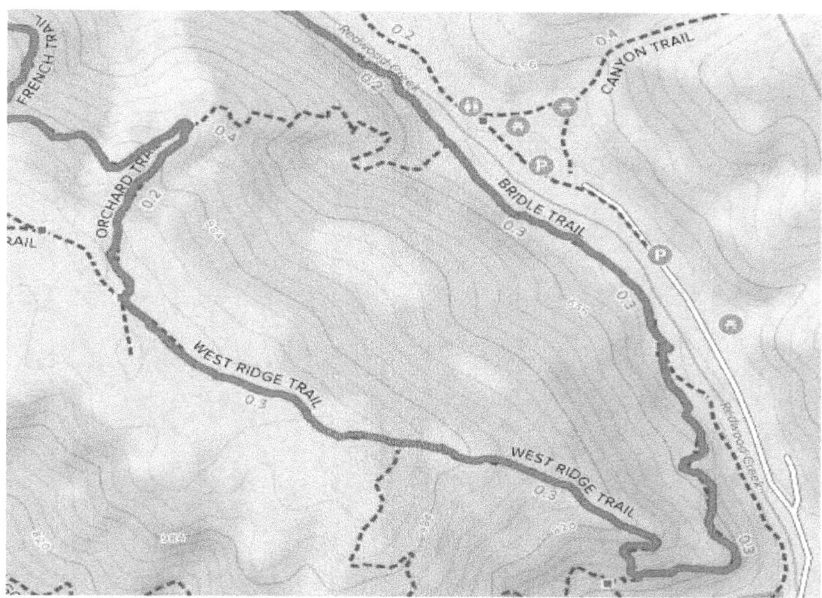

Stay on Stream Trail for 1.3 miles until you come to the junction with Eucalyptus Trail. Now turn right onto Eucalyptus Trail for 0.2 miles. At the next junction stay left to go on Philips Loop trail which ends at BART. Follow BART back to Huckleberry Reserve. At the first junction with Huckleberry Loop Trail, stay left to get on Upper Huckleberry Loop Trail. Stay on Upper Huckleberry Loop Trail and make no left or right turns until you arrive Huckleberry Preserve Staging Area parking lot at Winding Way. Continue along the trail parallels to Skyline Blvd until you arrive Sibley Volcanic Preserve main parking. Cross the parking and turn left on Bay Area Redge Trail on your left. Hike down the trail for 0.9 miles to go back to your car.

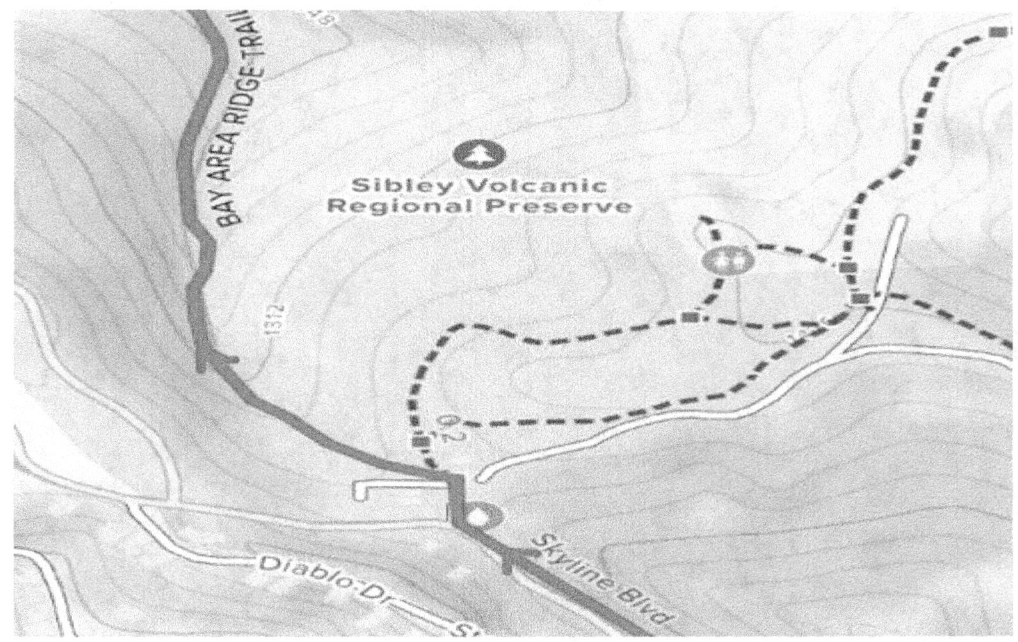

Hike Overview

Distance=13.5 miles

Elevation gain= 2943 feet

Parking: Old Tunnel Staging Area in Orinda

Shaded: 60%

Trail Map:

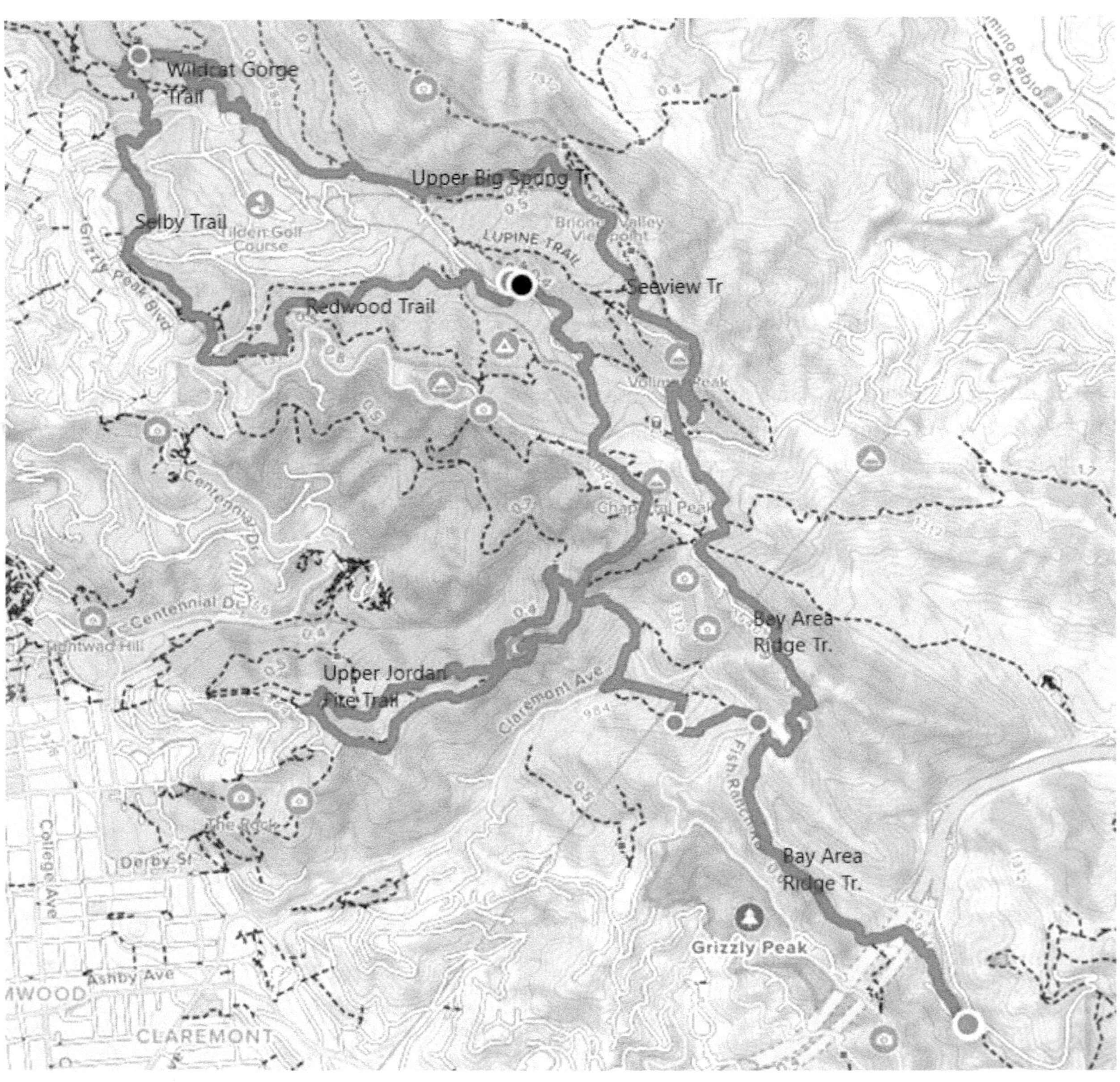

Detail Direction

Start this loop from the parking lot at Old Tunnel Road Staging Area by taking Bay Area Ridge Trail (BART) toward highway 24 direction. One mile late, you cross Fish Ranch Road and get into EBMUD property. Stay on the trail for another 1.5 miles before cross Loma Cantadas Road. Hike on the paved road toward the Vollmer Peak. The peak offers 360 degree view of the Bay Area. After snap a few pictures, retrace your steps and get onto the Seaview Trail. Keep slightly left to get on Arroyo Trail after only 0.1 miles on Seaview Trail. Follow Arroyo Trail downhill until the junction with Upper Big Spring Trail. Slightly right to hike on Upper Big Spring Trail. This trail ends at South Park Drive. Follow S Park Drive to visit the cute Regional Park Botanic Garden. Exit RPBG from the other side and walk on Wildcat Canyon Rd for a few hundred feet before get onto Wildcat Gorge Trail.

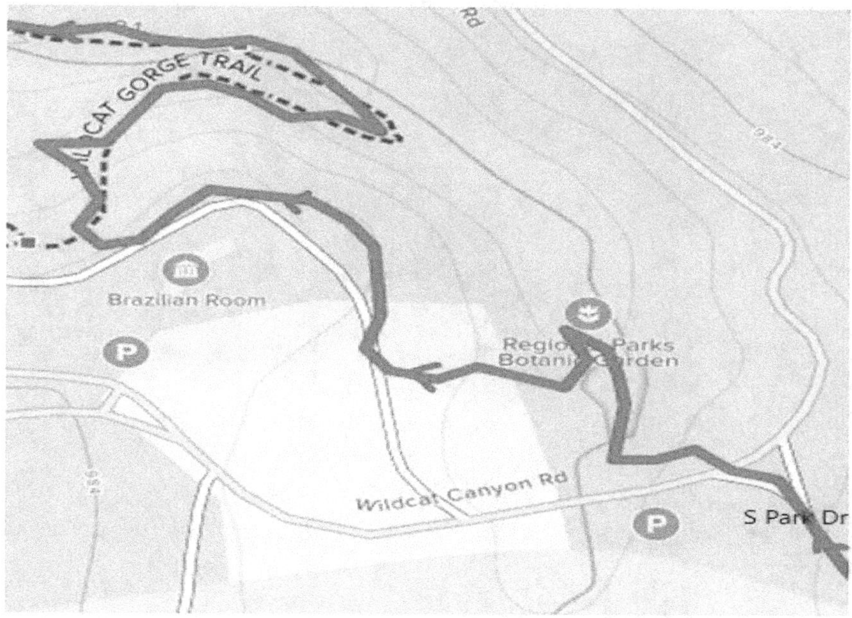

Turn left to get to Lake Anza Trail on the shore of Lake Anza. Very soon turn left onto Selby Trail. Selby Trail ends at Golf Course Drive. Cross the paved road and embark on Redwood Trail. Then turn right on Golf Course Trail. At the end of the trail, walk on paved road for a few hundred feet and then cross South Park Drive to access Vollmer Peak Trail. Turn right on Vollmer Peak Trail.

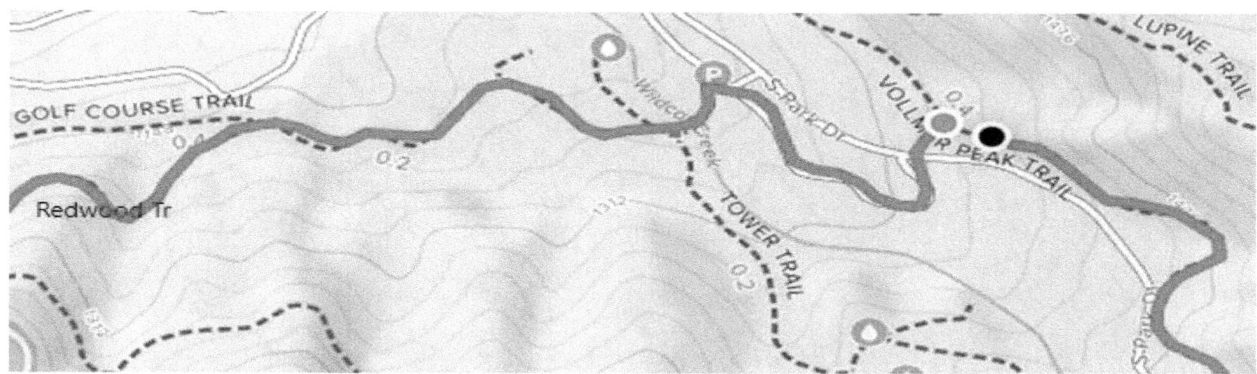

After VPT's ending at South Park Drive,continue on South Park Drive and then cross Grizzly Blvd. Get on the fire road across, stay on the main road to get an unknown peak where you have very nice view of Oakland and Berkeley. Hike down carefully a very steep section before you come upon a four way junction. Take the first trail on your right for 0.1 miles. Then turn left onto Upper Jordan Fire Trail. There is another trail that parallels with UJFT. Anytime you want to go back, just find a connecting trail and make two left turns to get on that trail. The trail will bring you back to the 4-way junction. Again you take the first right trail to the Claremont Canyon. Walk on Claremont Avenue for a few hundred feet before you turn left onto Willow Trail on your left. Willow Trail bring you up the ridge where Fish Ranch Road meets with Claremont Avenue and Grizzly Peak Blvd. Cross the intersection into the other side of the canyon, you see the BART you hiked earlier. Turn right onto BART and follow it all the way back to your car.

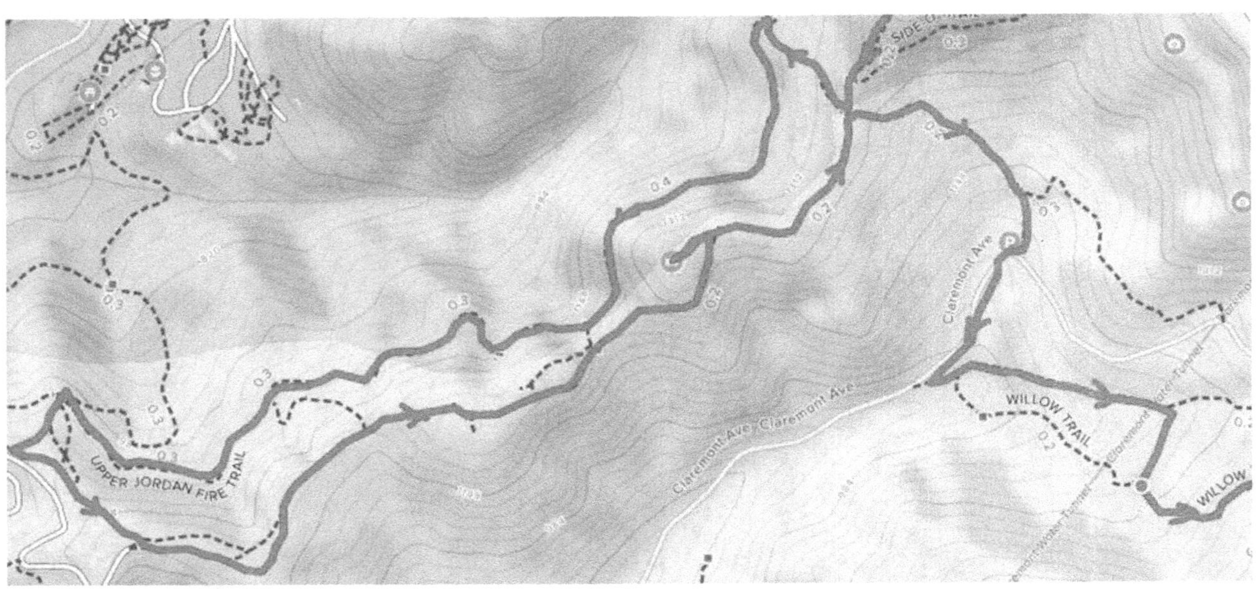

Hike Overview

Distance=15.3 miles

Elevation gain=2241 feet

Parking: Inspiration Point Parking Lot

Shaded: 30%

Trail Map:

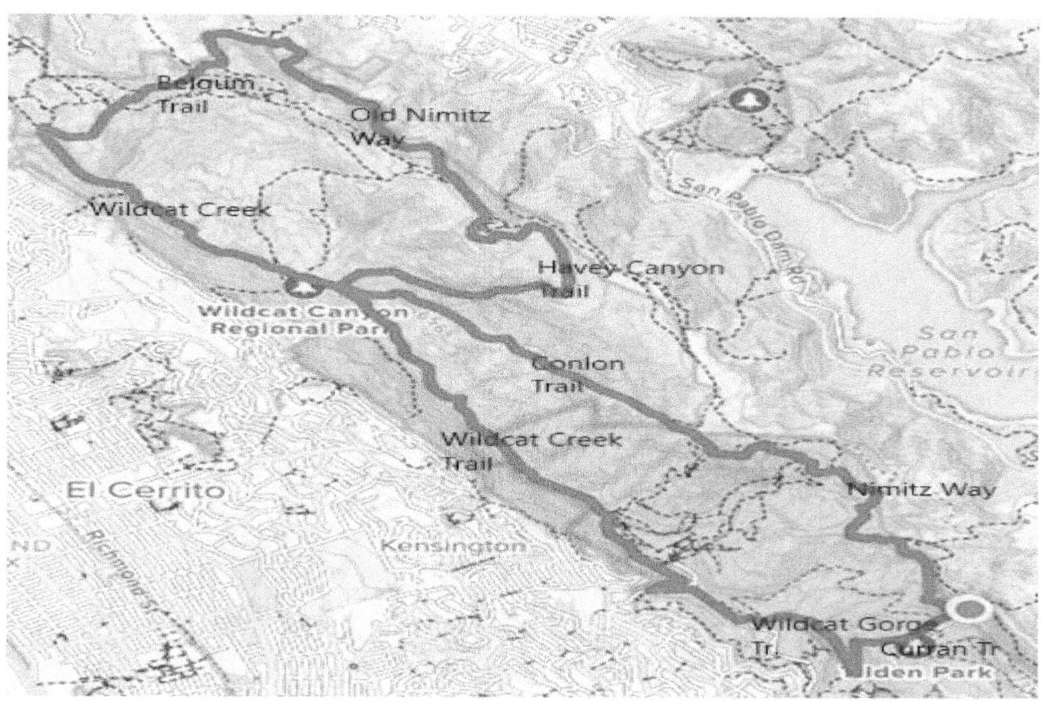

Detail Direction

You start the hike by taking Currant Trail downhill. Then turn right onto Wildcat Gorge Trail after 0.7 miles. Next turn right on Central Park Drive. At junction turn left onto Canon Drive for 0.3 miles. Keep eyes on your right to look for Memory Trail. Turn right onto Memory Trail and stay on Memory Trail for 0.3 miles. At Junction with Upper Packrat Trail, go ahead onto Packrat Trail. At the northern end of Jewel Lake, turn right onto Wildcat Creek Trail. Stay on Wildcat Creek Trail for 3 miles. Then begin to climb up the hills via Belgum Trail. At the junction with Old Nimitz Way, turn right onto Old Nimitz Way. ONW ends at San Pablo Ridge Trail. Continue onto SBRT for 0.2 miles before turn right onto Nimitz Way. Stay on Nimitz for 0.5 miles. Next turn right on Havey Canyon Trail for 1.5 miles. Next turn left onto Conlon Trail for 1.5 miles. At junction with Peak Trail, keep right to get on Peak Trail. Follow Peak Trail to the Wildcat Peak. Next continue on Peak Trail until the junction with Laurel Canyon Trail. Turn left onto Laurel Canyon Trail and turn right onto Nimitz Way. Follow Nimitz Way all the way to the parking.

Hike Overview

Distance=13.4 miles

Elevation gain=1923 feet

Parking: Crockett Ranch Staging Area

Shaded: No

Trail Map:

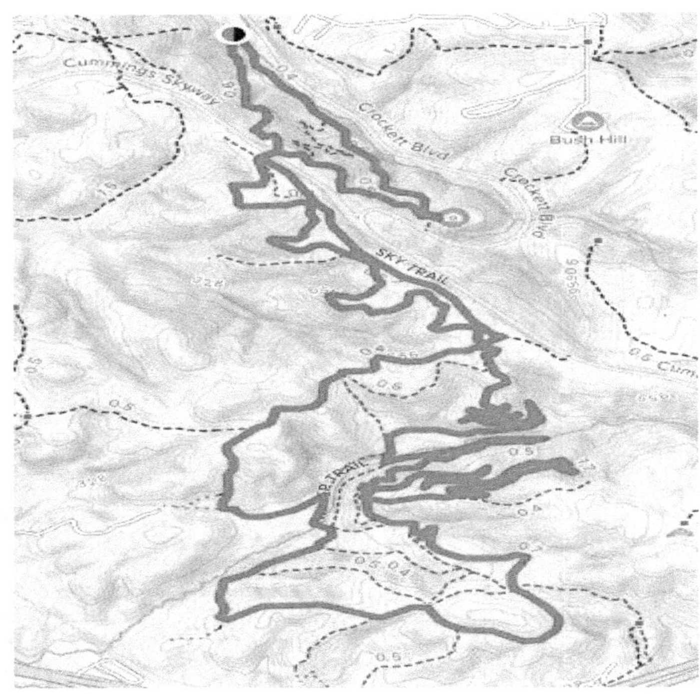

Detail Direction

You start the hike by tackling the Crockett Ranch Trail. At the end of the trail, go through the tunnel under Cummings Skyway. Then take Soaring Eagle Trail for two miles. At the end of the trail, stay right to be on Big Valley Trail for 0.4 miles. Turn right at the junction with Kestrel Loop for 0.7 miles before you turn right to get back on Big Valley Trail. Next you cross a seasonal creek and stay right on Back Ranch Loop. Stay on Back Ranch Loop for about 1.5 miles until you come to the junction with Goldfinch Trail. Take on Goldfinch Trail. And next turn right on Tree Frog Loop until its junction with Warep Trail. Stay on Warep Trail. Then cross a creek and back onto Big Valley Trail for a few yards. Next turn right on Sugar City Trail until its junction with Big Valley Trail. Turn right onto Big Valley Trail for 0.3 miles. Then keep right on Sky Trail. Sky Trail merges with Soaring Eagle Trail. Next you go through the same tunnel again. On the other side you turn right onto Edwards Loop Trail which ends at the staging area.

Hike Overview

Distance=10 miles

Elevation gain=2480 feet

Parking: park at road side of Gates Canyon Road. Parking area GPS Coordinates: 38.38138, -122.04299

Shaded: 30%

Trail Map:

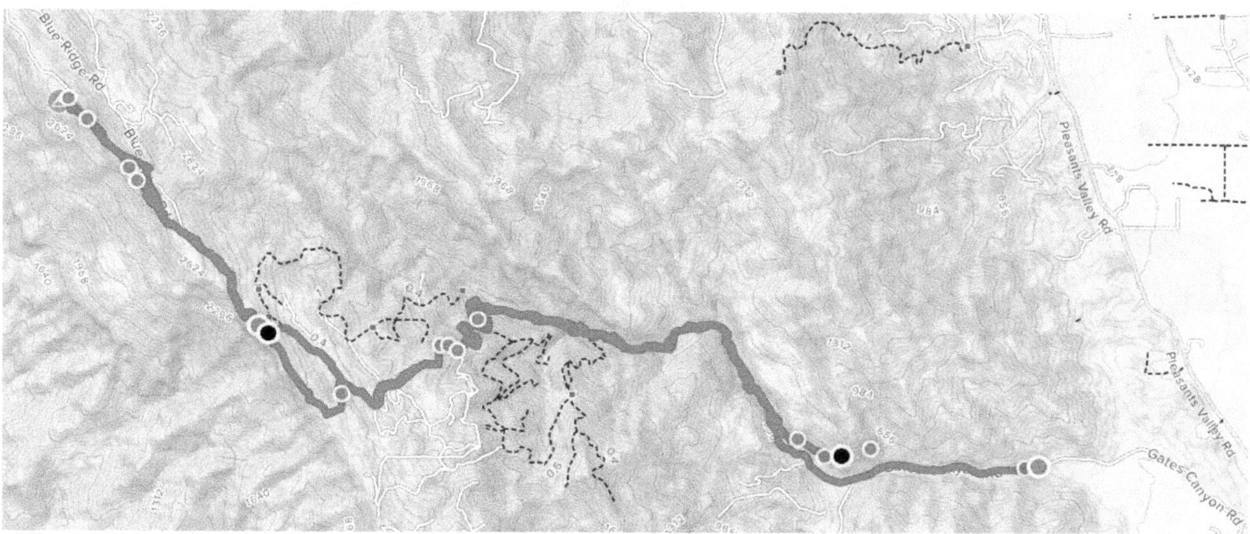

Detail Direction

This hike is straight forward: you follow Gates Canyon Road to the junction with Blue Ridge Road. Then turn slightly left to get onto Blue Ridge Road. Stay on Blue Ridge Road until the junction where you go left to Mount Vaca's Summit. Mount Vaca is the highest mountain in Solano County. At the summit, you have great view of both Napa Valley and Vaca Valley in Solano. After snap a few pictures, you continue to hike down the summit to the other junction with Blue Ridge Road. Then Turn right on Blue Ridge Road. At the junction with Gates Canyon Road, stay right and follow it all the way back to your parking.

Hike Overview

Distance=29.5 miles

Elevation=7365 feet

Parking: Oak Hill Trailhead in Calistoga (GPS: 38.58939, -122.57748)

Shaded: 35%

Trail Map:

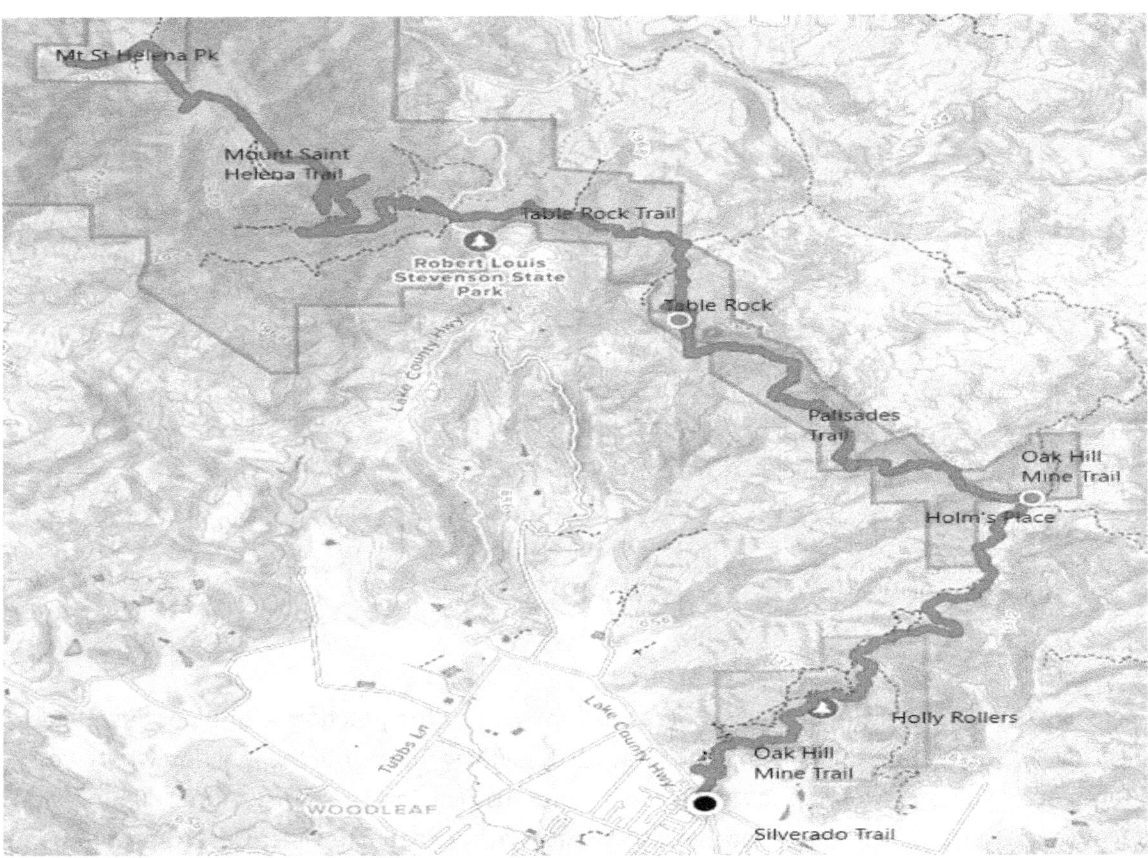

Detail Direction

Oak Hill Mine Trail starts right from the small parking lot at the trail head. Stay on OHMT for about 4 miles until you reach Holm's Place. Turn left at Palisades Trail for 3.6 miles until you are on top of Table Rock. Then follow Table Rock Trail all the way to the parking lot on the side of Hwy 29 or Lake County Hwy. Cross the Hwy and continue your journey on the trail toward Mt St Helena. You arrive Stevenson Memorial after one mile's climbing. Continue hike along Mount Saint Helena Trail all the way to the north Peak of Mt St Helena. The north peak stands at 4343 feet, the highest peak in the great bay area of San Francisco!

Hike Overview

Distance=18.2 miles

Elevation=5154 feet

Parking: Lower Parking lot at Sugarloaf Ridge Sate Park

Shaded: 50%

Trail Map:

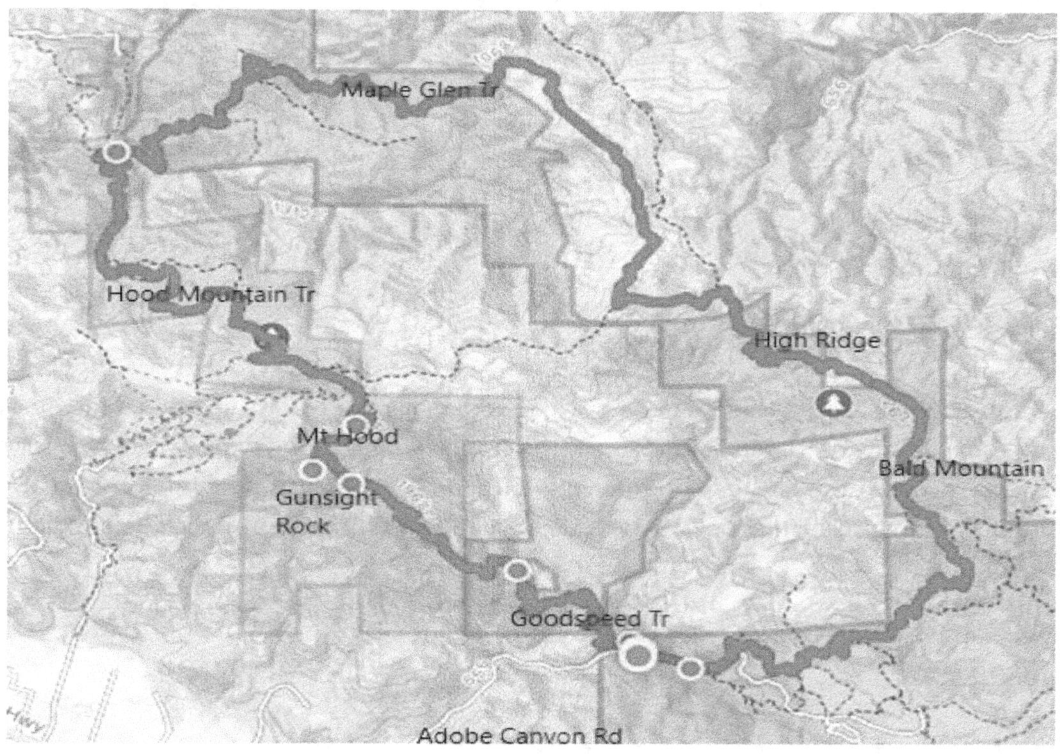

Detail Direction

Before you park your car at the said parking lot, you need go to the visitor center to get park permit which cost you $8(as of October 2018). The trail header of Goodspeed Trail is on your left. Follow this trail for 2.9 miles to the junction with Gunsight Rock Trail. Turn left on Gunsight Rock Trail to Gunsight Rock for 0.1 miles. You will be awarded with excellent views of Sonoma Valley, Santa Rosa and Pacific Ocean at the distance at Gunsight Rock.

Back track your steps to the junction and continue on Goodspeed Trail for another 0.2 miles to reach the junction of Hood Mountain and Summit Trails. Take the Hood Mountain Trail and stay on HMT for 3.1 miles until you reach the junction with Homestead Meadows at the bottom of the canyon. Turn right on

Home Meadows trail for 0.2 miles before turn left onto Quercus Trail. Stay on this trail for 0.6 miles before turn left onto Headwaters Trail. Hike Headwaters Trail for 0.5 miles. Then turn right onto Maple Glen Trail.

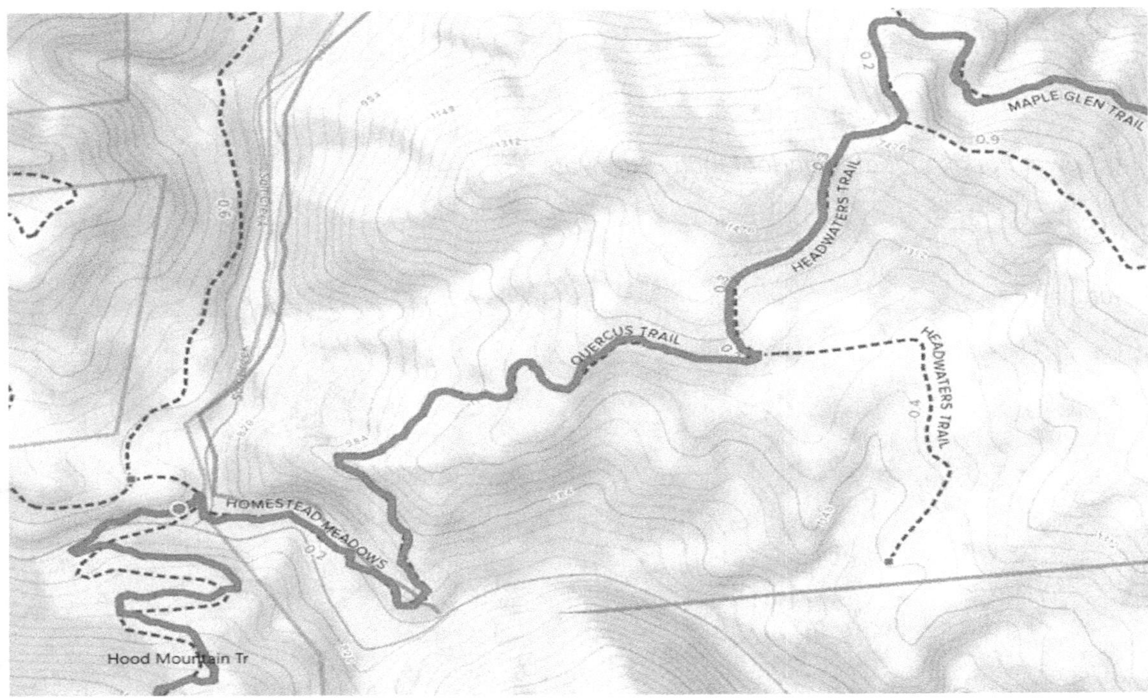

1.7 miles later you are facing at a locked gate which is right on the county line that separates Sonoma County and Napa County. With the permission of the grape yard manager, we climbed over the gate and turned right to following the fire road on the ridge for 1.5 miles. Don't turn right here. Stay on the road for another 0.5 miles to reach the junction with High Ridge Trail. Turn Right on High Ridge Trail

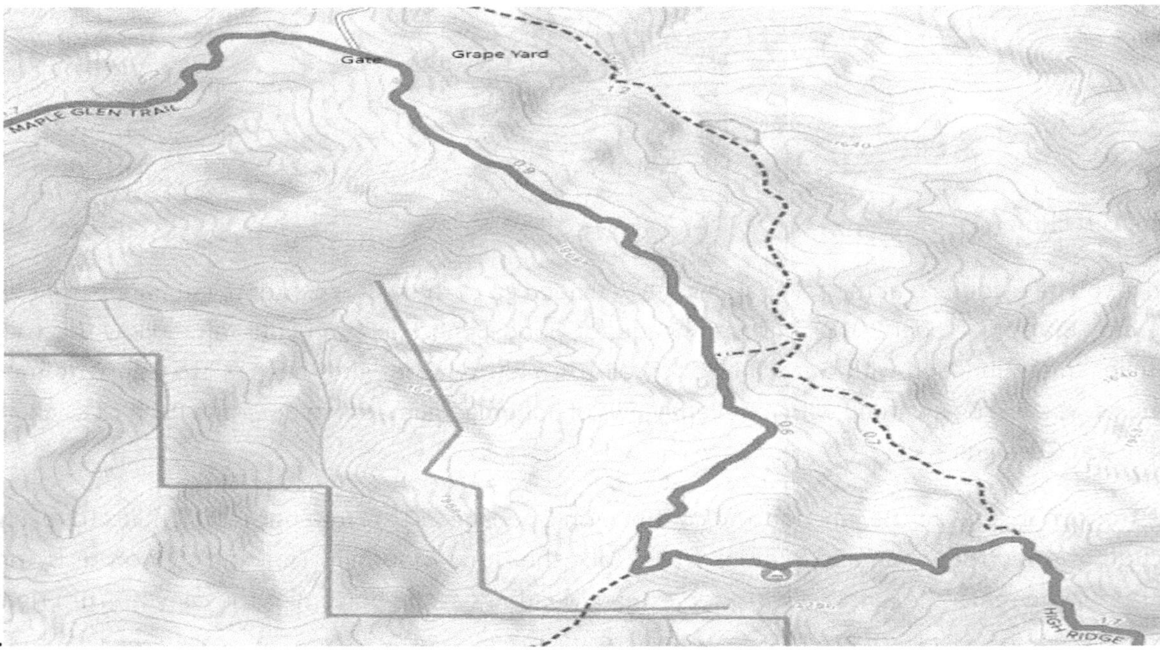

Hike High Ridge Trail for 1.7 miles. Then you come to Bald Mountain. After summiting Bald Mountain, take Bald Mountain Trail for 2 miles.

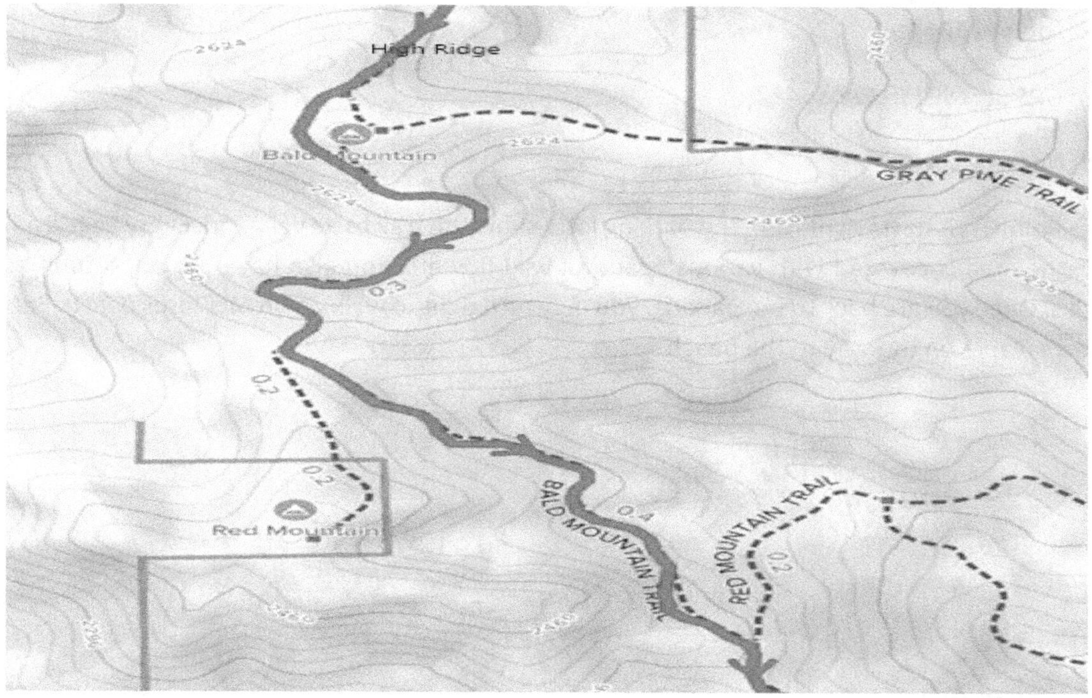

Then turn left on Stern Trail for 0.5 miles. There is a short cut on the right connecting Stern Trail to Pony Gate Trail. Take the shortcut and turn right on Pony Gate Trail. PGT ends at Adobe Canyon Road.

Turn right on Adobe Canyon Road to back to your car.

Distance=11 miles

Elevation gain=1274 feet

Parking: GPS 38.18913,-122.95427

Shaded: No

Tomales Point Trail starts right from the parking lot. Follow the trail to its very end. Every year from March to May, the area is covered with various beautiful wild flowers. You also have the opportunities to see many Elks. Once you are back to the parking, you may turn right to walk down McClures beach. Bathrooms are also available on the way to the beach.

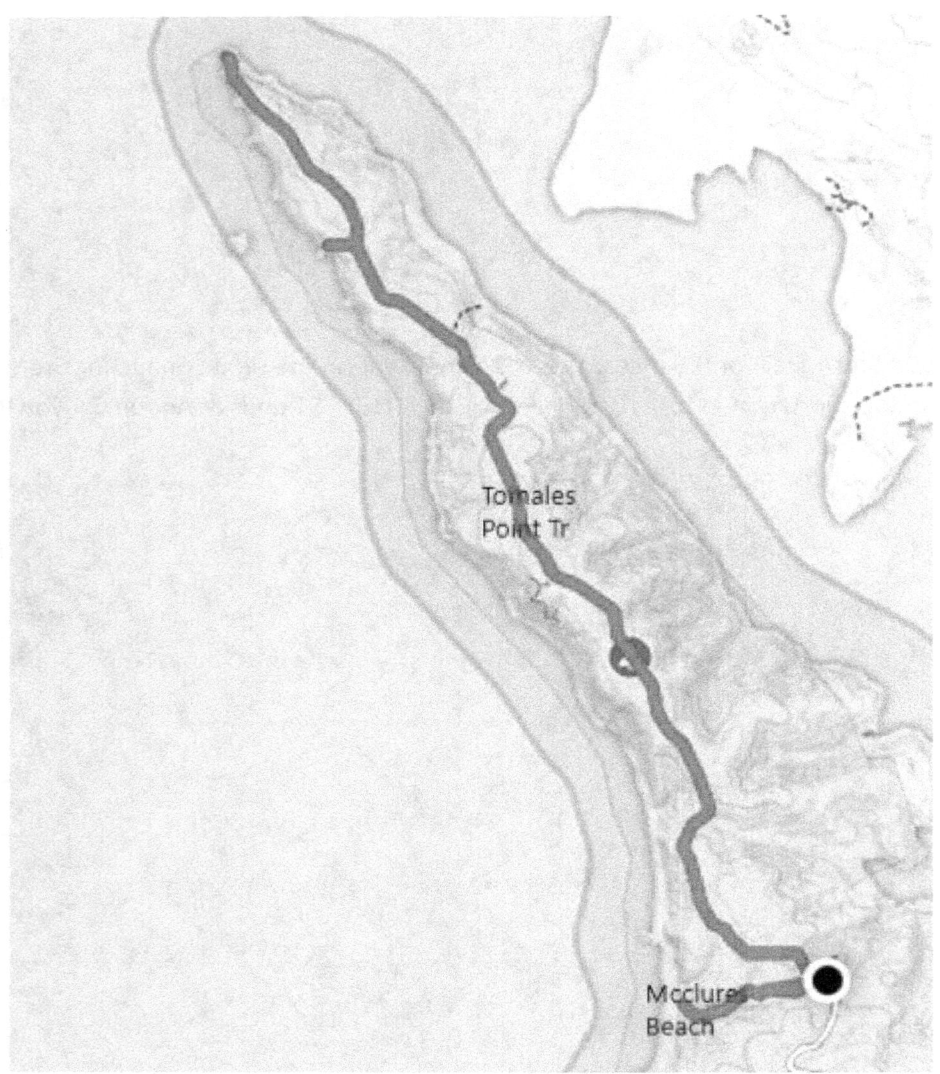

Hike Overview

Distance=18 miles

Elevation gain=2400 feet

Parking: Estero Trailhead Parking

Shaded: No

Trail Map:

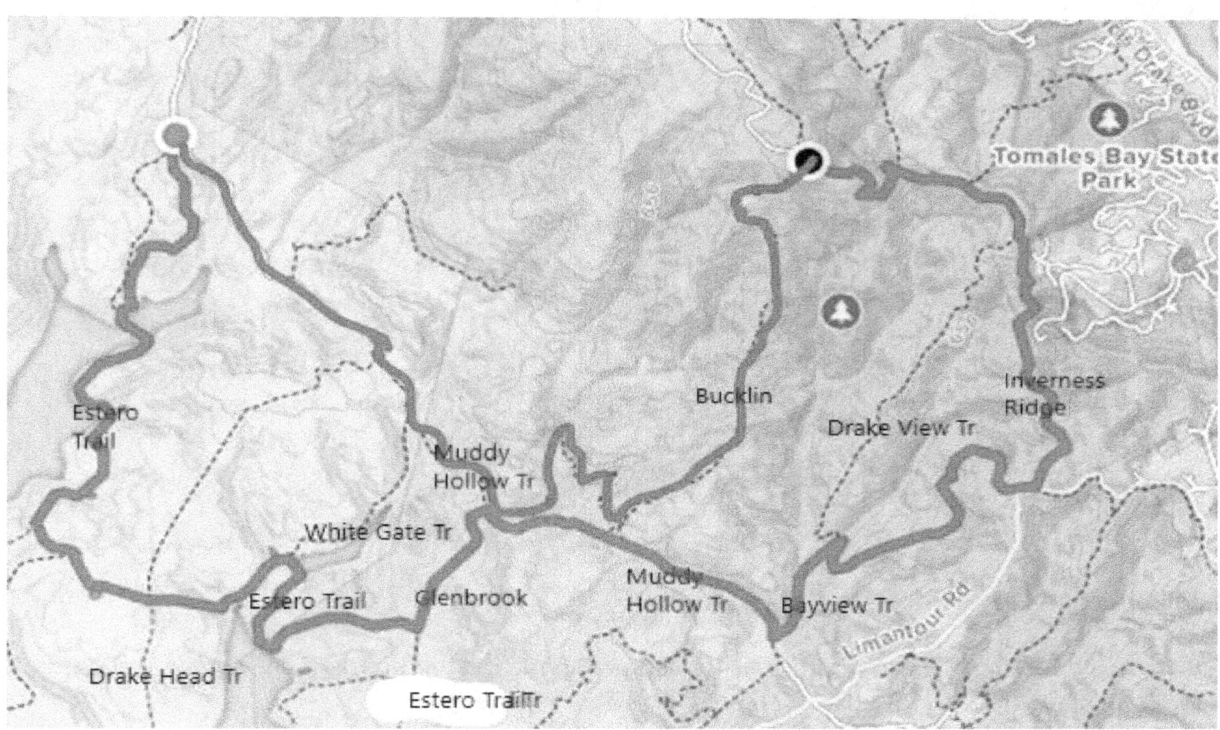

Detail Direction

Start with Estero Trail from the parking. The trail winds among rolling landscapes toward the bay for 2.3 miles. Then you come to the junction with Sunset Beach Trail. Turn left to stay on Estero Trail for 0.6 miles. Stay on Estero Trail at junctions with Drakes Head Trail and White Gate Trail. Finally you come to the junction with Glenbrook Trail. Turn left onto Glenbrook Trail. Turn right onto Muddy Hollow Trail. At the juction with Bayview Trail, take Bayview Trail for 2.1 miles before you turn left onto Inverness Ridge Trail. Inverness ends at Mt Vision Rd. Walk on the road for just a little bit before you turn left onto Bucklin Trail. At Bucklin's end at Muddy Hollow, turn right onto Muddy Hollow. Stay on Muddy Hollow until the end at the paved Estero Road. Follow the back to the trailhead.

Hike Overview

Distance=21.5 miles

Elevation gain=2756 feet

Parking: Bear Valley Visitor Center

Shaded: 50%

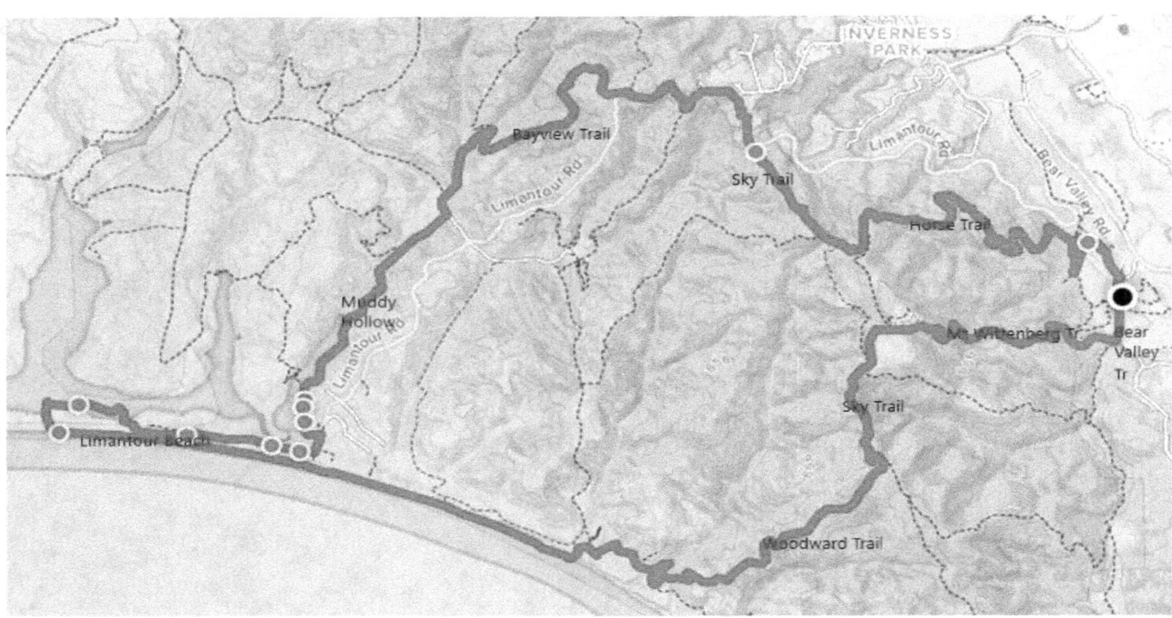

Detail Direction

You take Kule Loklo trail in front of the visitor center. 0.5 miles late, turn right on Morgan Trail. After 0.2 miles of downward slope, turn left on Horse Trail.

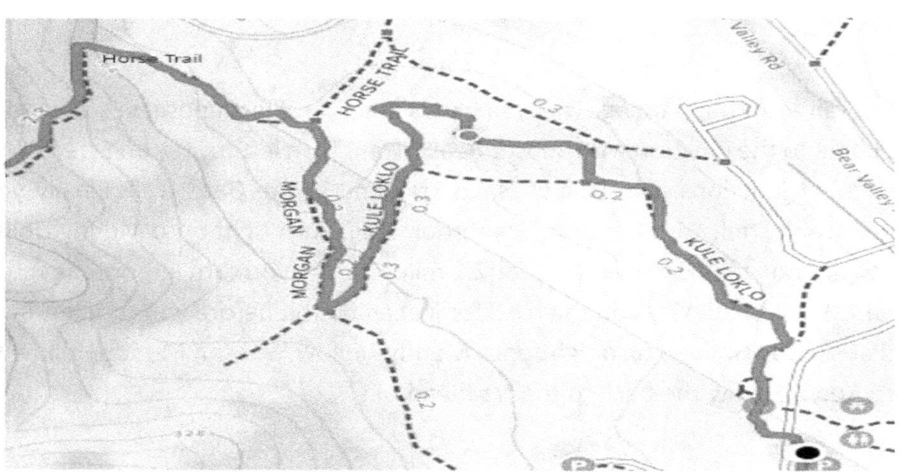

Stay on Horse Trail for about 3 miles, you reach the junction with Sky Trail on Inverness Ridge. Turn right on Sky Trail. Sky Trail becomes Bayview Trail when it is close to Limantour Road. Follow Bayview Trail for about 2.5 miles. You reach the junction with Muddy Hollow Road. Turn left on Muddy Hollow Rd and go all the way toward the beach.

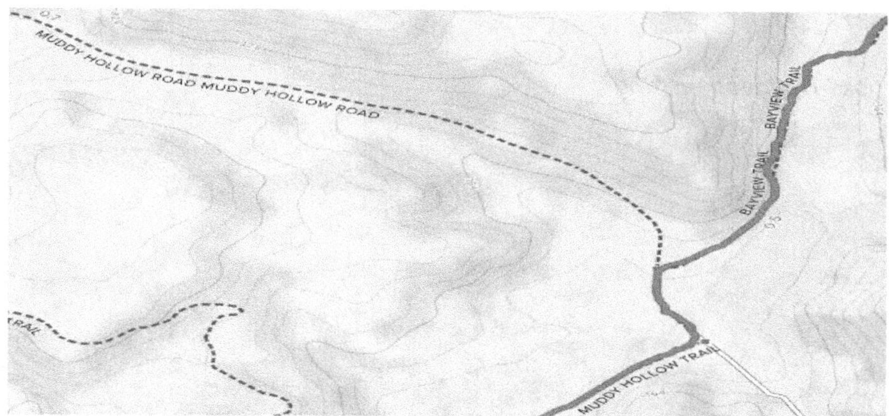

Then turn right on Limantour Spit Trail for one mile. When you reach the end of trail, you turn left and walk on the beach. The beach is 5 mile long. After enjoy beach walk as much as you like, you walk south toward the Coast Camp of Point Reyes National Seashore in the south. There are restroom and fresh water at the camp. Follow the Coast Trail south for half mile and then turn left on Woodward Trail to climb up the ridge.

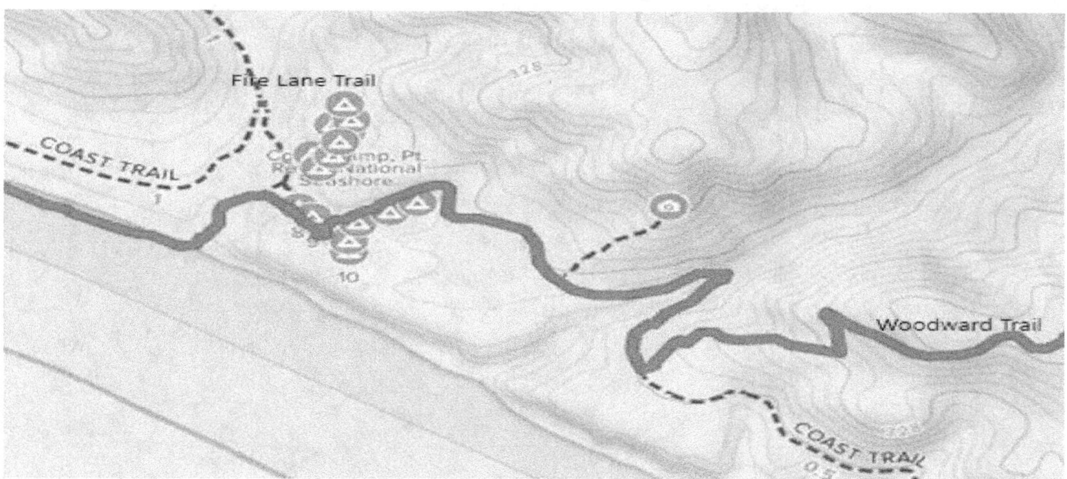

Turn left on Sky Trail after you climb 2 miles. Stay on Sky Trail for only 0.8 miles. At next 4 way junction, you choose Mount Wittenberg Trail. Staying on this trail for 2 miles, you reach junction with Bear Valley Trail. Turn left on Bear Valley Trail and your car is only 0.2 mile away from you.

Hike Overview

Distance=26.6 miles

Elevation gain=4272 feet

Parking: Five Brooks Trailhead Parking

Shaded: 50%

Trail Map:

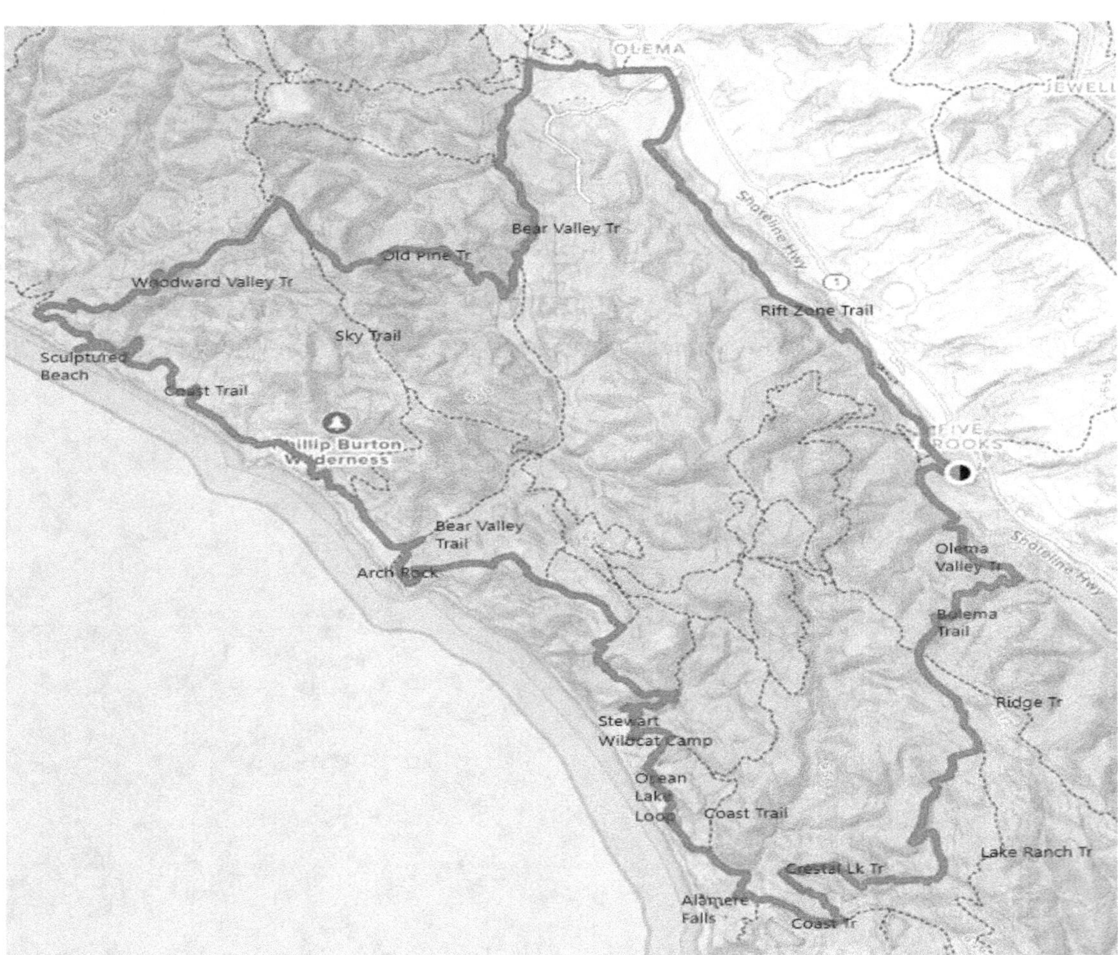

Detail Direction

The hike starts from Olema Valley Trail. Stay on OVT until the junction with Bolema Trail. Turn right onto Bolema to climb up the ridge. At the junction with Ridge Trail and Lake Ranch Trail, choose Lake Ranch Trail. Next turn right on Crystal Lake Trail. Next turn right on Coastal Trail. Watch out for Alamere Falls Trail on your left. You have the option to see this beautiful waterfalls all year long.

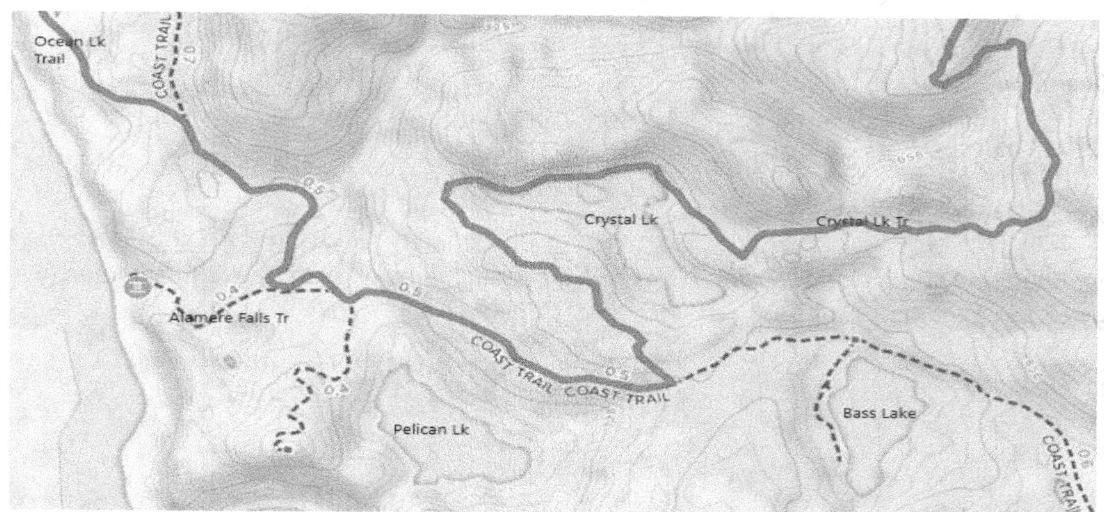

At the junction with Ocean Lake Loop, stay left to get on Ocean Lake Trail. When Ocean Lake rejoin Coastal Trail, turn left on Coastal. Almost immediately, turn left on Stewart to go Wildcat Camp and Wildcat Beach. After spend quality time at the beach, get back on Stewart Trail. Stay on Stewart for 0.8 miles before you turn left on Coastal Trail. Stay on Coastal Trail for a few miles until you pass junctions with Bear Valley, Sky Trail etc. At the junction with Sculptured Beach Trail, turn left on Sculptured Beach Trail. There are interesting rock formations at Sculptured Beach. When it is low tide, you can explore some of the caves.

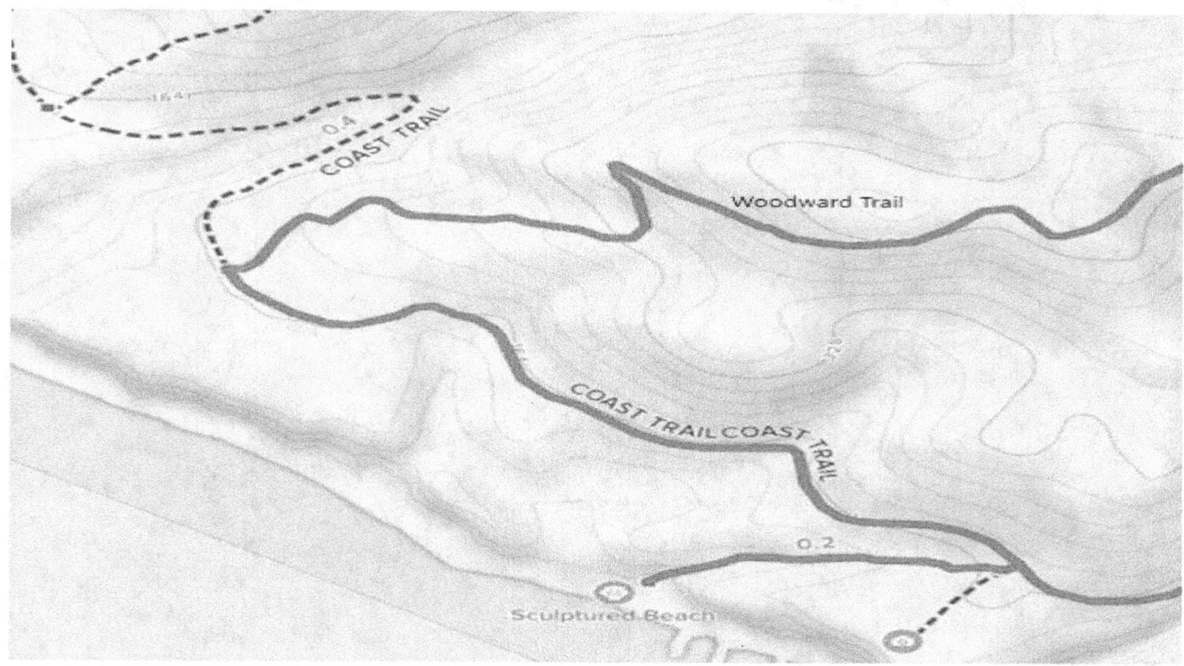

When you get back from Sculptured Beach, turn left on Coastal Trail. Next turn right on Woodward Trail. At the junction with Sky Trail, turn right on Sky Trail. At the junction with Old Pine Trail, turn left on Old Pine Trail. OPT ends at Bear Valley Trail. Turn left on BVT. Turn right onto Rift Zone. Follow Rift Zone Trail all the way to Stewart Trail. Turn left on Stewart Trail for only 0.1 miles and you have arrived Five Brooks parking lot.

Hike Overview

Distance=33 miles

Elevation gain=6401feet

Parking: Road side parking on Sir Francis Drake Blvd near the junction with Devil's Gulch Road (GPS: 38.02912, -122.73628)

Shaded: 60%

Trail Map:

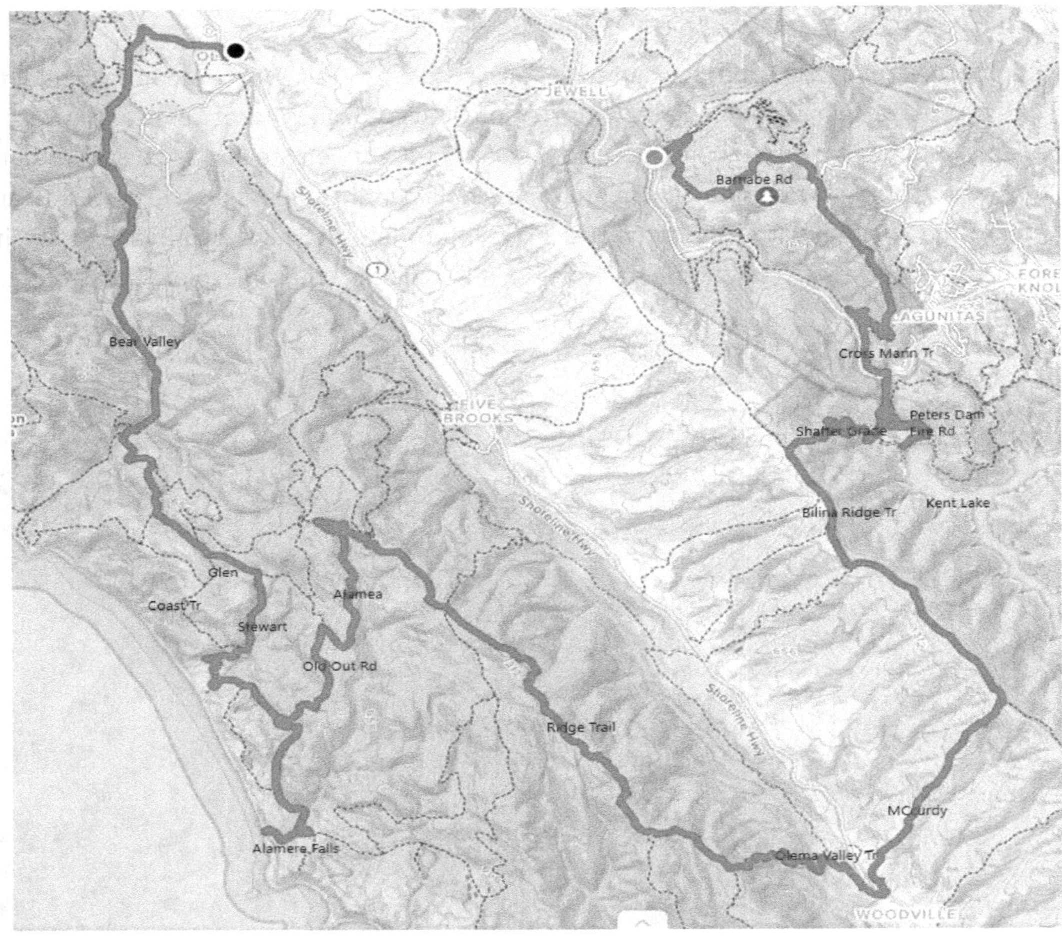

Detail Direction

Cross Sir Francis Drake Blvd to hike on Devil's Gulch Road for 0.1 miles before you get on the trail on your right side. Stay on the trail for only 0.1 miles. Then turn right onto Garvestone Road. At the junction with Barnabe Road, turn left to continue uphill climbing. Turn right at the junction with Bill's Trail to stay on Barnabe Rd. Then turn left to go the summit of Barnbe Mountain.

Retracing steps from summit to Barnabe Rd and stay on the fire road to descend the mountain on the other side. Turn left at the junction with Cross Marin Trail onto CMT. Cross Sir Francis Drave Blvd and continue on Peters Dam Fire Road. PDFD leads you to Kent Lake. Continue on Upper Peters Dam Road for 0.7 miles. Then turn left on Continental Cove Road for 0.8 miles. Stay left on the next two junctions. Now you are on San Geronimo Ridge Road which brings you back to PDFD.

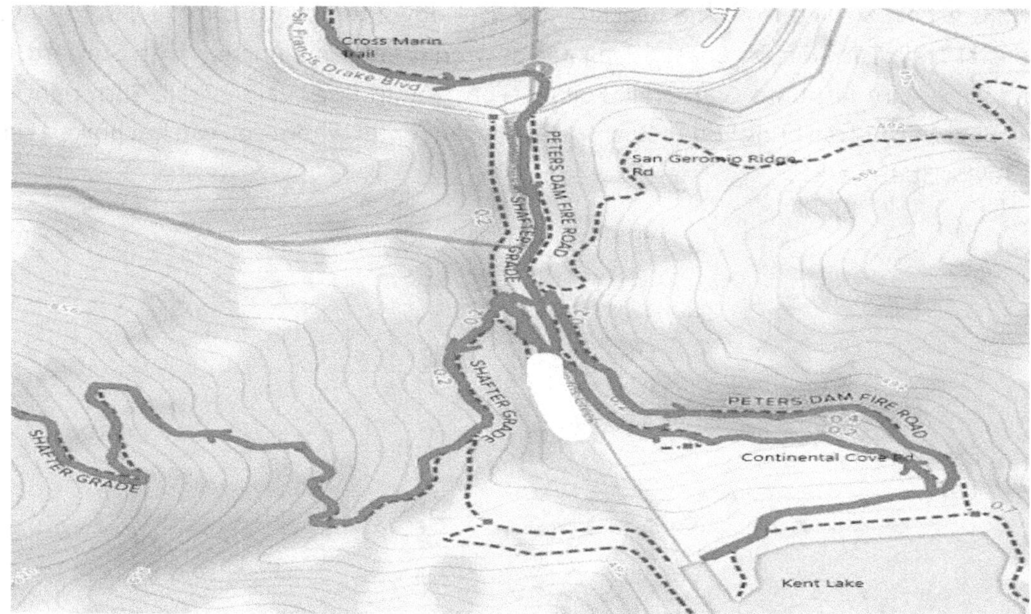

Cross Lagunitas Creek and get onto Shafter Grade road. If the creek is not easy to cross, please turn right on PDFD and walk to Sir Francis Drake Blvd, turn left SFDB and turn left on Shafter Grade road. Shafter Grade ends at Bolinas Ridge Trail. Turn left on BRT. Next you turn right on McCurdy Trail to get down to Olema Valley. McCurdy ends at Shoreline Hwy. Cross the Hwy and turn right onto Olema Valley Trail. Turn left at the junction with Teixeira Trail. Stay on Teixeira Trail for 1.8 miles. Next stay right at the junction with Ridge Trail. Stay on Ridge Trail for 3.8 miles. Turn left on Alamea Trail to go toward the ocean. Alamea ends at Old Out Road. Turn left onto Old Out Road. Turn left again on Coastal Trail. Stay left on next junction to stay on Coastal Trail. Watch for Alamere Falls trail on your right. It is a tiny trail with overgrown bushes. Turn right on Alamere which leads you to Alamere Falls.

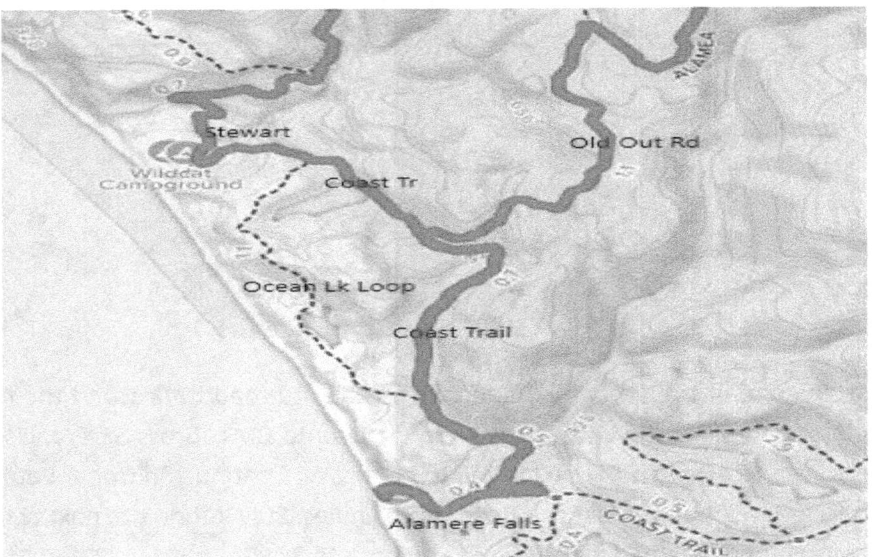

The waterfalls is best viewed from the beach below. Get down the beach carefully. Retrace your steps back to Coastal Trail. Turn left on Coastal Trail and stay on it until the junction with Steward Trail. Turn right on Steward. Turn left onto Glen Trail. Follow Glen Trail to Bear Valley Trail. Turn right onto Bear Valley Trail. Bear Valley Trail bring you to Bear Valley Visitor Center where you can hitchhike a ride to back to Samuel Taylor State Park.

Hike Overview

Distance=17.3 miles

Elevation gain=3609 feet

Parking: Tennessee Valley Rd parking lot

Shaded: No

Trail Map:

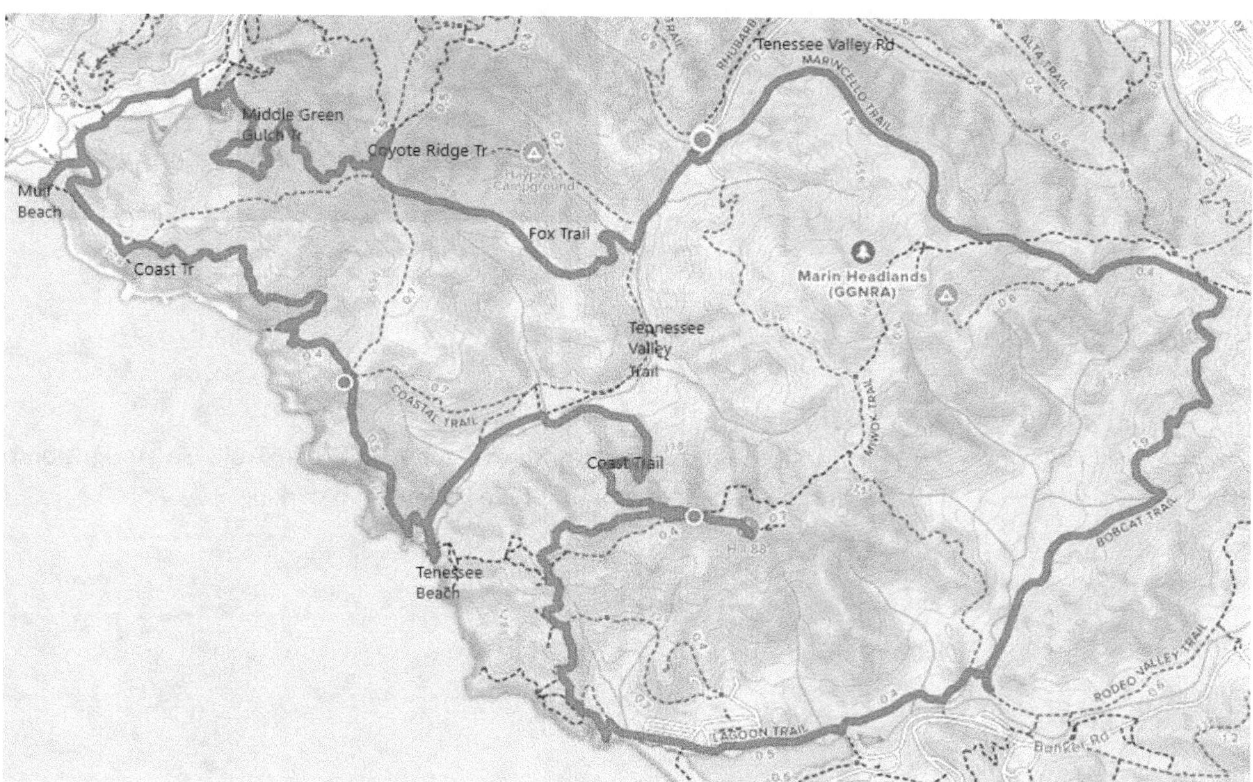

Detail Direction

Hike down Tennessee Valley Trail toward the ocean for 0.3 miles. Turn right onto Fox Trail for 1.1 miles. Next you turn right at Coastal Fire Road for 0.1 miles. At the junction with Coyote Ridge Trail, turn right onto Coyote Ridge Trail for 0.2 miles. Then turn left onto Middle Green Gulch Trail for 1.8 miles to go down the hills. At the bottom of the hills, there are some organic vegetable fields. Stay on trail when cross the fields. Then turn left toward the ocean. At the junction with Coastal Trail, turn right to see beautiful Muir Beach. Retrace your steps back to the junction with MGGT. Stay right on the junction to continue on Coastal Trail. At the junction of Coastal Trail and Tennessee Valley Trail, turn right to get on Tennessee Valley Trail. TVT ends at Tennessee Beach. Next you get back on TVT. At the junction with Lower Tennessee Valley Trail, stay right for 0.3 miles. Next you turn right onto Coastal Trail. And climb up Hill 88. The summit of Hill 88 is only 0.2 miles away from the junction of coastal Trail and Wolf Ridge Trail. Using the road that ends at Hill 88 summit to go the summit. Retrace your steps back to the last junction and turn left onto Coastal Trail. Follow Coastal Trail to Rodeo Beach and Rodeo Lagoon. Turn left onto Bunker Road at the far end of the lagoon. Then turn right onto Miwok Trail for 0.5 miles. Watch out a short connector that connects Miwok Trail with Bobcat Trail and Rodeo Valley Trail. Turn right onto the connector and turn left onto Bobcat Trail.

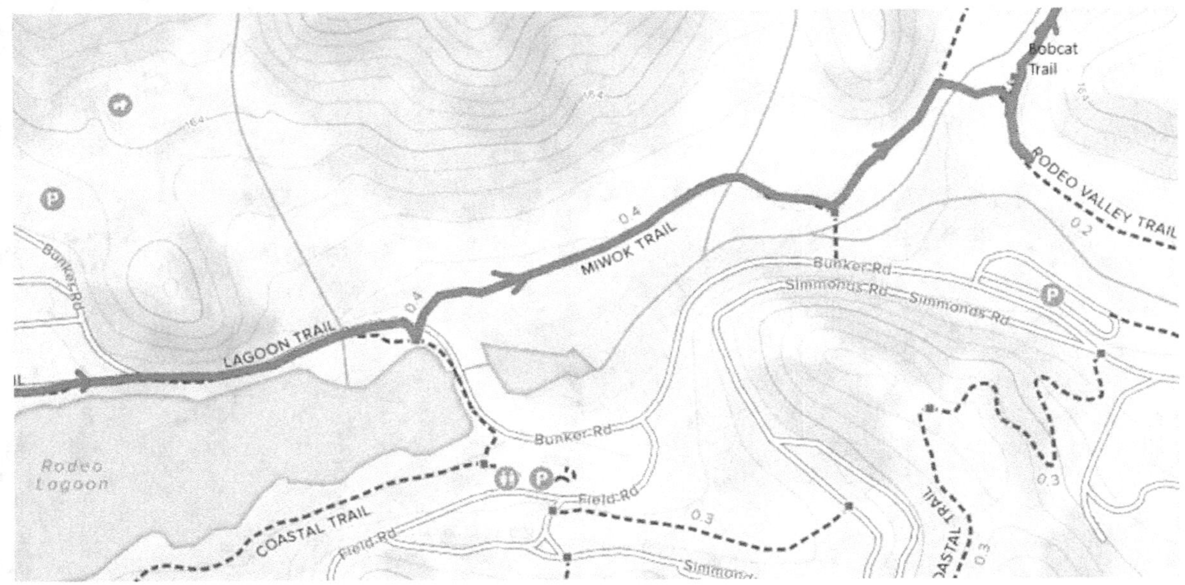

Stay on Bobcat Trail for 2.5 miles until the junction with Miwok and Marincello Trail. Go straight onto Marincello Trail for 1.5 miles. Marincello Trail ends at Tennessee Valley Road parking.

Hike Overview

Diatance=24.9 miles

Elevation gain=5735 feet

Parking: Muir Woods National Monument parking lots

Shaded: 50%

Trail Map:

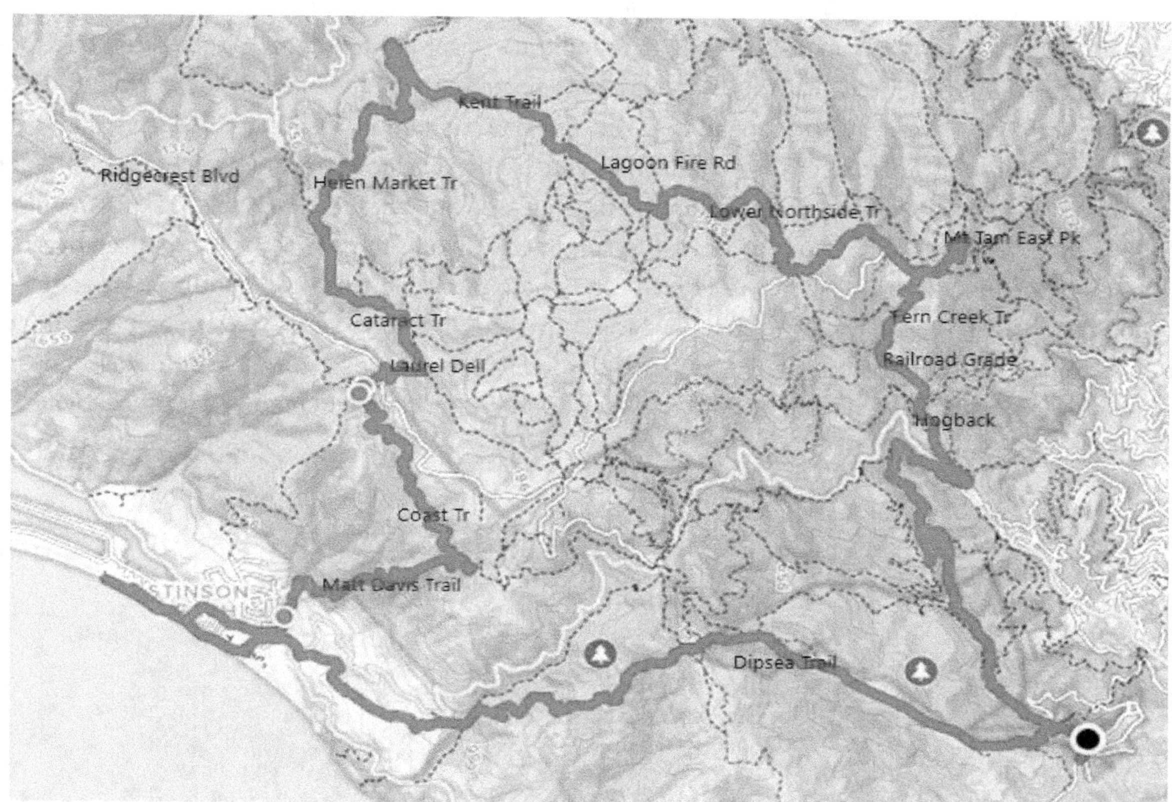

Detail Direction

You start the hike by finding the Dipsea Trail Head on the west side of the parking. Follow Dipsea Trail to cross Redwood Creek and stay on it all the way to Stinson Beach. After spend quality time at Stinson Beach, cross Shoreline Highway to get on Belvedere road. Straight ahead for a short distance, you will find the start of Matt Davis Trail. Stay on Matt Davis for 2.1 miles. Next you turn left onto Coastal Trail for 1.5 miles. Then you turn right on Willow Camp Fire Road for only 0.1 miles. Cross Ridgecrest Blvd and take on Laurel Dell Fire Road for 0.6 miles. Note that Laurel Dell Fire Road turn abruptly left at 0.3 mile mark. Next turn left on Cataract Trail to see the namesake waterfalls. Then turn right onto Helen Market Trail before you turn right again on Kent Trail. Stay on Kent Trail for 1.2 miles.

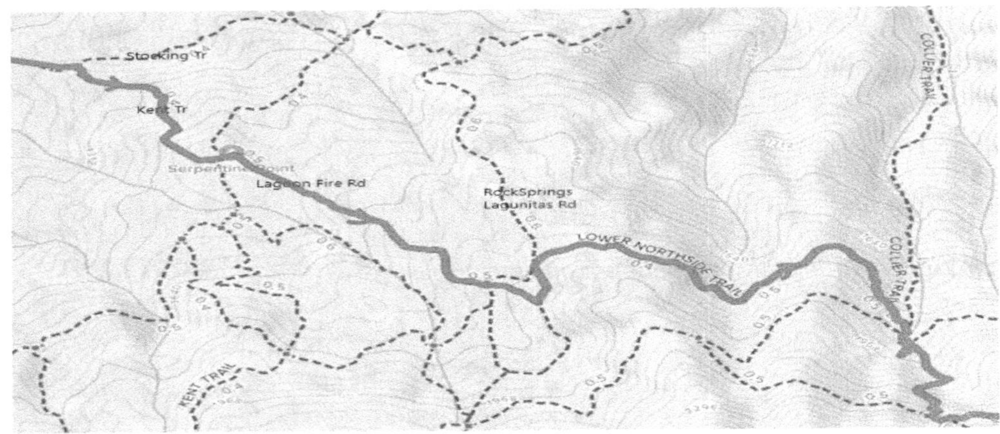

Then take a user trail to climb up Serpentine Point and then turn right to get on Lagoon Fire Road for 0.5 miles. Then turn left on CC Boys Trail for 0.1 miles and then straight ahead to get on Lower Northside Trail. At junction with Collier Trail, straight ahead to follow Collier Trail uphill. CT ends at E Ridgecrest Blvd. Stay on it for only a very short distance. Then slightly left you are on Lakeview Trail. LT ends soon on the same drive way. Walk along the driveway, cross summit parking area and get on Plank Walk Trail to summit the East Peak of Mount Tamalpais. Come down the summit by taking the Plank Trail and circumvent the summit by following Verna Dunshee Trail which offers panoramic view of Marin and San Francisco Bay. Next you back to the driveway and keep an eye for Fern Creek Trail on your left. You need take this trail downhills. At the junction of Fern Creek Trail and Railroad Grade Fire Road, turn left onto Railroad Grade Fire Road for 0.3 miles. Then turn right onto Hogback Road. Hogback Road ends at Panoramic Hwy.

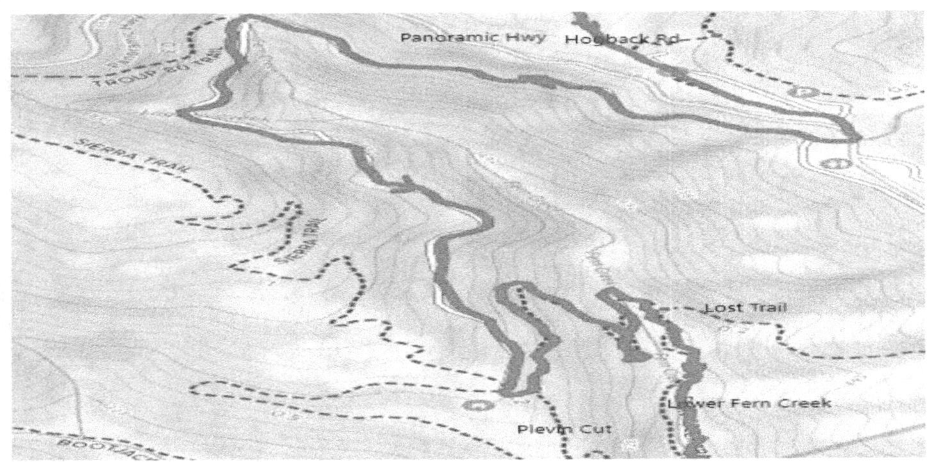

Cross Panoramic Hwy and continue downhill on Trestle Trail. Then turn right onto Alice Eastwood Road. At its junction with Lower Fern Creek Trail, turn left onto Lower Fern Creek Trail. Stay on Fern Creek Trail until it ends on the main trail of Muir Woods National Monument. Then follow the main trail out of the gate and go to your car.

Hike Overview

Distance=13.8 miles

Elevation gain=3392 feet

Parking: Old Mill Park in Mill Valley

Shaded: 60%

Trail Map:

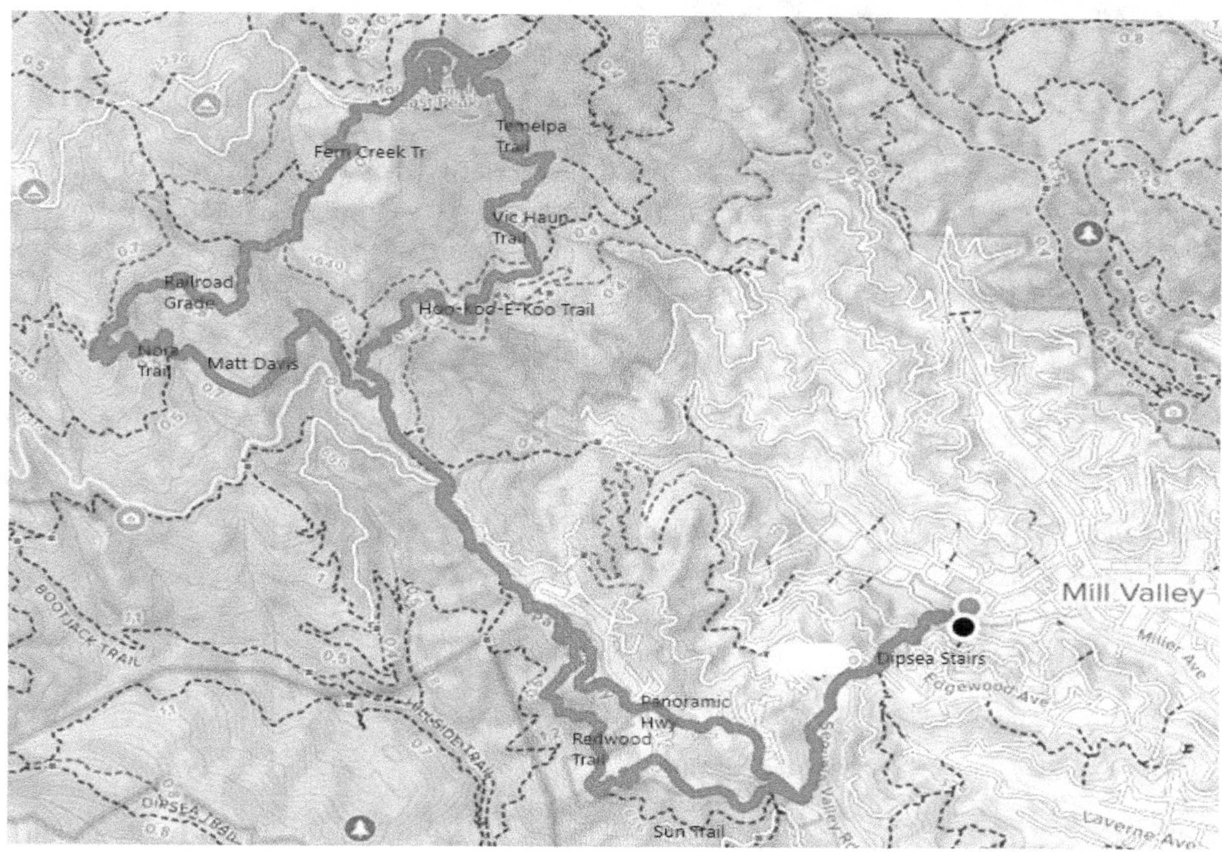

Detail Direction

Follow Cascade Way to the historical Dipsea Stairs. There are three sets of nearly 700 wooden and stone stairs. After you climb the first two sets of stairs, slightly left to find the third set of stairs. With a traffic circle on your right, you pass Sequoia Valley Road and turn left through a gate to start the real Dipsea Trail. At the junction with Sun Trail, you slight right to go uphill by taking Sun Trail. Sun Trail will end soon (0.8 miles) at Redwood Trail. When Redwood Trail ends, continue ahead on Panoramic Trail. Then turn right on Ocean View Trail. After passing Mountain Home Inn and crossing Panoramic Highway, you continue your climb on Hogback Road. Then turn right on Hoo-Koo-E-Koo Trail.

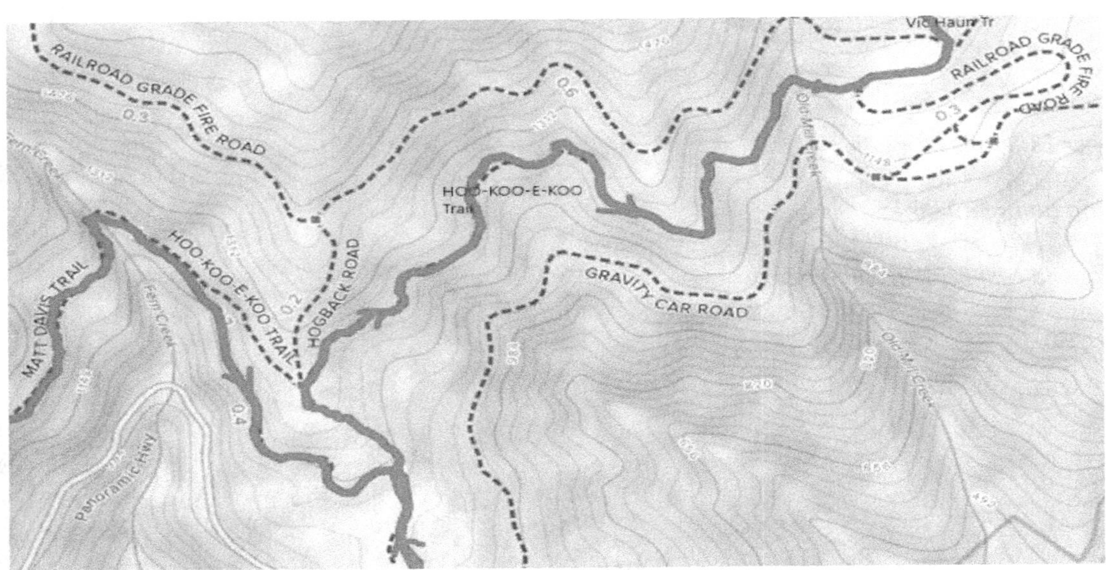

At the junction with Temelpa Trail, turn left on Temelpa Trail which climbs about 1000 vertical feet to join Verna Dunshee Trail. Turn right to go around the east Peak until you get on Plant Walk Trail. Follow Plant Trail to the summit of Mt Tam. After enjoying the 360 degree view of the bay area, retrace your steps back to Verna Dunshee Trail. Go straight and turn left on Fern Creek Trail.

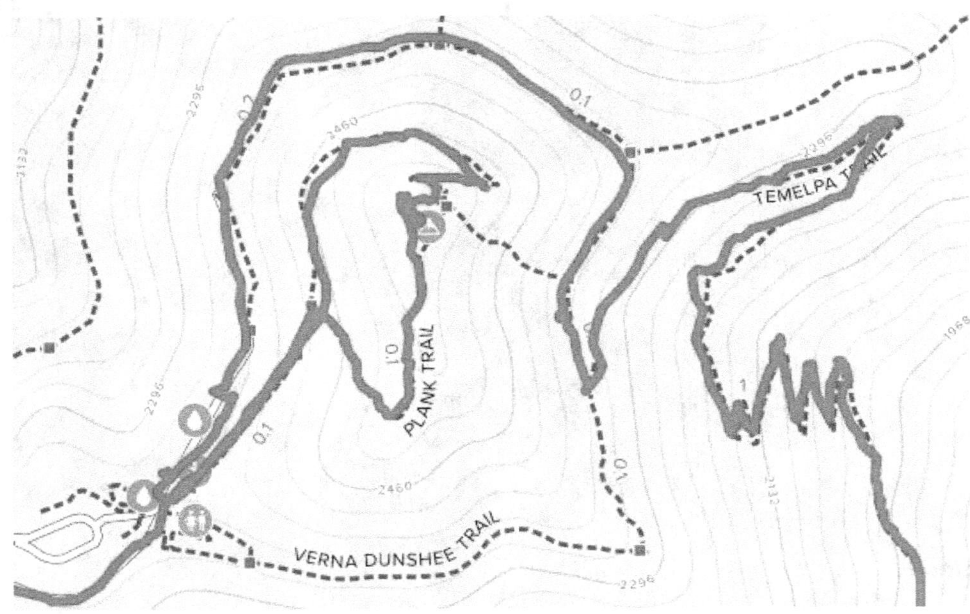

At the junction with Railroad Grade Fire Road, turn right on RGFD. In front of West Point Inn, take Nora Trail to go down the hill. Nora trail ends at Matt Davis Trail. Turn left onto Matt Davis Trail. Matt Davis Trail ends at Hogback Road. Turn right on Hogback Road and follow the trails you have taken earlier to go back to your car.

Hike Overview

Distance=19 miles

Elevation gain=2782 feet

Parking: Chrissy Field parking lot

Shaded: No

Trail Map:

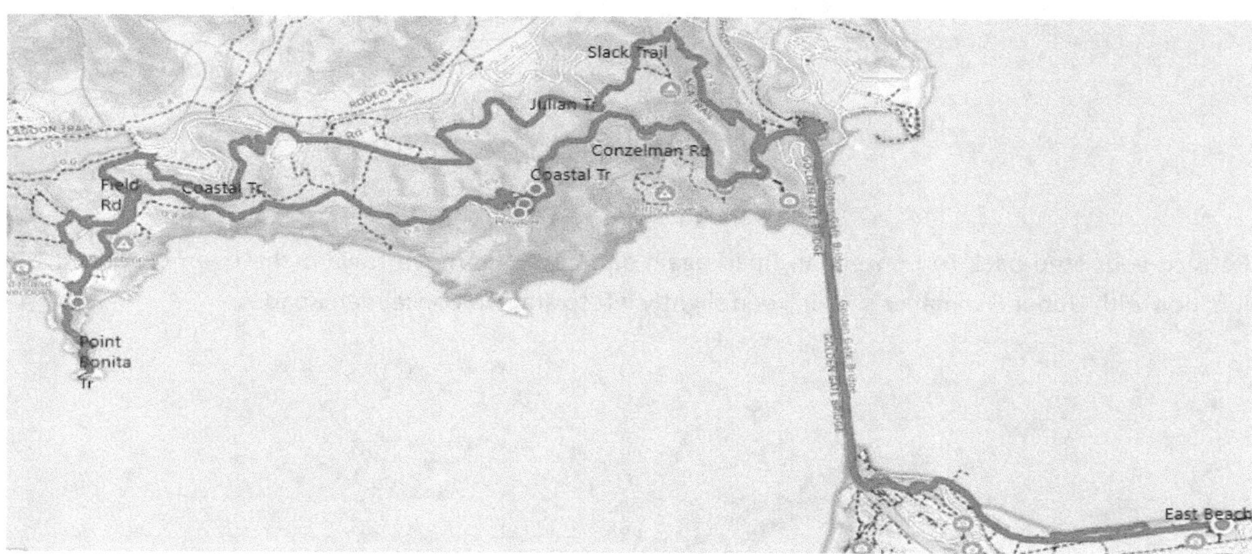

Detail Direction

We started our hike on East Beach across from Palace of Fine Art toward Golden Gate Bridge. After passing the pier (on the right), there is a climbing up trail on your left. Follow this trail to get on Golden Gate Bridge.

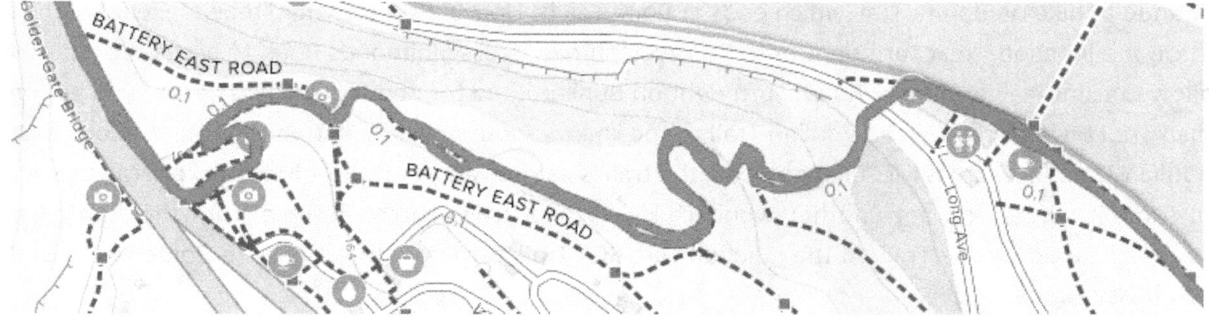

After cross the bridge, there is a vista on your right where you can get close-up view of the bridge. Use the trail underneath the bridge to cross the busy highway. When you emerge from the other side of the bridge, you are actually on SCA Trail. Stay on SCA for 0.2 miles and then turn left onto Conzelman Road. Next you turn left on Battery Spencer Trail to go Battery Spencer. At Battery Spencer, you have the best view of Presidio. Get back to Conzelman Road until you arrive at a round-about. Stay left to get on Coastal Trail which leads you to Hawk Hill and Battery Construction 129.

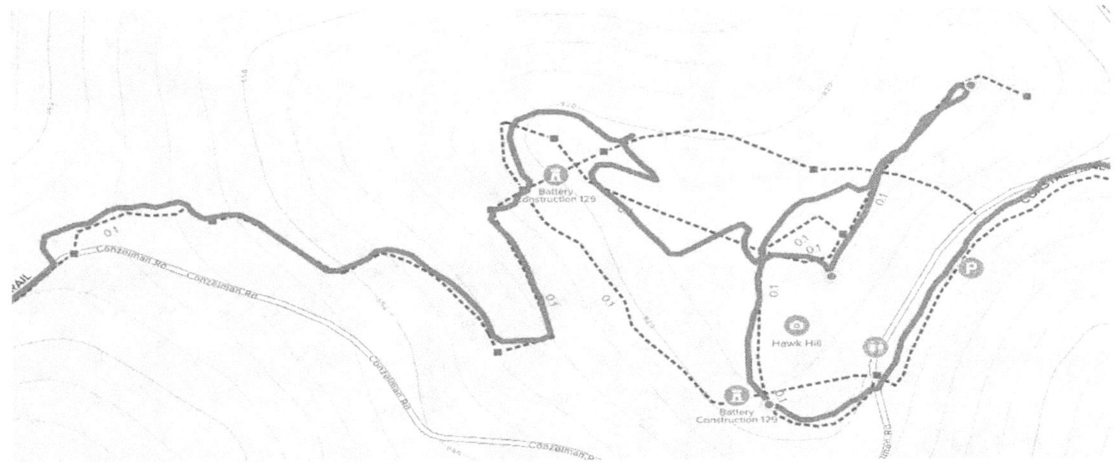

Retrace your step back to Conzelman Road again and continue move toward the open ocean. At the junction with Upper Fishmaner's Trail, keep slightly left to stay on Conzelman Road.

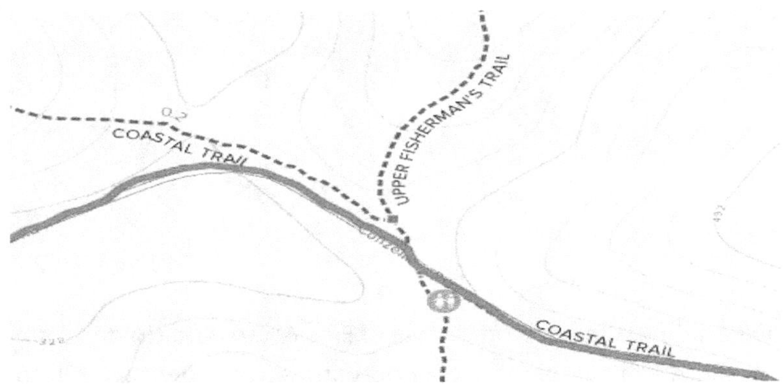

When Conzelman Road ends at Field Doad, turn left onto Field Road. When reach the end of Field Road, continue to hike on Bonita Trail which ends at Bonita Light House. Retrace your steps to Field Road. Stay left on the junction. Next turn right onto Bodsworth Road, cross Simmonds Road to access Coastal Trail. Follow Coastal Trail to Bunker Road. Turn right on Bunker Road for about 200 yards before you get onto Julian Trail on your right. Follow Julian Trail to the round-about and stay left on the round-about to stay on Julian Trail. After cross McCullough Road, the trail is named Slacker Trail. Follow Slacker Trail to Slacker Hill summit where you get another wonderful view of San Francisco. Retrace from the summit and continue hike on Slacker Trail. At the junction with SCA Trail, turn right to get back to Golden Gate Bridge and Chrissy Field.

Hike Overview

Distance=15.4 miles

Elevation gain=1385 feet

Parking: Ocean Beach parking lot

Shaded: 10%

Trail Map:

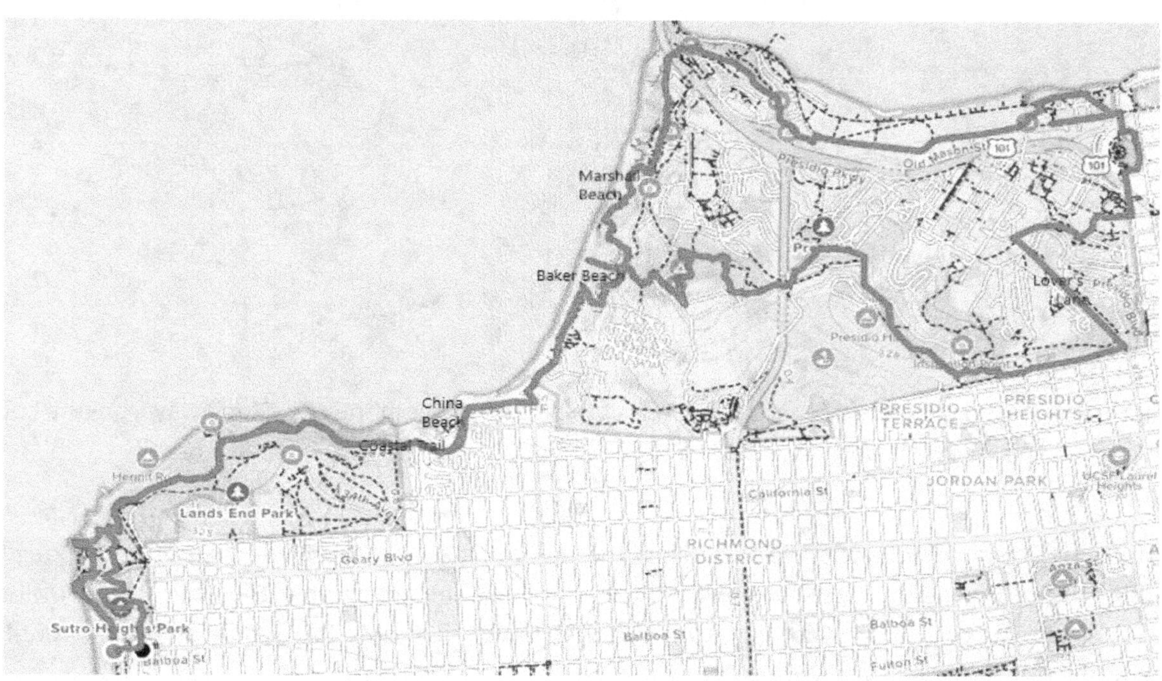

Detail Direction

Park your car close to Cliff House and walk on Ocean Beach toward Sutro Baths. Next you follow Coastal Trail until the junction with El Camino del Mar Road. Turn left on the road. At the junction with Sea Cliff Avenue, turn left onto Sea Cliff Avenue. At the junction with 25th Avenue, turn left onto 25th Avenue. Next turn right to stay on the right branch of 25th Ave.

There is a gate that leads you to Baker Beach and back to Coastal Trail. Stay on Coastal Trail all the way to Golden Gate Bridge. Use tunnel to go the other side of the bridge and get on Battery East Road for 0.1 miles. Next stay left to get on Presidio Promenade. At junction with Crissy Field Avenue, turn left to get on Crissy Field Avenue. Then cross over to Old Mason Street. Follow the road to East Beach. Next you turn right to walk to Palace of Fine Art. Near the corner of Lyon and Chestnut St, turn right for two blocks. Then turn left at the corner of Starbucks to walk to Letterman Drive. Turn right onto Letterman Drive. After cross Lincoln Blvd, the road name changes to Presidio Blvd. The start of Lover Lane is near the junction with Martinez St.

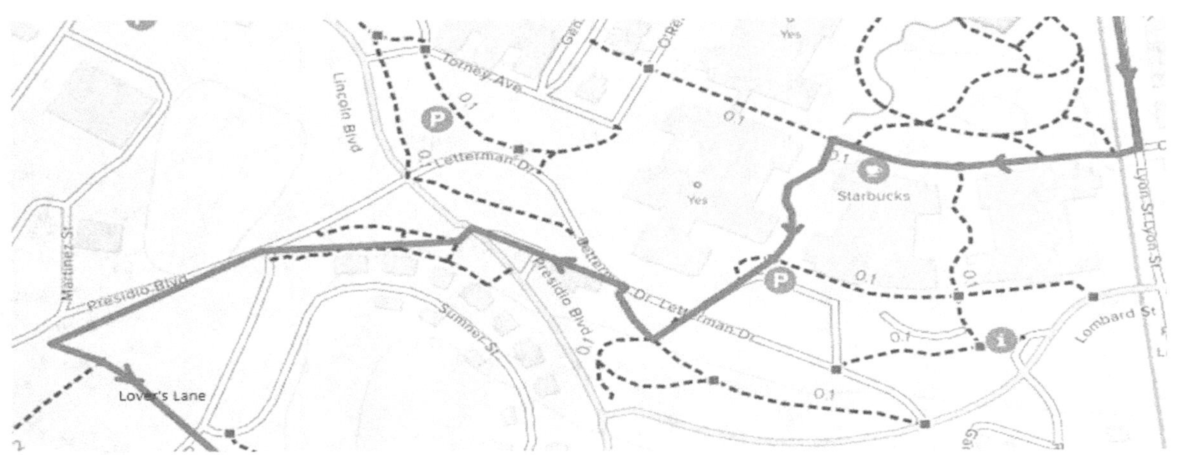

Soldiers from the Presidio used Lover's Lane to visit their loved ones in the city. Step away from the Lover's Lane is the iconic Andy's Wood Line. Made up of eucalyptus trunks, the structure is more than 1,200 feet in length.

Next turn right before W Pacific Ave and follow the trail to cross Arguello Blvd. The trail runs along with the edge of Presidio Golf Course for a while. Next you leave the golf course and get on Park Trail near Nauman Road. At the junction with Bay Area Ridge Trail, turn right onto BART. Stay on the trail until you come to the junction with Washington Blvd.

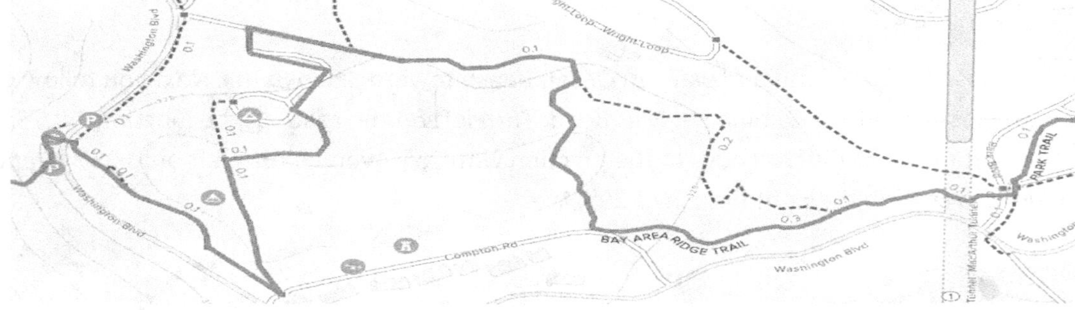

Turn left and stay for 0.1 miles. Now you cross Washington Blvd to Immigrant Point Overlook. Follow the trail and stay right at next junction. After cross Lincoln Ave, turn left onto Coastal Trail. Once you are on Coastal Trail, you can simply reverse what you did earlier to get back to your car or you can change the route as much as you like to explore beaches along the way.

Hike Overview

Distance=14.6 miles

Elevation gain=2516 feet

Parking: roadside parking on Crocker Avenue near trailhead in Daly City

Shaded: 10%

Trail Map:

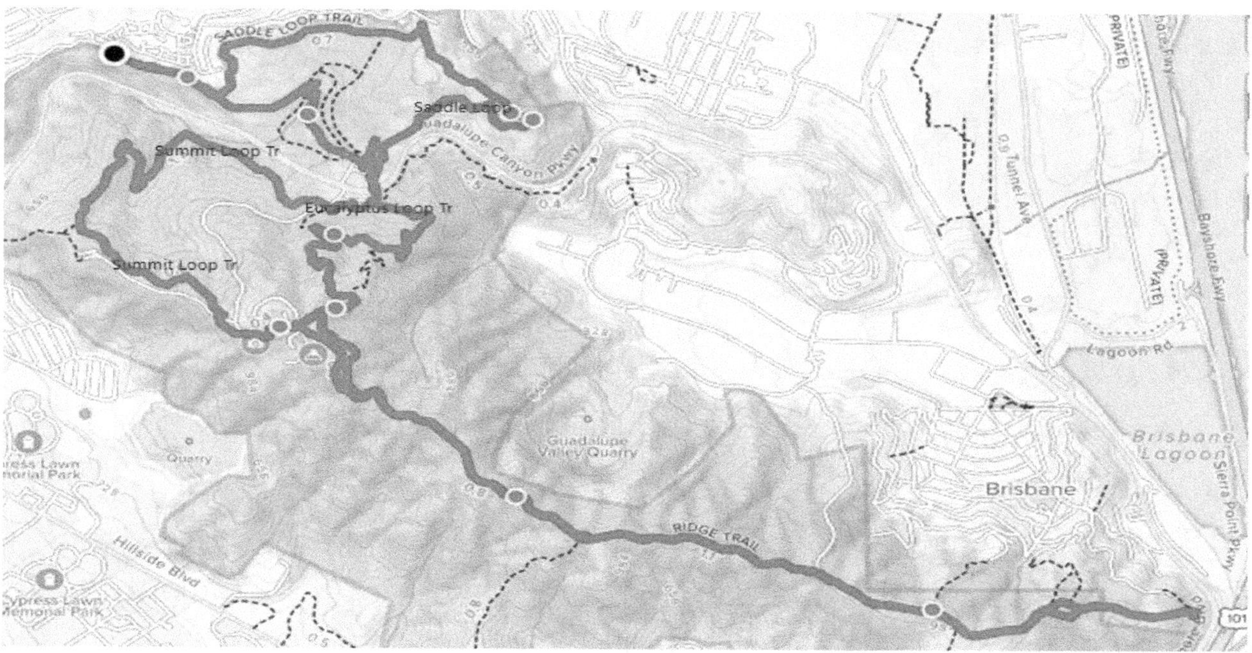

Detail Direction

Park your car near the junction of Crocker Avenue and Rampart Way and walk up hill until you see eucalyptus forest on your right side. Turn right on the fire road that leads to the forest. Merely 0.1 miles later, you come to the junction with Saddle Loop Trail. Turn right on Saddle Loop Trail for another 0.3 miles. Then you arrive a picnic area with parking and bathrooms. Stay on right branch of the Saddle Loop Trail for 0.1 miles, go underneath the Guadalupe Canyon Pkwy and then turn right onto Eucalyptus Loop Trail for another 0.1 miles. At the junction with Summit Loop Trail, you turn right. Stay on Summit Loop Trial for 1.9 miles. Cross the summit drive way and the Summit Loop Trail continues on the other side. Hike another 0.5 miles before you turn right onto Ridge Trail. Hike the 2.8 mile long Ridge Trail all the way to its end near Highway 101. Trace your way back to Summit Loop Trail. At the junction with Eucalyptus Trail, turn right on to ET for 0.7 miles. Go underneath Guadalupe Canyon Pkwy again and you are back to the Saddle Loop Trail. Turn right onto Saddle Loop Trail for 2 miles. Then turn right on the fire road and follow the fire road for 0.1 miles to back Crocker Avenue.

Hike Overview

Distance=12.5 miles

Elevation gain=2536 feet

Parking: Skyline College parking lot

Shaded: No

Trail Map:

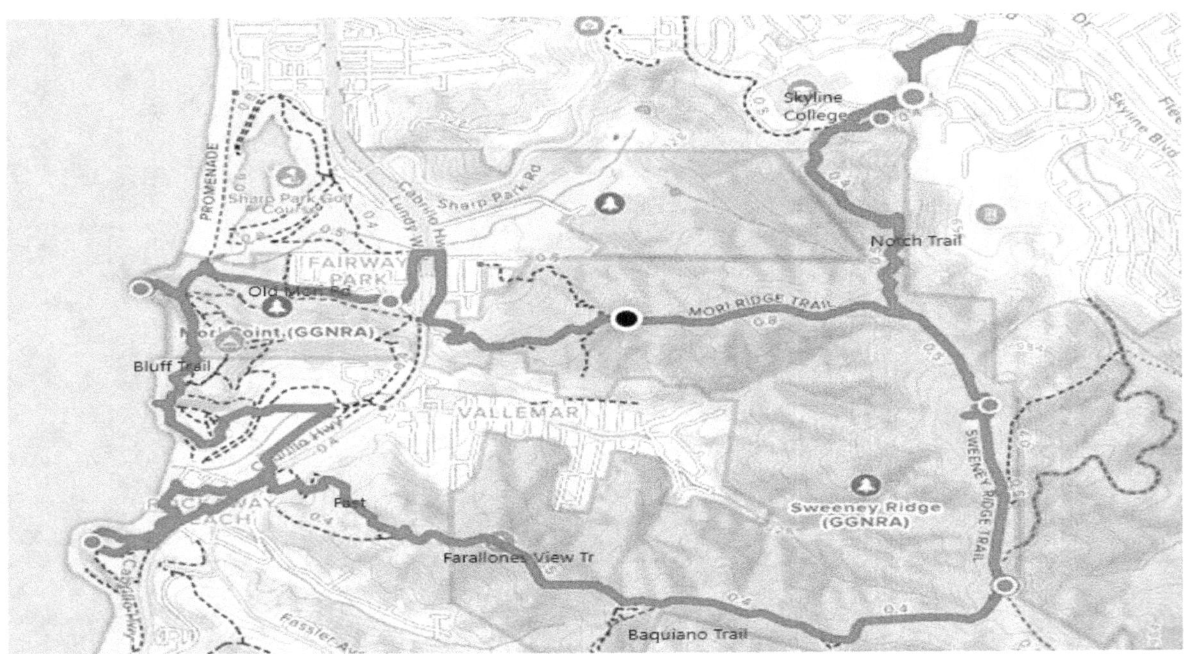

Detail Direction

A trail starts from the Parking on the west side of College Loop Drive. Take the trail to the junction with Mori Ridge Trail and Sweeney Ridge Trail. Then turn right onto Mori Ridge Trail. Follow MRT all the way to residential area where you walk on Lindy Way toward a golf course. There is an underground tunnel on the edge of the golf course to get you safely to the other side of Hwy 1. Next you turn left on Bradford Way and turn right on Old Mori Road to go to Mori Point. There are many trails on Mori Point. Feel free to explore it. Last time I was there, we visited Sharp Park Beach, The Point and Rockaway Beach. They are all so unique and beautiful. When you are ready to go to the mountain, cross Hwy 1 at Fassler Avenue and follow Harvey Way to go behind Our Savior's Lutheran Church. A small trail will bring you uphill to the junction with Farallone's View Trail. Turn left on Farallone's View Trail and continue to climb up. At the junction with Baquiano Trail, turn left. Baquiano Trail ends at Portola Discovery Site of San Francisco Bay. There is a monument there. Finally, you follow Sweeney Ridge Trail to the junction with Mori Ridge. Keep right at the junction to get back to the parking at Skyline College.

Hike Overview

Distance=10.8 miles

Elevation gain=2241 feet

Parking: Gray Whale Cove Parking Lot on Hwy 1

Shaded: No

Trail Map:

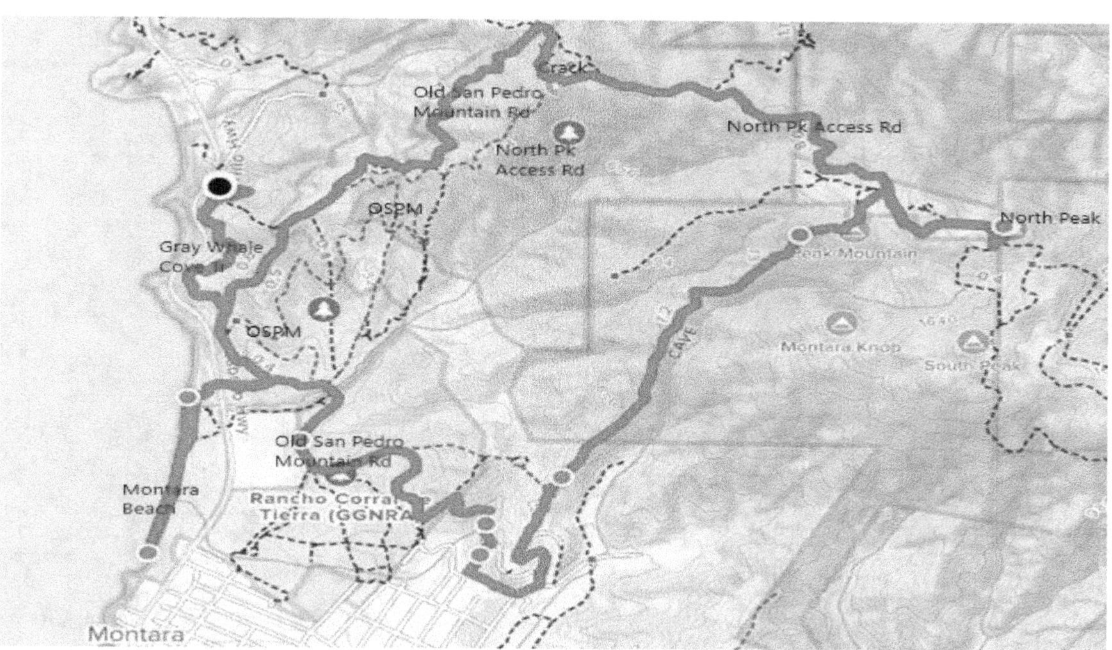

Detail Direction

The Gray Whale Cove Trail starts right from the parking area. Follow the trail for 0.8 miles before you turn left onto Old San Pedro Mountain Road. Stay on OSPMD for over a mile before you take right turn onto Crack and Up Crack trails. The Crack trails climb steeply and end at North Peak Access Road. Turn left onto North Peak Access Road which leads you to the North Peak of Mount Montara. After enjoy the 360 degree view at the peak, retrace the North Peak Access Road until the junction with Cave Trail. Turn left onto Cave trail. This trail ends at Alta Vista Road. Continue on Alta Vista Road until it meets with Elm Street. Turn right on Elm Street. Turn right on Drake Street next. Then turn right on Cedar Street. In about 100 yards, you will see a use trail on the left. Take this trail for 0.2 miles before turn left on another use trail for 0.1 miles. That bring you to the junction with Old San Pedro Mountain Road. Turn right onto OSPMD for 0.7 miles. When the trail is close to the highway 1 near the junction with Gray Whale Cove Trail, cross the highway to access the mile long Montara State Beach. Finally, back to the last junction and turn left onto Gray Whale Cove Trail to go back to your car.

Hike Overview

Distance=17.5 miles

Elevation gain=4426 feet

Parking: North Ridge Trailhead at PCO1 parking (GPS coordinates: 37.45005, -122.33865)

Shaded: 70%

Trail Map:

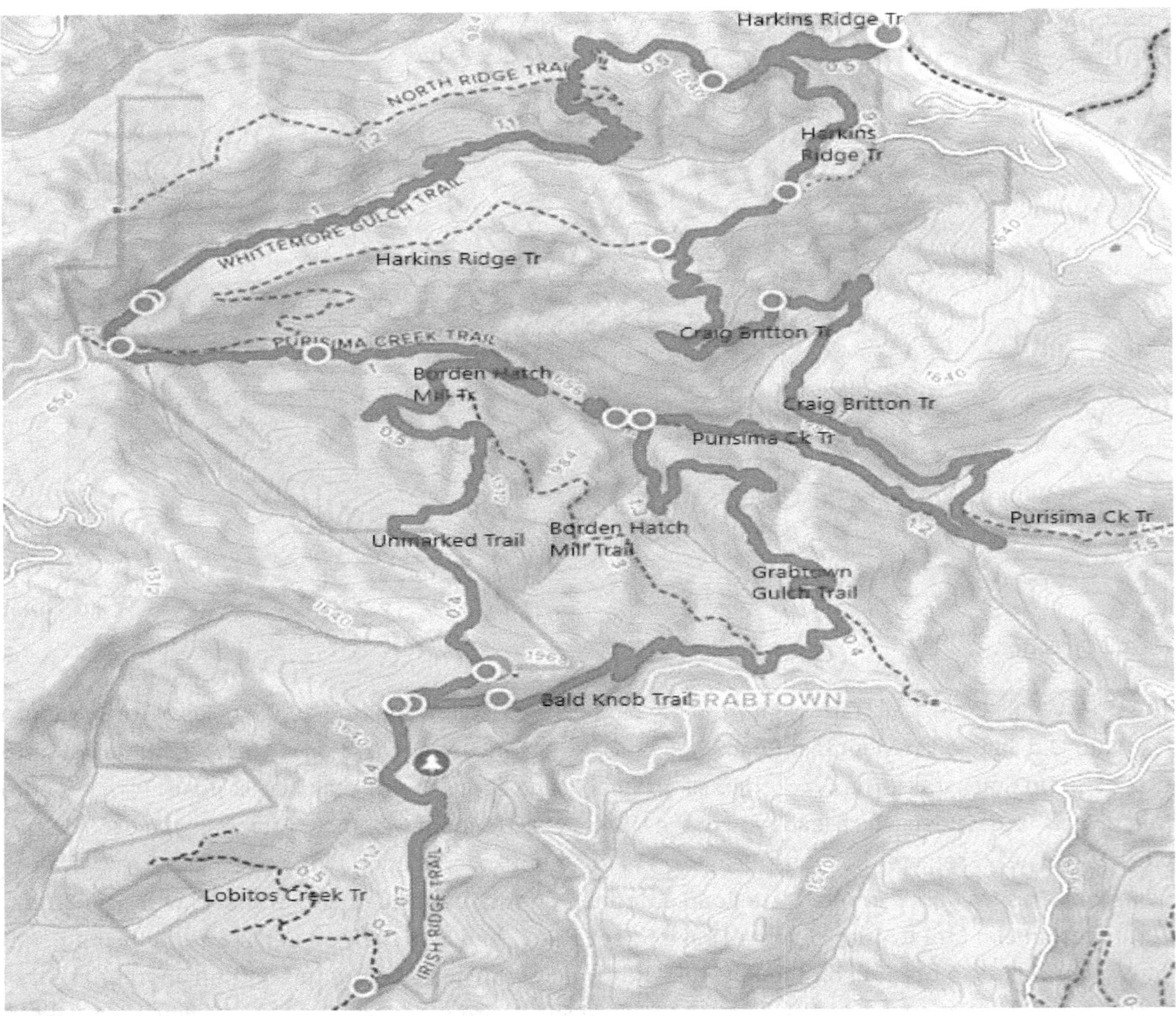

Start from the west side of the parking, keep right to get onto Harkins Ridge Trail. After just 0.5 miles, turn right onto North Ridge Trail. After walking for another 0.5 miles, turn sharply left onto Whittemore Gulch Trail. You need take the lower branch of Whittemore Gulch Trail.

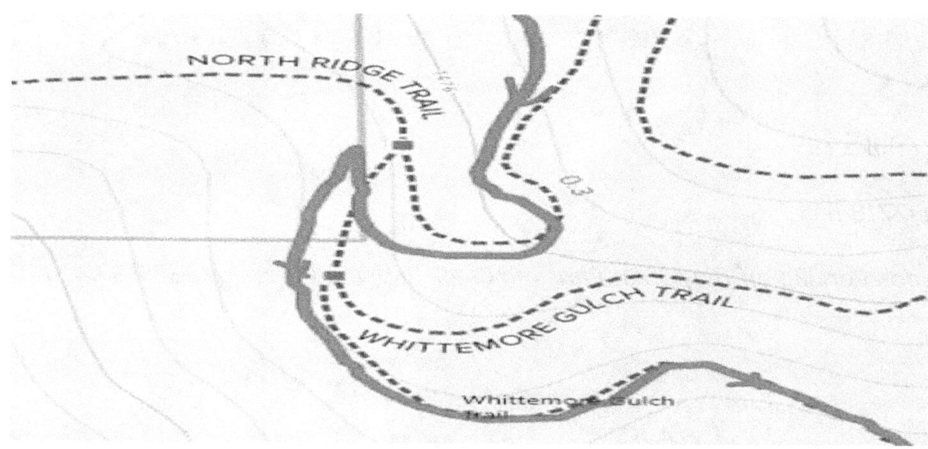

Stay on Whittemore Gulch Trail for 2.7 miles. Then turn right on Harkins Ridge Trail. Almost immediately, turn left on Purisima Creek Trail for 1 mile. Then you leave PCT by turning sharply right onto Borden Hatch Mill Trail. As February, 2019, this junction is not marked.

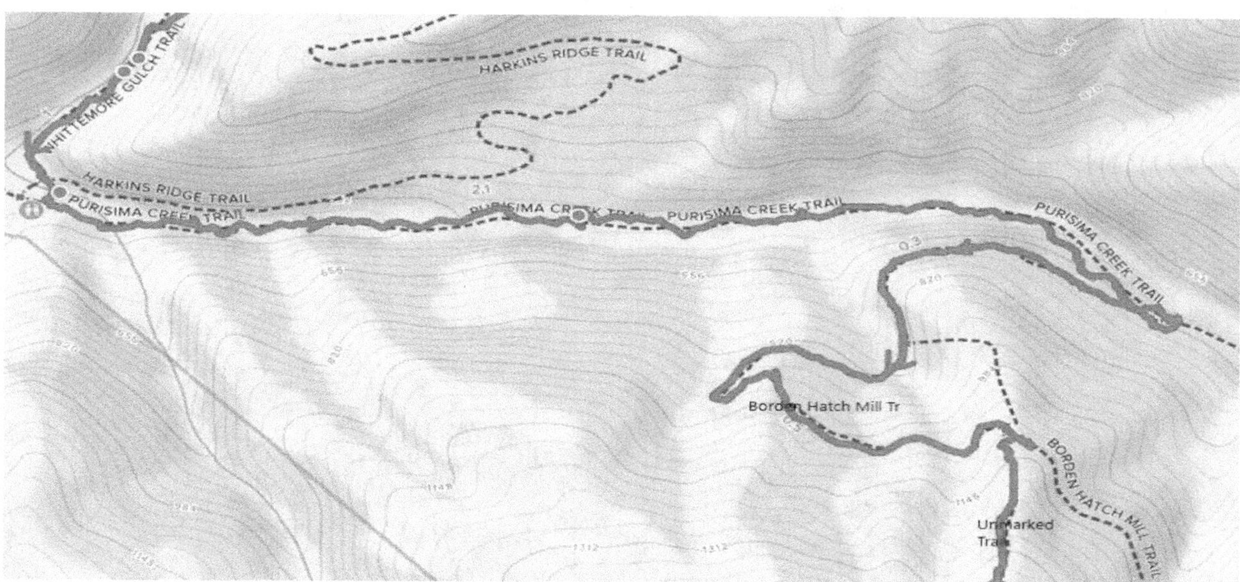

Stay on Borden Hatch Mill Trail for only 0.8 miles. Then you will see another unmarked trail on your right. Turn right here to go straight up for 0.8 miles. You just arrive the highest point of the open space: Bald Knob. After descending from the knob for 0.2 miles, you come to the junction with Bald Knob Trail and Irish Ridge Trail. Continue hike ahead on Irish Ridge Trail for one mile. Then you arrive the junction with Lobitos Creek Trail. It is time to go back now. Retrace your way back to the junction with Bald Knob Trail. Turn right onto Bald Knob Trail. At the junction with Crabtown Gulch Trail, turn left. After 1.5 miles, you are back to Purisima Creek Trail. Turn right onto PCT for 1.2 miles. Then turn left onto Craig Britton Trail for 2.6 miles. At junction with Harkins Ridge Trail, turn right. 0.9 miles later, you are back to North Ridge Trail. Turn right onto North Ridge Trail for 0.3 miles and you arrive at your parking.

Hike Overview

Distance = 11.7 miles

Elevation gain=2713 feet

Parking: Redwood Parking off Hwy 35 at Purisima Creek Redwood Preserve (GPS: 37.42941, -122.31278)

Shaded: 80%

Trail Map:

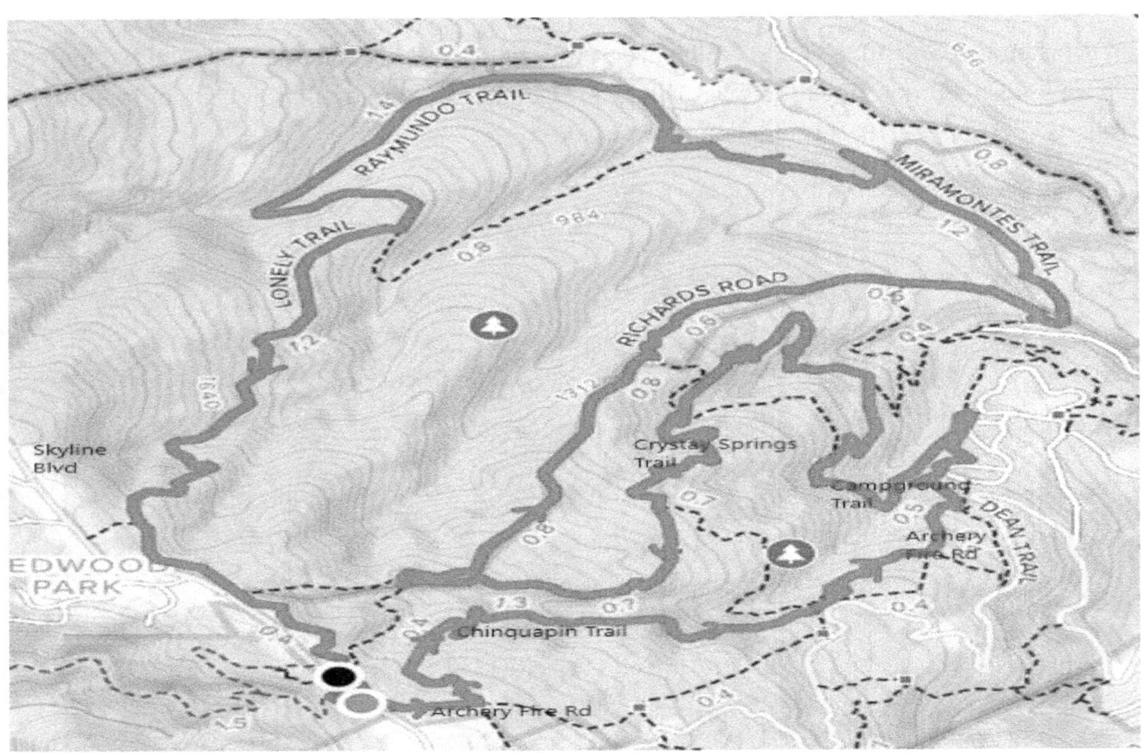

Detail Direction

You start the hike from Redwood Trail in Perisima Creek Open Space. Then cross Skyline Blvd to access Archery Fire Road in Phleger Estate. Turn left on the junction of Archery and Chinquapin Trail. Stay on Chinquapin Trail for 1.3 miles before turn right for Dean Trail. Stay on Dean Trail for about 1 mile. At the junction with Campground Trail, turn sharply left on Campground Trail. At junction with Canyon Trail, turn right onto Canyon Trail. Canyon Trail is only 0.5 miles long. It ends at Crystal Springs Trail. Turn left on CST and stay CST for 2.4 miles. When it finally meets with Summit Springs Trail, turn right. Summit Springs ends very soon at Richards Road. Turn right onto Richards Road. Stay on Richards Road for 1.7 miles before turn left onto Miramontes Trail. At next junction, turn right onto Raymundo Trail for 1.4 miles. Next you stay right to get onto Lonely Trail which becomes Skyline Trail after 1.5 miles. At the junction with Archery Fire Rd, you turn right to cross Skyline Blvd to get back to your car.

Hike Overview

Distance=11.2 miles

Elevation gain=2240 feet

*Parking: Sierra Morena Trailhead off Skyline Blvd(*on the right side of Skyline Blvd, if you are driving south, between Reids Roost Road and Mountain Meadow Road)

Shaded: 80%

Trail Map:

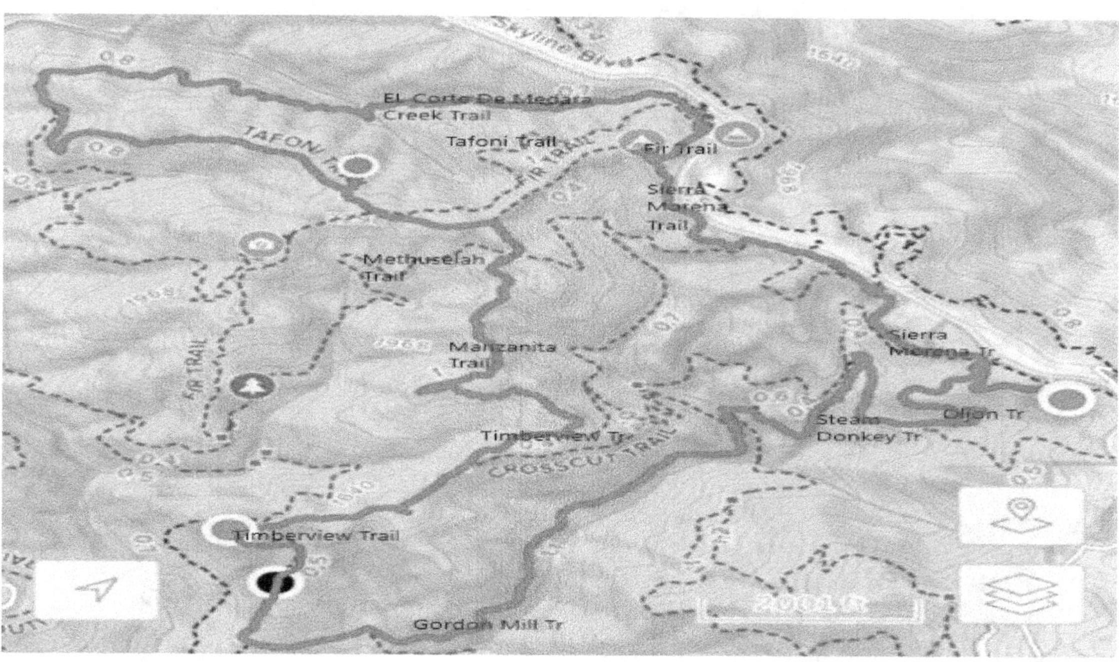

Detail Direction

This hike starts from Sierra Morena Trail off Skyline Blvd. It basically parallels with Skyline Blvd. When it ends at Fir Trail, turn right onto Fir Trail. Then sharp left on to Tafoni Trail and then right on EL Corte De Madera Creek Trail only 100 feet late. Stay on this trail for 1.5 miles. At next junction with Tafoni Trail, turn left to get on Tafoni Trail. Hike Tafoni Trail for 0.8 miles before make a left turn for 0.1 miles to see an old growth redwood. Back to the main trail and continue another 0.1 miles to get the junction with Fir Trail. Go straight to get on Fir Trail. Only 0.2 miles late, turn right onto Manzanita Trail. Stay on this trail for 1.1 miles before you make right turn onto Timberview Trail. Stay on TT for about 1.5 miles. At junction with Gordon Mill Trail and Lawrence Creek Trail, you choose Gordon Mill Trail. Stay on GMT for 1.1 miles. Then slightly right to get onto Spring Board Trail. At the next junction, turn left to go Steam Donkey Trail. At junction with Oljon Trail, Stay left to take on Oljon Trail. Finally turn right on Sierra Morena Trail to get back to the trail head.

Hike Overview

Distance=11.7 miles

Elevation gain=2218 feet

Parking: Bear Gulch Parking in Woodside

Shaded: 80%

Trail Map:

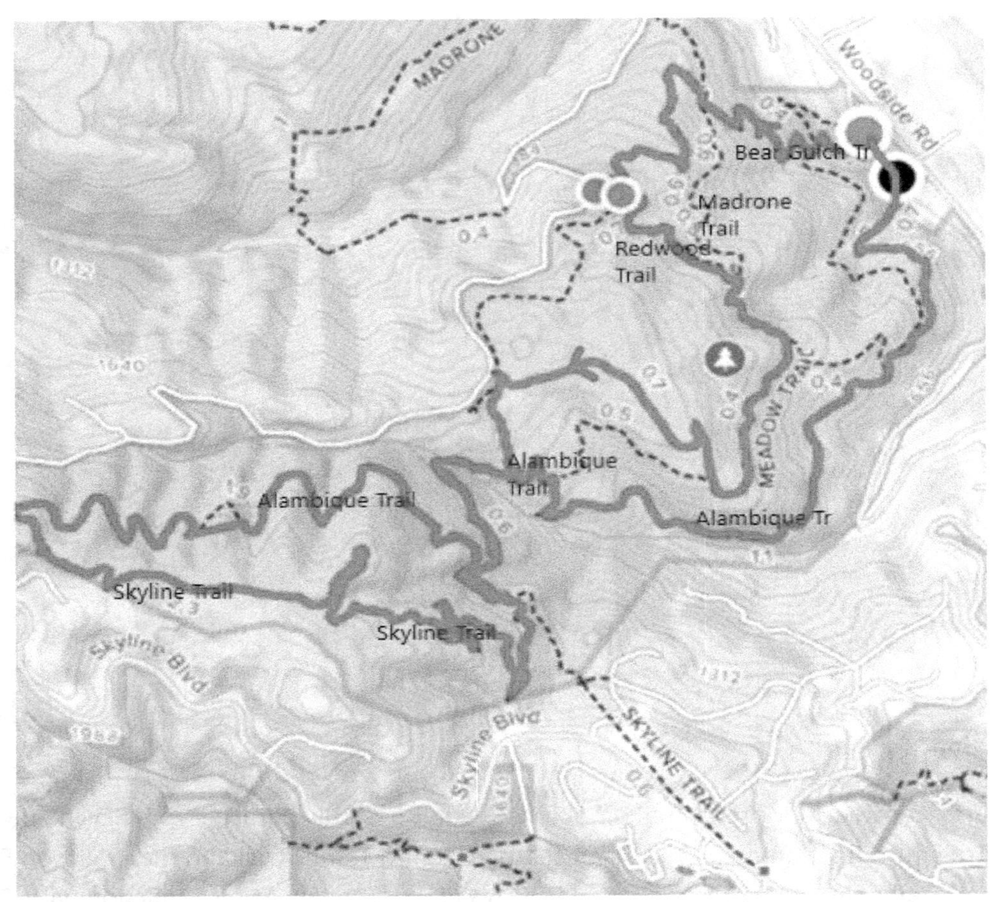

Detail Direction

There are three trails leave the parking lot: Loop Trail, Bear Gulch Trail and Alambique Trail. I took the middle trail: Bear Gulch Trail. After climbing for 1.2 miles, turn left onto Redwood Trail. Redwood Trail ends at Meadow Trail. Turn right on Meadow Trail for 1.1 miles. Then turn left on Bear Gulch Trail and right on Alambique Trail. At junction with Skyline Trail, take sharp right to stay on Alambique Trail. This trail ends at Skyline Trail. Take sharp left turn to get on Skyline Trail. Stay on Skyline Trail for 2.3 miles before you take on the right fork of Alambique Trail. Stay on Alambique Trail all the way to the parking.

Hike Overview

Distance=15 miles

Elevation gain=2950 feet

Parking: Betsy Crowder Trailhead off Portola Road

Shaded: 70%

Trail Map:

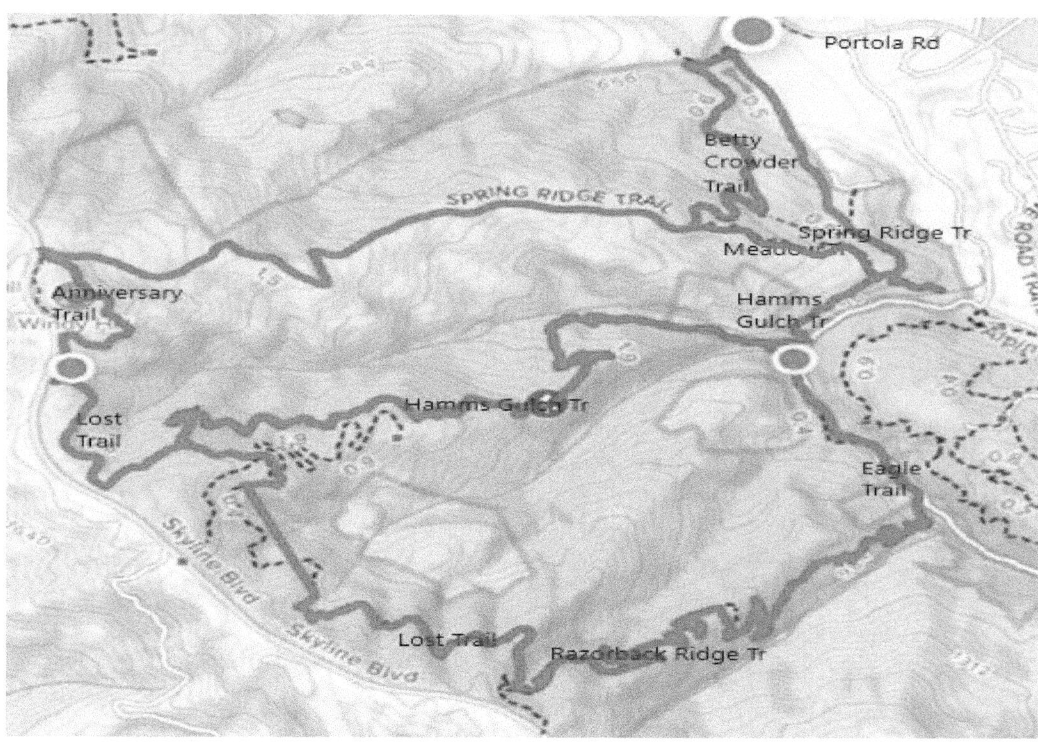

Detail Direction

Windy Hill Preserve is a beautiful small open space in Portola Valley. Hike toward the hills for 0.2 mile before turn left at fork. With Sausal Pond on your right, hike another 0.5 mile. At the junction with Spring Ridge Trail, turn left again for 0.2 miles. At the next junction, turn right onto Hamms Gulch Trail. Stay on Hamms Gulch Trail for 2.5 miles. At the junction with Lost Trail, turn right onto Lost Trail for 0.6 miles. Then turn right onto Anniversary Trail for 0.5 miles. At the junction with Spring Ridge Trail, turn right onto SRT. SRT bring you down the hills. At the junction with Meadow Trail, turn right onto Meadow trail for 0.5 miles. Meadow Trail ends at Hamms Gulch Trail. Turn right onto HGT for 0.3 miles before you turn left onto Eagle Trail. At the end of Eagle Trail, turn right on to Razorback Ridge Trail. After multiple switchbacks, you come to the junction with Lost Trail. Turn right on Lost Trail. Then turn right on Hamms Gulch Trail and left on Spring Ridge Trail to back to your car.

Hike Overview

Distance=13.6 miles

Elevation gain=2280 feet

Parking: Los Trancos Open Space Preserve parking lot

Shaded: 50%

Trail Map:

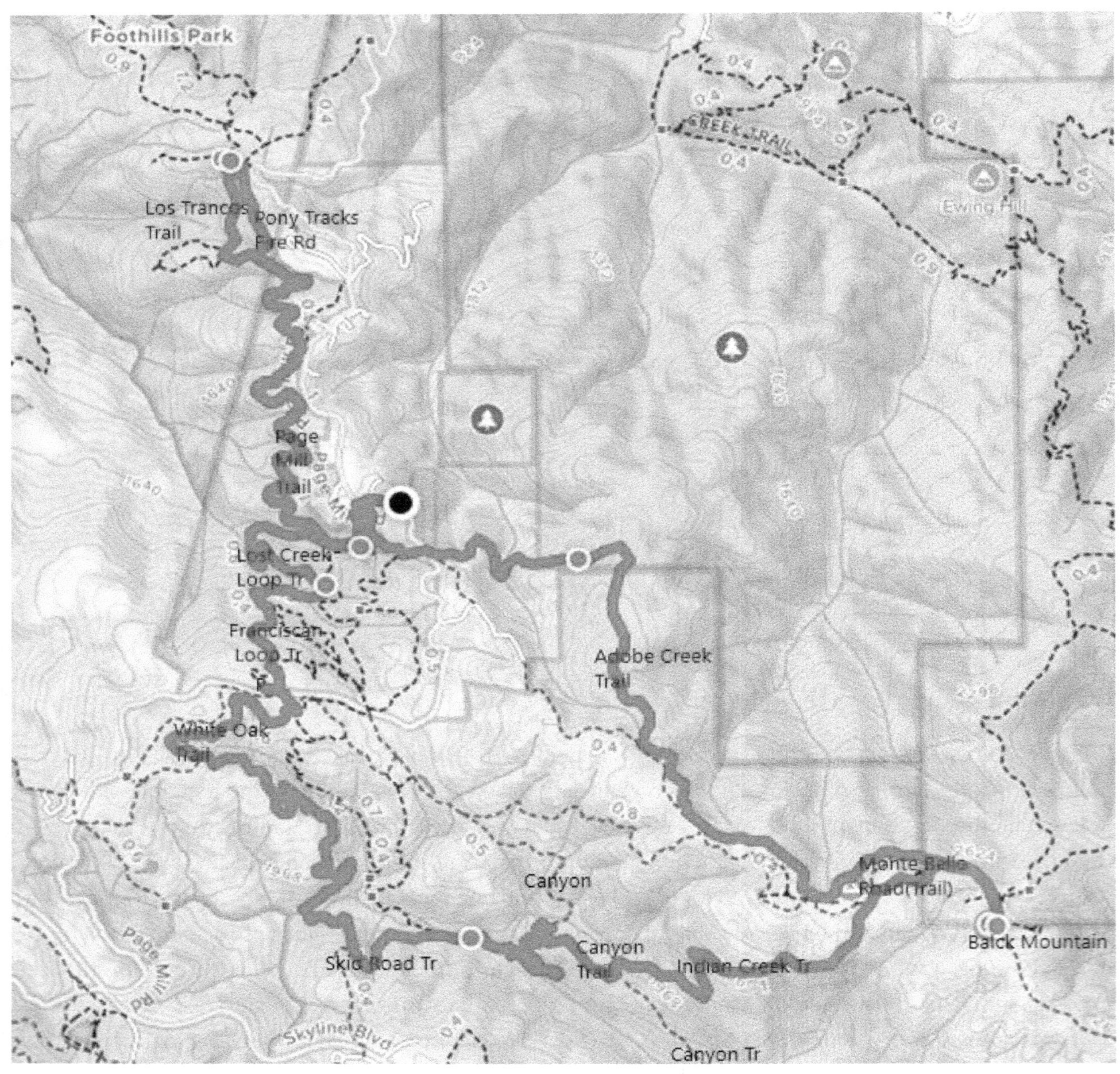

Detail Direction

Start from the parking lot and hike down Franciscan Loop Trail downhill. At the junction with Lost Creek Loop Trail, turn left onto LCLT. At the junction with Page Mill Trail, turn left again to continue downhill for one more mile. At one mile's end, stay left at the fork. The right fork bring you to Page Mill Road. The left fork ends at the junction with Pony Tracks Fire Road and Los Trancos Trail. You stay right to get onto Pony Tracks Fire Road for 0.3 miles. Then you turn left on Shotgun Fire Road. Very quickly you need turn left again to go uphill on Los Trancos Trail. Follow Los Trancos Trail to Page Mill Trail. When you are back to the junction with Lost Creek Loop Trail, take the left branch of Page Mill Trail to go to Page Mill Road. Walk on the side of Page Mill Road for a few dozen yards before cross the road to access Adobe Creek Trail. Adobe Creek Trail ends at Monte Bello Road. Turn left on Monte Bello Road. Stay on MBR until you reach the junction with Black Mountain Trail. Stay right to reach Black Mountain summit where you can see all major peaks in the bay area. Retrace your steps to the junction of MBR and Indian Creek Trail and stay slightly left to go downhill on Indian Creek trail for 1 mile. At the junction with Canyon Trail, you turn right to get on Canyon Trail for 0.3 miles. Then turn left onto Stevens Creek Nature Trail for 0.5 miles. At the junction with Skid Road Trail, keep left to get on Skid Road Trail for 0.3 miles. At the next junction, turn right onto White Oak Trail. White Oak Trail ends at Monte Bello Open Space Preserve parking lot. Walk across Page Mill Road to get back to your car.

Hike Overview

Distance=23.60 miles

Elevation gain=4140 feet

Parking: parking lot at the corner of Skyline Blvd and Alpine Road

Shaded: 50%

Trail Map:

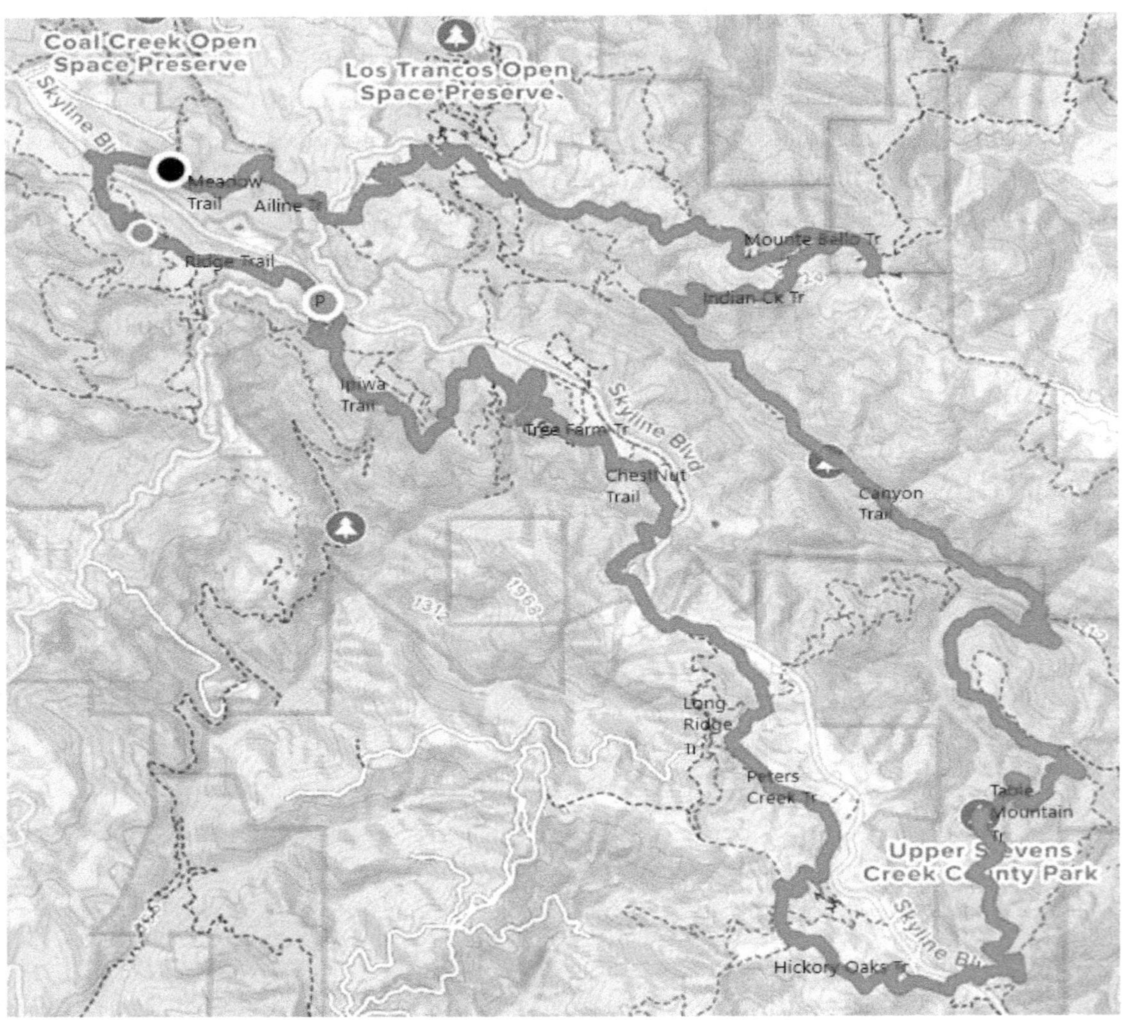

Detail Direction

Park your car at the small parking lot at the corner of Skyline Blvd and Alpine Road and follow Ipiwa Trail. Ipiwa Trail is also part of Bay Area Ridge Trail. Continue onto Sunny Jim Trail. Sunny Jim Trail connects with Horseshoe Lake Trail. Continue on Horseshoe Lake Trail. Then turn sharply left onto Tree Farm Trail.

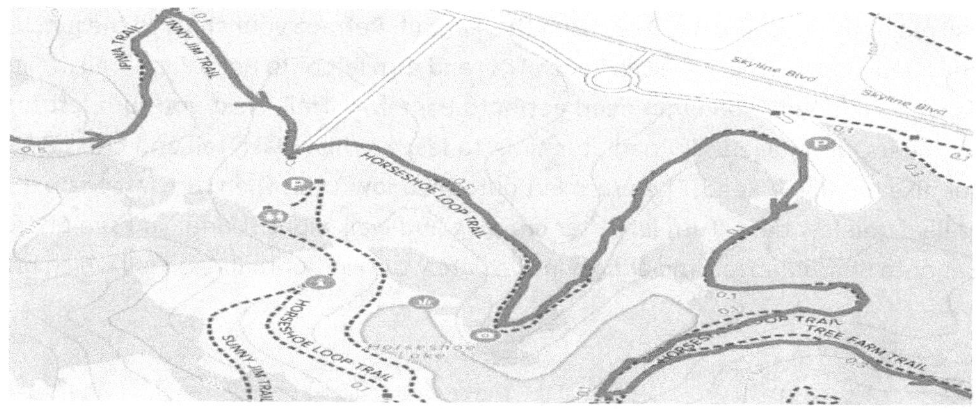

At the junction with Chestnut Trail, turn slightly right onto Chestnut Trail. Then turn slightly right on Ridge Trail. Ridge Trail becomes Chestnut again soon. At three-way junction with Long Ridge Trail and Peters Creek Trail, go straight onto Peters Creek Trail. PCT ends at the junction with Long Ridge Trail and Ward Road. Take 1st left onto Ward Road for only 0.1 miles. The Stay left to get onto Bay Area Ridge Trail for 0.2 miles. Next turn left onto Hickory Oaks Trail. Stay on Hickory Oaks Trail until it ends at Skyline Blvd.

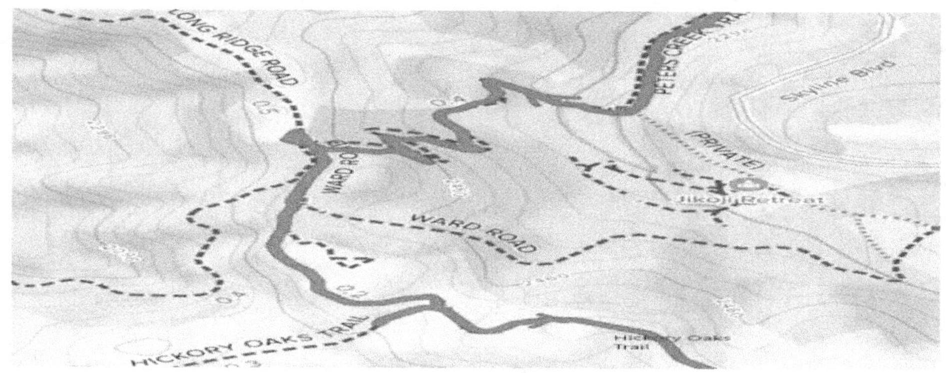

Cross Skyline Blvd and following Saratoga Gap Trail to the junction with Charcoal Road and Table Mountain Trail. Turn left onto Table Mountain Trail and follow the trail all the way to Table Mountain and the junction with Canyon Trail. Turn left onto Canyon Trail for 2.5 miles. Then turn right onto Indian Creek Trail. Stay on it until it ends at Monte Bello Road. Follow Monte Bello Road for 0.2 miles to the Black Mountain summit.

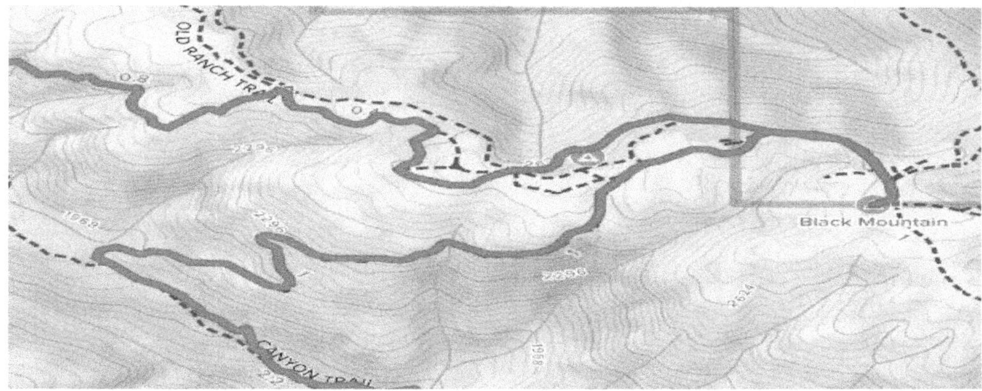

You can see all major peaks of the Bay Area from the summit. Retrace your steps to the junction of Monte Bello Road and Indian Creek Trail. Take Old Ranch Trail and turn left onto Bella Vista Trail. Next turn slightly right onto Canyon Trail. Very soon you need get onto Page Mill Trail. Next you turn left for White Oak Trail. When it meets with Page Mill Road, it is time to leave White Oak Trail and cross Page Mill Road. Continue your hike on Alpine Road. Then turn left onto Meadow Trail. Then turn left again on Cloud Rest. Cross Skyline Blvd one last time. Turn left after crossing and walk along it until you see Charquin Trail on your right. Get onto Charquin Trail and almost immediately turn left onto Ridge Trail which bring you back to your car.

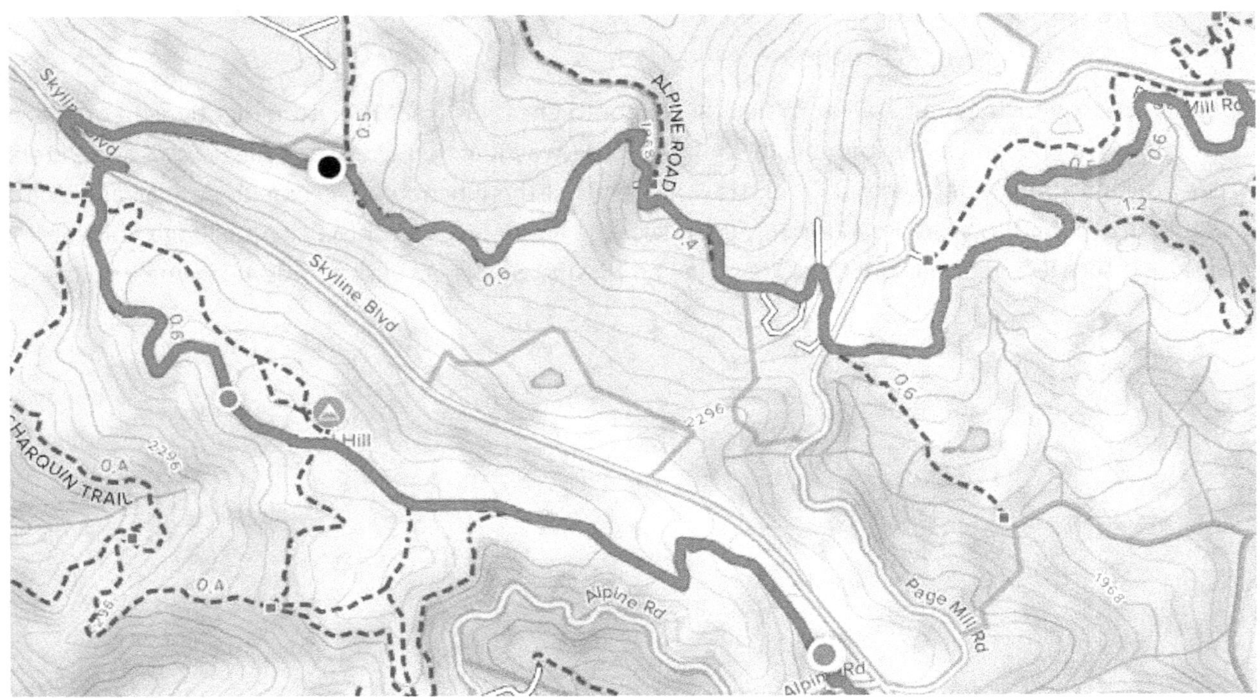

Hike Overview

Distance=15.7 miles

Elevation gain=3219 feet

Parking: Rancho San Antonio Open Space Preserve parking

Shaded: 50%

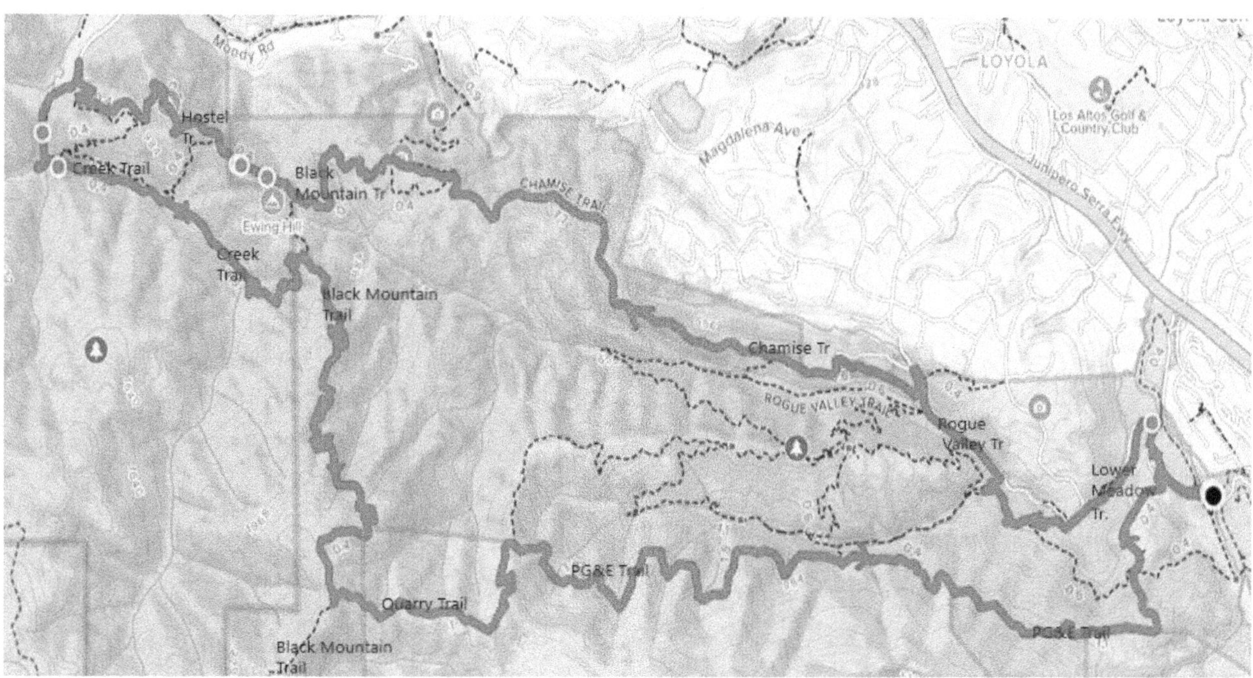

Detail Direction

You start this hike from Lower Meadow Trail near the bathroom in Rancho San Antonio Open Space Preserve. Take left on Farm Bypass trail before join Coyote Trail. Then take sharp right onto Connect to Deer Hollow Park. At the junction with Wildcat Canyon Trail, take right turn for 0.1 miles. At its end, turn left onto Rogue Valley Trail. Take right at the next junction with Ravenbury Trail for 0.2 miles. Turn sharp left for Chamise Trail. Chamise Trail becomes Black Mountain Trail after about 2 miles. Stay on BMT for 0.3 miles and then turn left on Hostel Trail which takes you all the way down to garden and picnic table at Hidden Villa. After visit the garden and the villa, walk toward the valley and turn left Creek Trail. Creek Trail will take you back to Black Mountain Trail at top of the ridge. Climbing 2 miles on BMT before you arrive the junction with Quarry Trail. Now you have two choices: climb along BMT for 0.9 miles and summit the Black Mountain or turn left on Quarry Trail. I decided to take QT because of time constraint. One mile late, stay right at junction to take PG&E Trail. Follow PG&E Trail all the way to the parking.

Hike Overview

Distance=14 miles

Elevation gain=2398 feet

Parking: Stevens Canyon Road side or Stevens Creek County Park parking lot

Shaded: 40%

Trail Map:

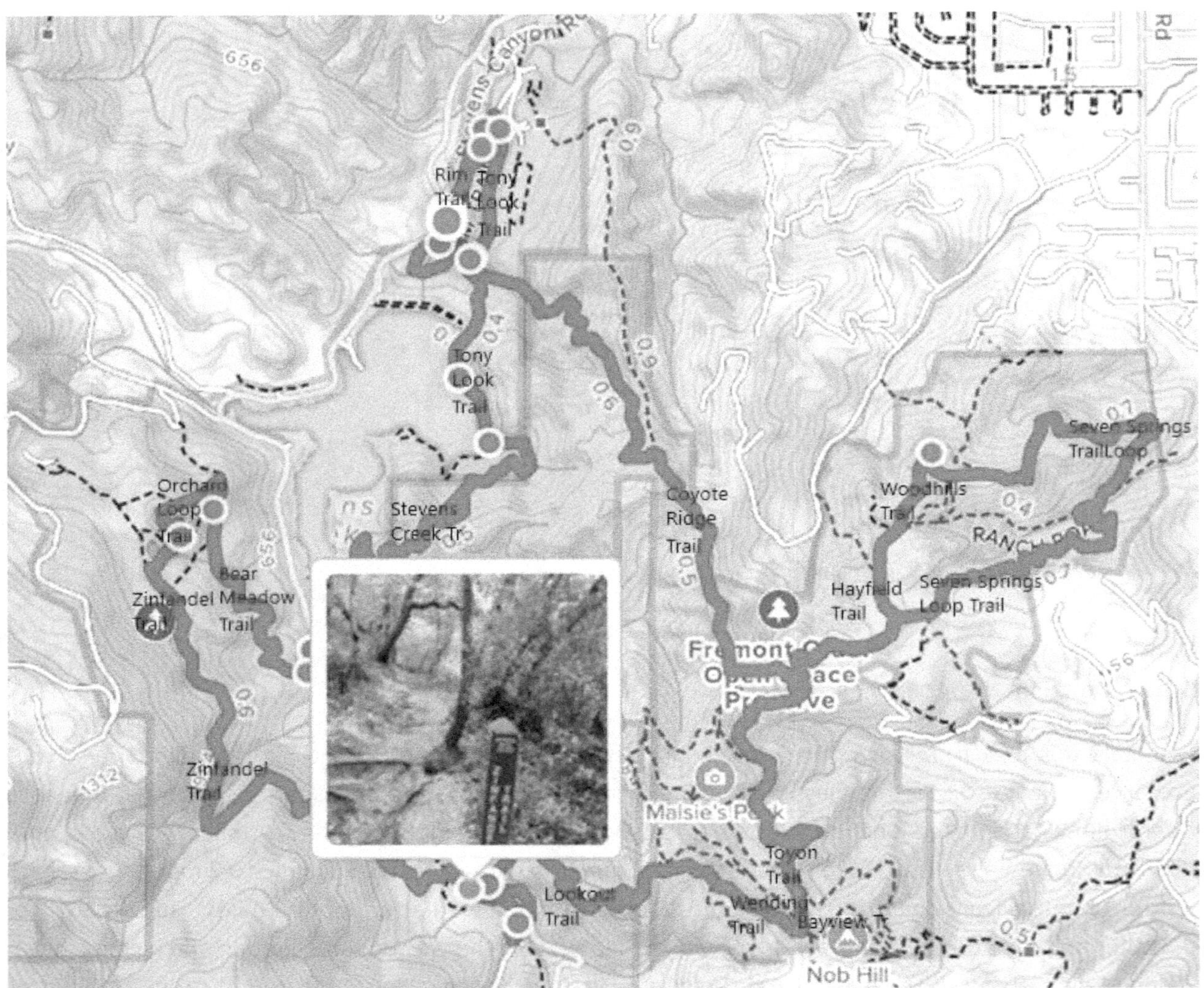

Detail Direction

Start the hike on Rim Trail from where you park. Turn right onto Tony Look Trail when you arrive at the junction. Tony Look Trail goes around Stevens Creek Reservoir initially. It starts to climb uphill after the junction with Loop Trail. But it comes down when it is close to Stevens Canyon Road. Cross Stevens Canyon

Road and walk on the shoulder for a few hundred yards until you see sign for Bear Meadow Trail on your left.

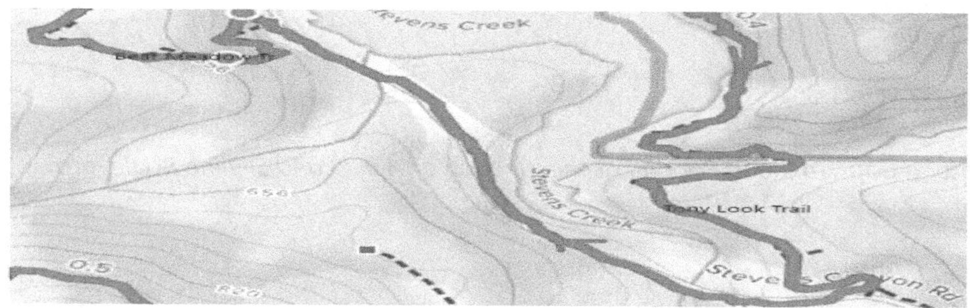

Hike on Bear Meadow Trail until the second junction with Orchard Loop Trail. Turn left on Orchard and left on Zinfandel Trail. Zinfandel Trail ends at Creek Trail in Cooley Picnic Area. Turn left on Creek Trail, cross Stevens Canyon Road one more time and turn left to hike to Sycamore Group Area. Look Out Trail is on the right side (hill side). Using Outlook Cut Off Trail (0.1 miles) to gain access of Look Out Trail. Turn right onto Lookout Trail. Stay on Lookout Trail till its junction with Wedding Trail. Turn right onto Wedding Trail. Then turn left on Bay View Trail. At its junction with Toyon Trail, get on the left branch of Toyon Trail.

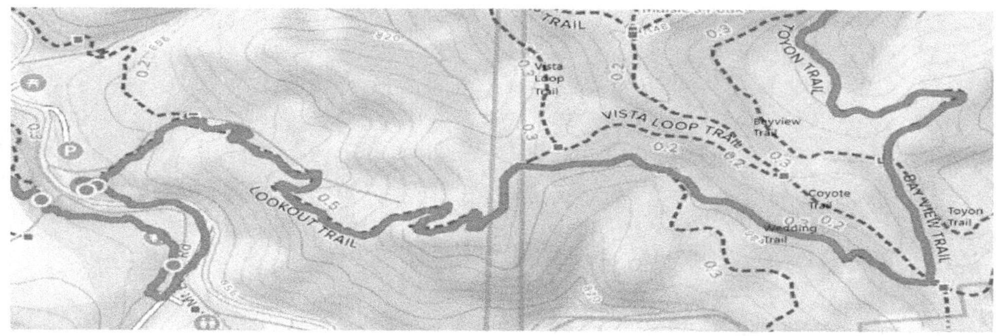

At the junction with Hayfield Trail, turn right. Next, you need get on Seven Springs Loop Trail. Stay on Seven Springs Loop Trail until its junction with Woodhills Trail. Stay right to get on Woodhills Trail. Woodhills Trail brings you to Hunter Point where you have a nice view of Saratoga and nearby areas. Woodhills Trail ends at Hayfield Trail. Stay on Hayfield Trail until the junction with Coyote Ridge Trail. Turn right onto Coyote Ridge Trail and follow it all the way to Rim Trail and back to your car.

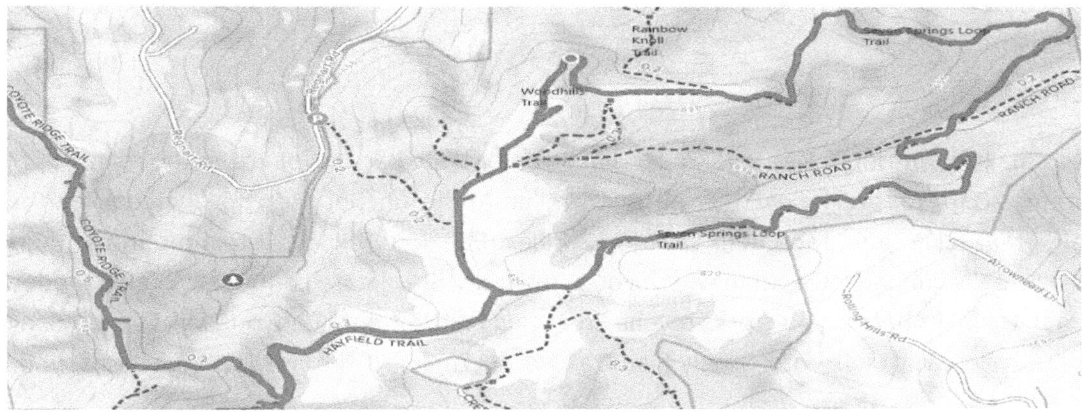

Hike Overview

Distance=14.9 miles

Elevation gain=2605 feet

Parking: Saratoga Gap Trailhead Parking at the junction of Hwy 9 and Skyline Boulevard

Shaded: 85%

Trail Map:

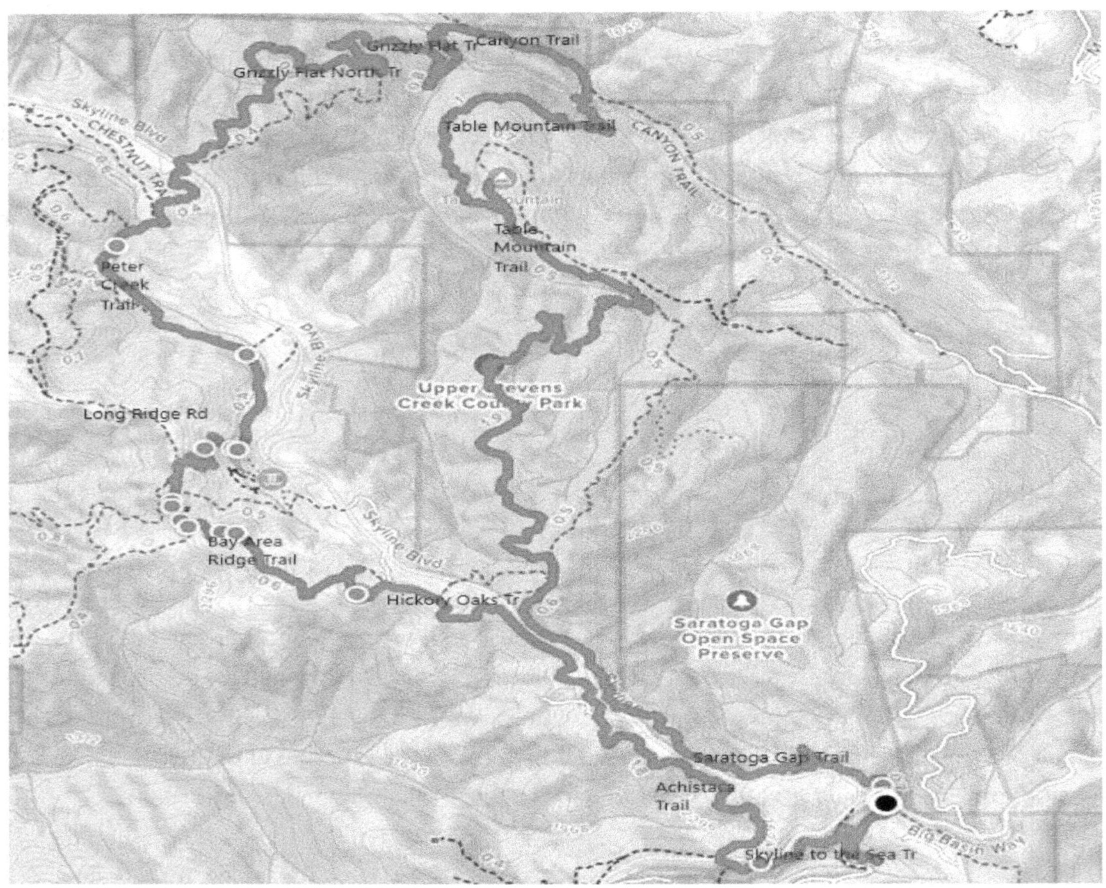

Detail Direction

There is a small parking lot at Saratoga Gap trailhead and a large parking lot across the road. Start the hike from Saratoga Gap Trail and follow the trail for 1.7 miles. At the junction with the Charcoal Road and Table Mountain Trail, take Table Mountain Trail for 2 miles. But don't expect a real mountain there. Table Mountain is really flat and lower than where you come from. Stay left to continue on Table Mountain Trail for another 1.2 miles before you cross Stevens Creek and turn left onto Canyon Trail. Stay on Canyon Trail for only 0.3 miles. Turn left onto Grizzly Flat Trail for one mile. At the next two junctions, you have to choose you want to go Grizzly Flat Trail North or Grizzly Flat Trail South. Either way is fine because they meet again and again. But I chose Grizzly Flat Trail North each time.

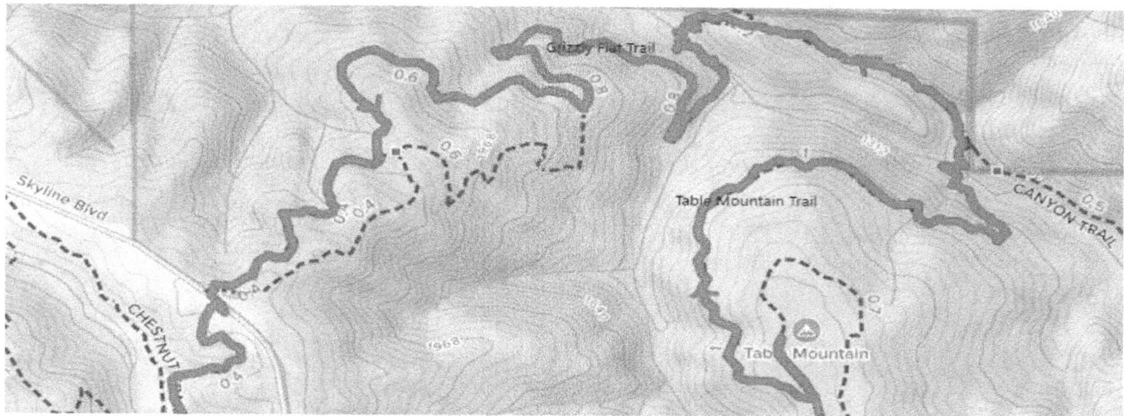

Grizzly Flat Trail North (or South) ends at a gate. Exit the gate and cross Skyline Blvd. Grizzly Flat Trail continues on the other side of Skyline Blvd and end at the junction with Chestnut Trail and Peters Creek Trail. Turn left onto Peters Creek Trail for 1.2 miles. Then you come to the side of Two Moon Lake. Don't trespass since the lake is privately owned by Jikoji Retreat. Peters Creek Trail turns right there and goes uphill. Next you are at the junction with Long Ridge Road and Ward Road. Take the 1st left onto the upper branch of Ward Road for just 0.1 miles before you stay right to get onto Bay Area Ridge Trail for 0.2 miles.

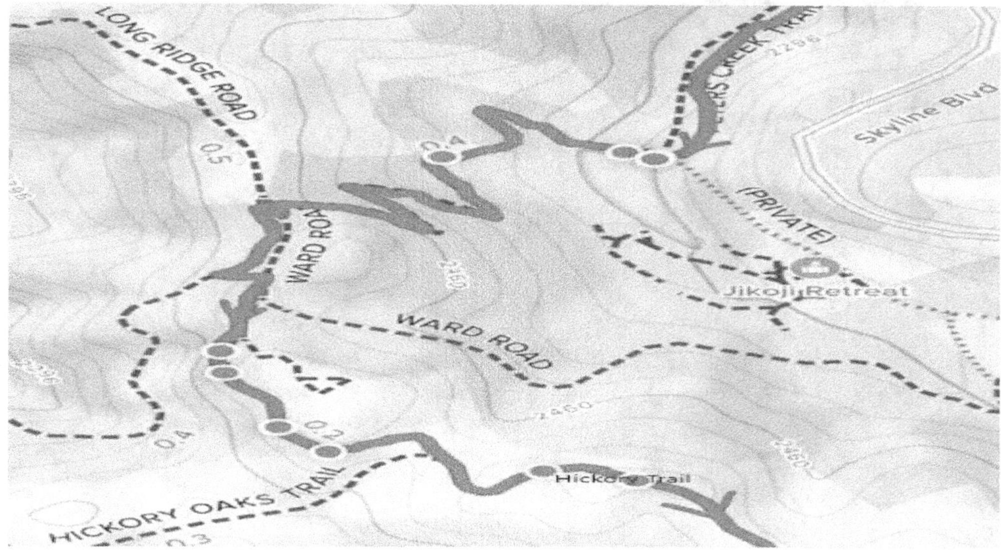

Then turn left onto Hickory Oaks Trail for 0.6 miles. There is a vista on your right. Leave Hickory Trail briefly and turn right to access the vista which offers panoramic views all the way to the Pacific. After resting at the bench and snapping a few pictures, you come down the vista and rejoin Hickory Trail. Hickory Trail connects with Achistaca Trail. Continue your hike on Achistaca Trail for 1.8 miles. The trail ends at the junction with Skyline to the Sea Trail at Big Basin Way. Cross Big Basin Way and turn left onto Skyline to the Sea Trail. Slightly right onto Saratoga Gap Trail and turn sharply left onto Indian Trail Road. Indian Trail Road ends at Skyline Blvd. Cross Skyline Blvd and you are back to the parking.

Hike Overview

Distance=15.4 miles

Elevation gain=2546 feet

Parking: Castle Rock State Park parking lot at the junction of Hwy 9 and Skyline Boulevard

Shaded: 100%

Trail Map:

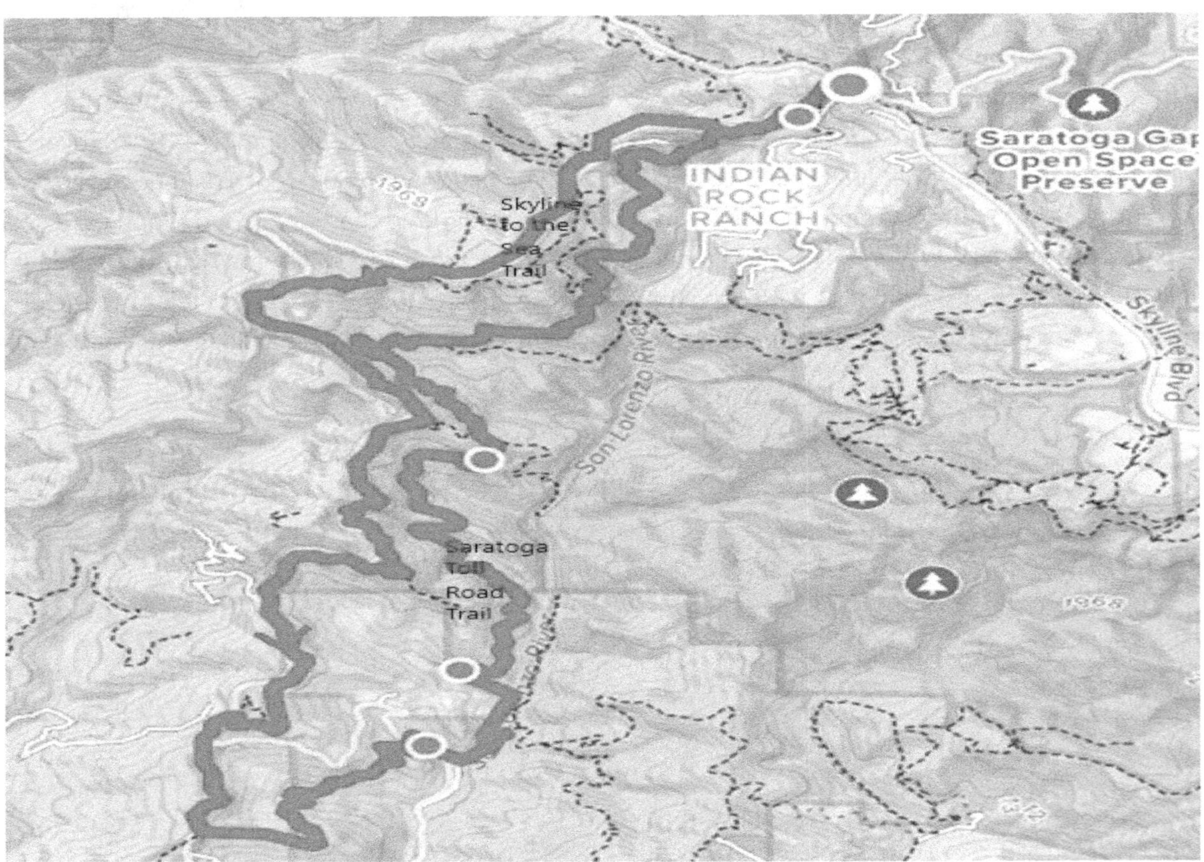

Detail Direction

You cross Skyline Boulevard from the parking and get on Skyline-to-the-Sea Trail. In about 1 mile, you come to the junction with Saratoga Toll Road Trail. You just keep right to stay on Skyline-to-the-Sea Trail. The trail crosses Big Basin Way soon after. Continue hiking on the famed trail until you pass Waterman Gap. Then watch out for Skyline-to-the-Sea/Toll Road Interconnector Trail on your left. Turn left onto the connector. Then turn left again on next junction with Saratoga Toll Road Trail. Stay on STRT all the way until it ends at Skyline-to-the-Sea Trail. Turn right onto Skyline-to-the-Sea Trail. You are back to the parking in about 0.5 miles.

Hike Overview

Distance=18 miles

Elevation gain=3652 feet

Parking: Castle Rock State Park parking lot at the junction of Hwy 9 and Skyline Boulevard

Shaded: 95%

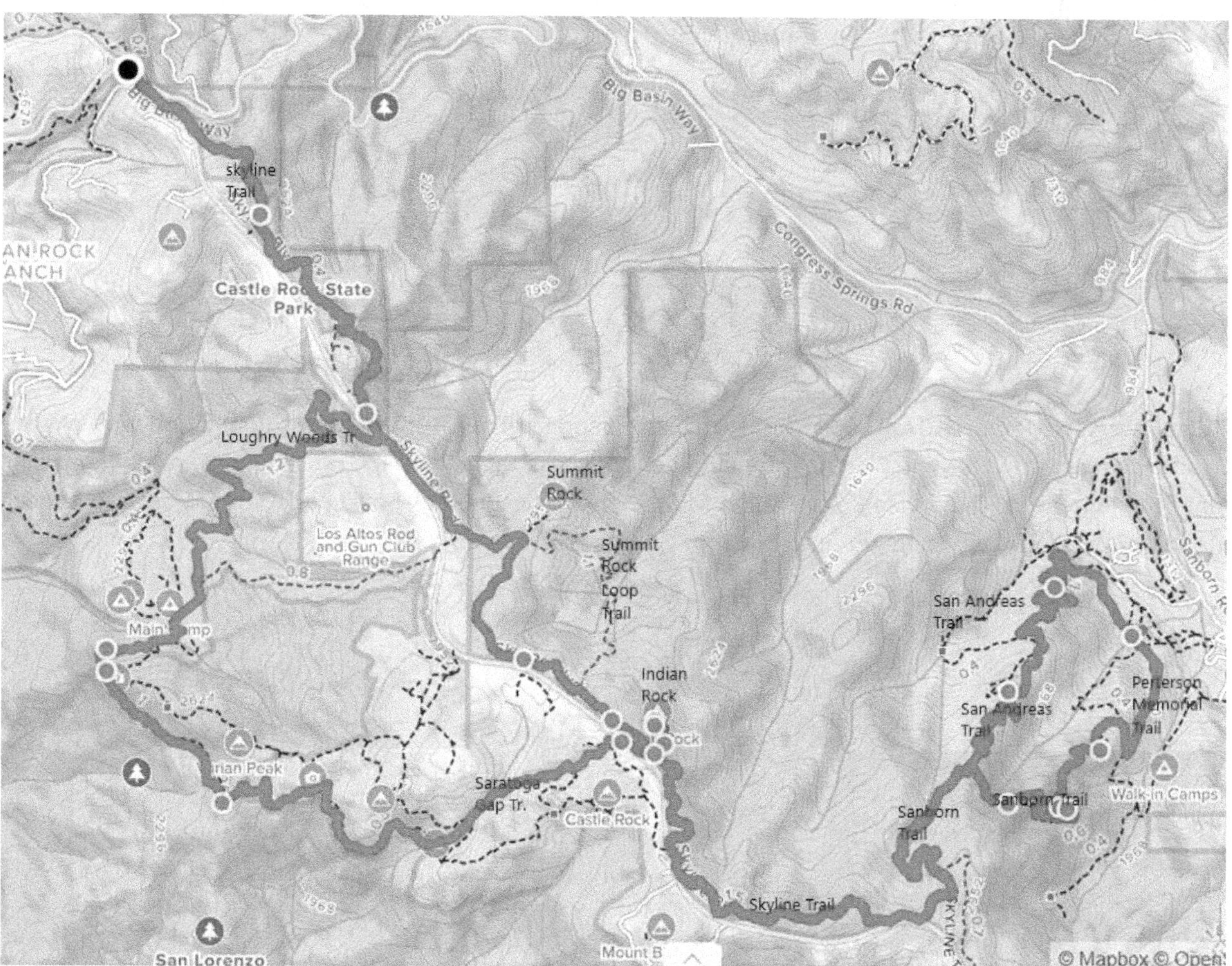

Detail Direction

You leave the parking by following the Skyline Trail in the South-East direction. Follow Skyline Trail which parallels Highway 35 (or Skyline Blvd) all the way until its junction with Sanborn Trail in Sanborn County Park. Turn left (downhill) onto Sanborn Trail. Stay on it until it meets with San Andreas Trail. Turn left onto San Andreas Trail. At next two junctions, go straight. At the junction with San Andreas Trail, take the right branch of San Andreas Trail to climb up the hills again. Stay on San Andreas Trail until its junction with Peterson Memorial Trail.

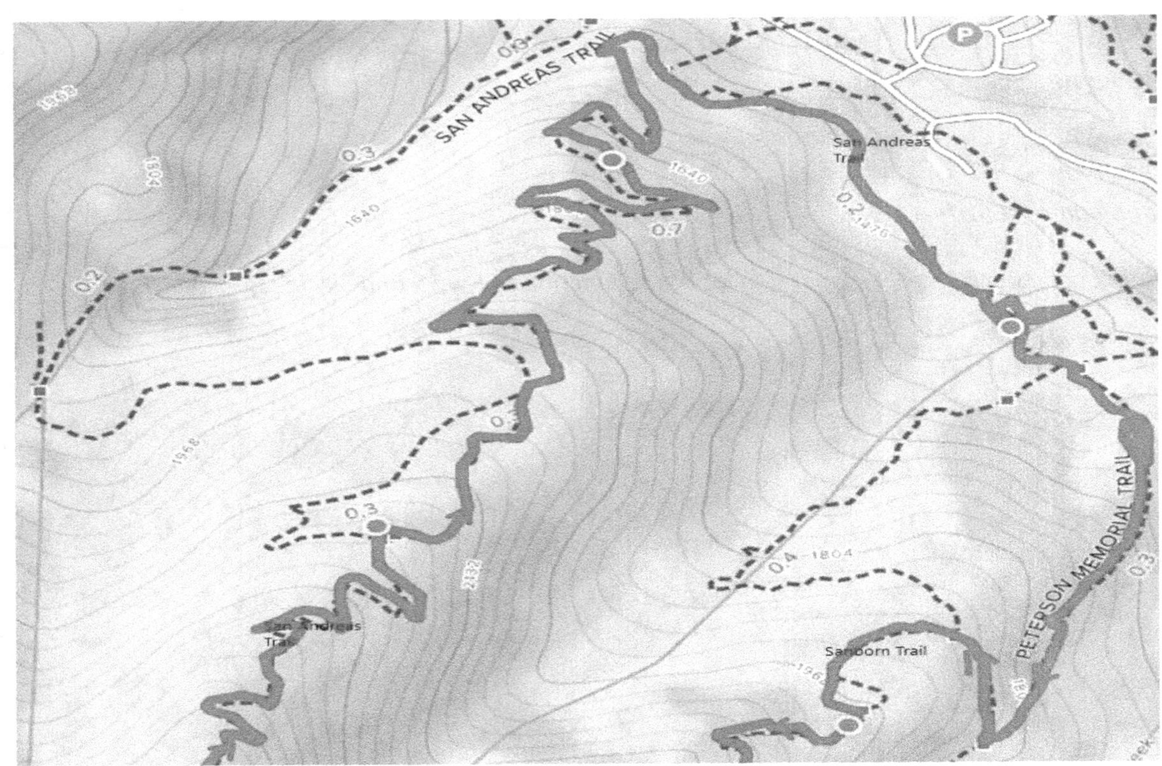

Take Peterson Memorial Trail. Then turn right onto Sanborn Trail. Turn right at the junction with Skyline Trail. You need cross Skyline Blvd near Indian Rock to access Saratoga Gap Trail. Follow Saratoga Gap Trail until the junction with Service Road Trail at Main Camp in Castle Rock State Park. Turn right onto Service Road for just 0.1 miles. Then get onto Loughry Woods Trail on your left .

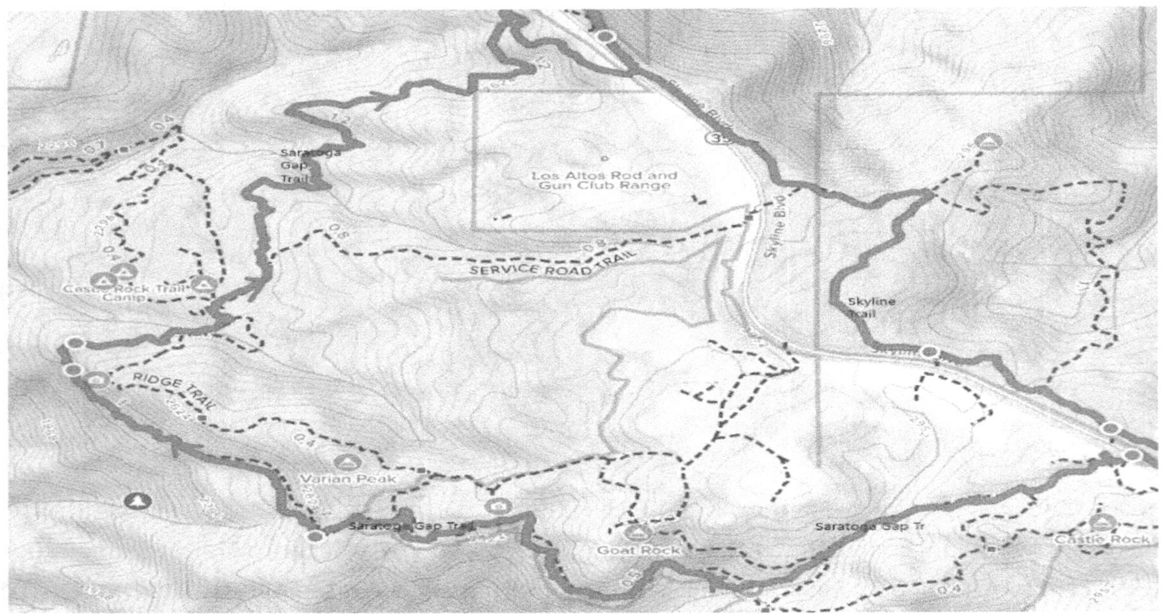

The trail ends Skyline Blvd at Summit Rock Parking. Cross Skyline Blvd one last time to get back onto Skyline Trail. Finally turn right on Skyline Trail and the trail brings you back to the parking.

Hike Overview

Distance=13 miles

Elevation gain=2130 feet

Parking: roadside parking at China Grade and Big Basin Way junction

Shaded: 90%

Trail Map:

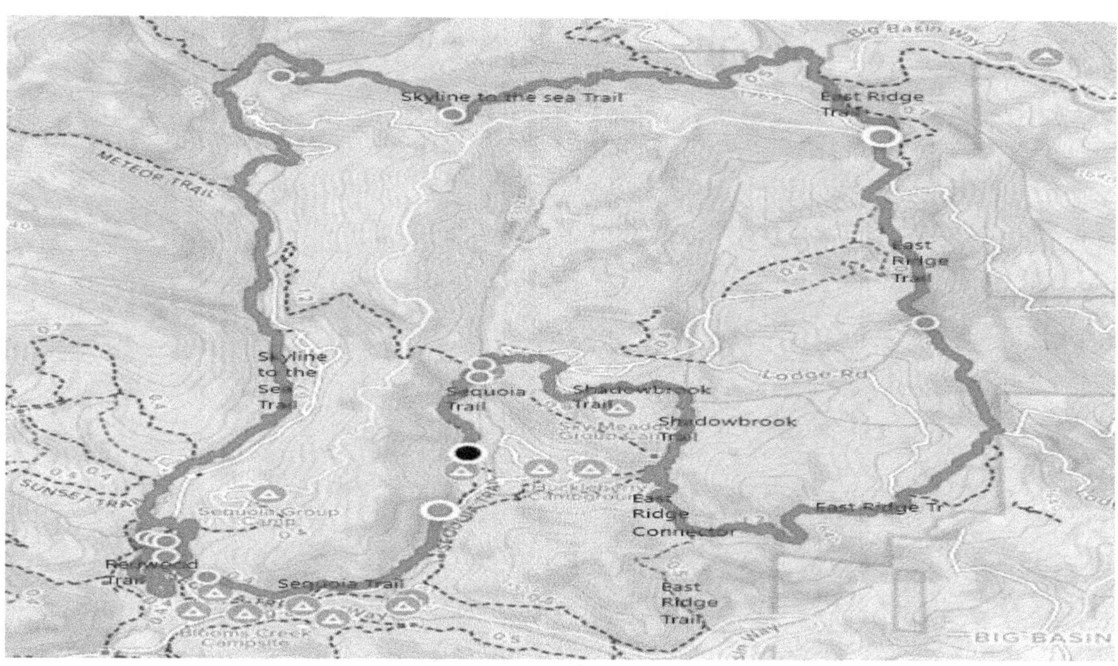

Detail Direction

Walk down China Grade Road from your car at the junction of China Grade and Big Basin Way. Watch out the sign for East Ridge Trail. Turn right onto East Ridge Trail for next few miles. Next you turn right onto East Ridge Connector Trail for 0.3 mile. At next junction with Shadowbrook Trail, turn right onto Shadowbrook Trail. Follow the trail to Sequoia Trail. Then turn left on Sequoia Trail. A side trail that goes to Sempervirens Falls is on your left very soon. Take the short side trip to the small, but beautiful waterfalls before continue on Sequoia Trail. When you are near the park headquarters, watch out for Redwood Trail on your left. The short Redwood Trail loops through some of the biggest trees in the world. Then go to find Skyline-to-the-Sea Trail nearby. Then turn right onto Skyline-to-the-Sea Trail to climb up toward China Grade. When you finally reach China Grade Road, cross the road and continue on Skyline-to-the-Sea Trail. After you cross Big Basin Way, you come to the junction of Skyline and East Ridge Trail, turn right to get onto East Ridge Trail. Watch for a shortcut on your right to get back to Big Basin Way and back to your car.

Hike Overview

Distance=15.7 miles

Elevation gain=2989 feet

Parking: roadside parking at China Grade and Big Basin Way junction

Shaded: 85%

Trail Map:

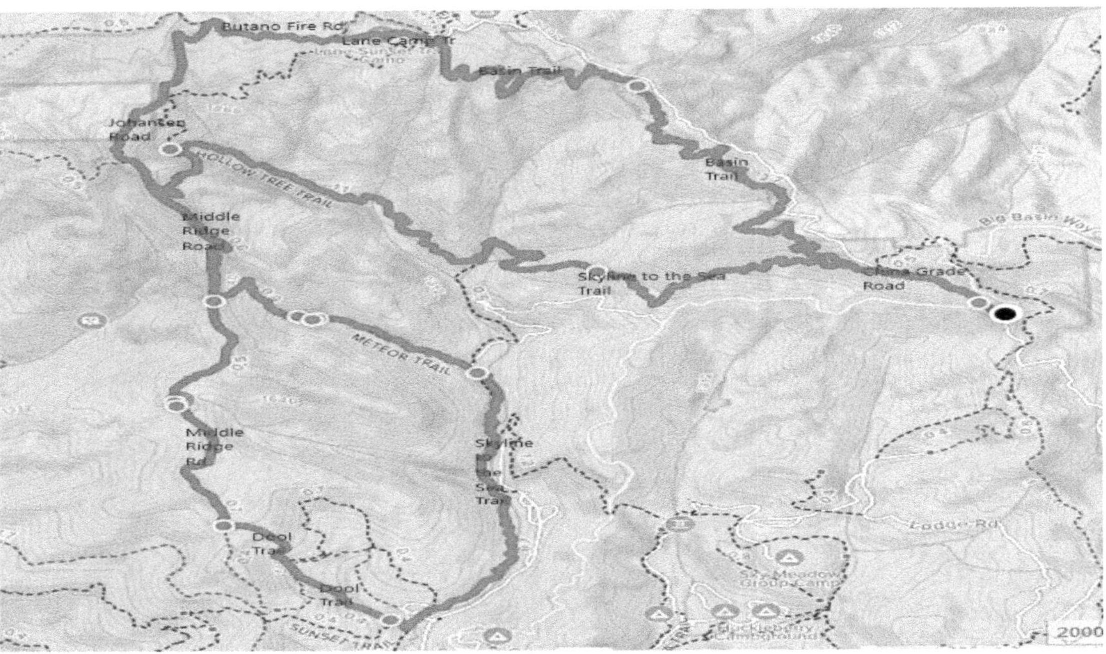

Detail Direction

Walk up China Grade Road from your car at the junction of China Grade and Big Basin Way for 0.3 miles. Watch out for sign for Skyline-to-the-Sea Trail. Turn left onto the famed trail for 1.9 miles. Next you turn right onto Hollow Tree Trail for 1.7 mile. At next junction, you choose a connector trail on the left to go up Middle Ridge Road for 0.3 miles. Then turn left on Middle Ridge for 0.7 miles before turn left onto Meteor Trail. You will see some giant redwood along Meteor Trail. At the end of Meteor Trail, turn right onto Skyline-to-the-Sea Trail. When you are near the park headquarters, watch out for Dool Trail on your right. Get onto Dool Trail to get back to Middle Ridge Road. Turn right onto Middle Ridge Road. Follow Middle Ridge Road to its end at Johansen Road. Then turn right. When Johansen Road ends at Butano Fire Road, turn right on Butano Fire Road. Stay Right to get on Lane Camp Trail. At next junction, take the second trail on your right: Basin Trail. This segment of Basin Trail is over 3 miles long and ends at Skyline to-the-Sea Trail. Then turn left onto Skyline-to-the-Sea Trail for 0.1 miles. Finally turn right on China Grade to get back to your car.

Hike Overview

Distance=15.70 miles

Elevation gain=2769 feet

Parking: Waddell Beach (3600 CA-1, Davenport, CA 95017)

Shaded: 80%

Trail Map:

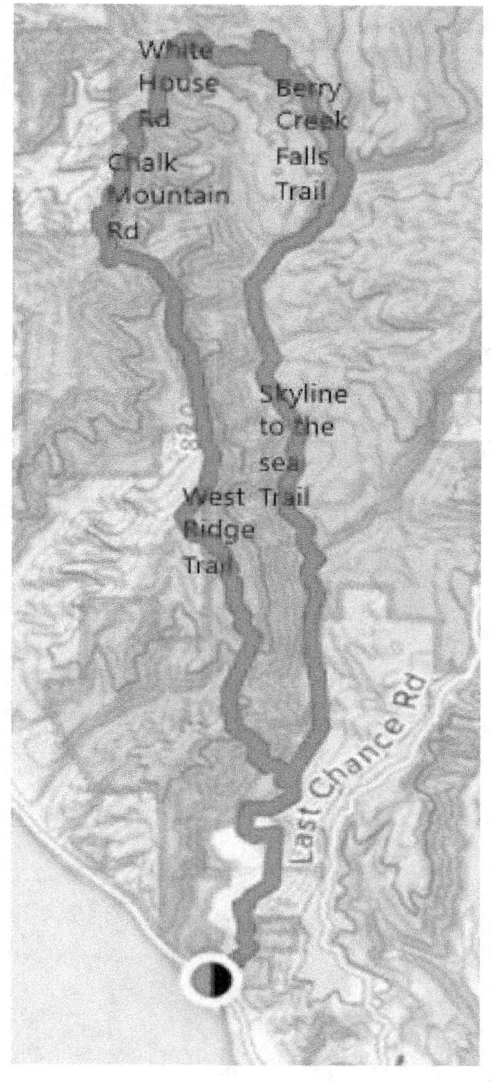

Detail Direction

You can park your car at Waddell Beach for free. Then cross HWY-1 with care to get onto Big Basin State Park Road. Watch out sign for Clark Connector Trail on your left after walk the flat road for 1 miles. The connector will ends at West Ridge Trail. Turn right on West Ridge to continue uphill. West Ridge Trail brings you to the Chalk Mountain. Turn right on Chalk Mountain Road. It ends at White House Road. Continue ahead on White House Road for half miles before turn right onto Henry Creek Trail for only 0.2 miles. Watch out for unmarked trail on your left. Get onto this trail to go down to Berry Creek. After crossing Berry Creek, you turn right to stay on Berry Creek Falls Trail. Berry Creek Falls is about 70 feet tall and the most beautiful waterfalls in the San Francisco Bay Area. Next you turn right onto Skyline-to-the-Sea Trail and following it all the way to Big Basin State Park Road and Waddell Beach.

Hike Overview

Distance=23.8 miles

Elevation gain=4239 feet

Parking: Mockingbird Hill Entrance Parking Lot

Shaded: 20%

Trail Map:

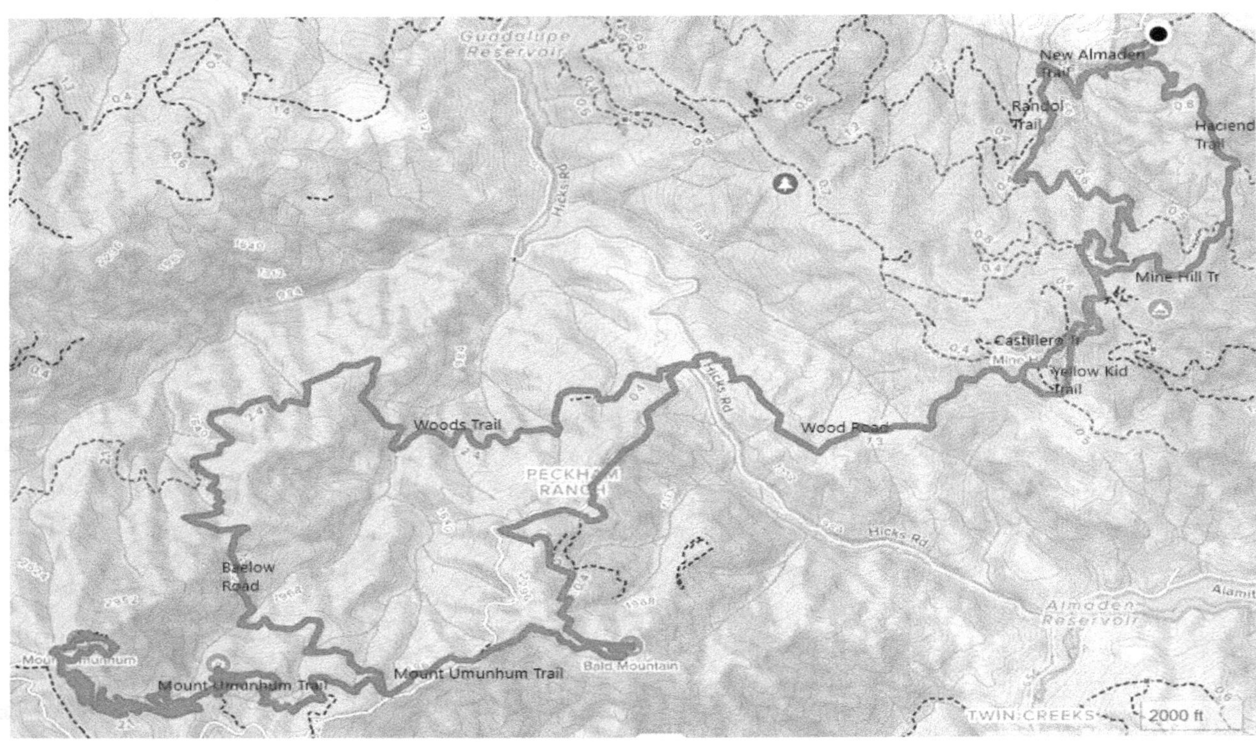

Detail Direction

From the parking lot, you choose New Almaden Trail next the bulletin board for 0.2 miles. At the junction with Hacienda Trail, turn left onto Hacienda Trail for 0.8 miles to climb up.

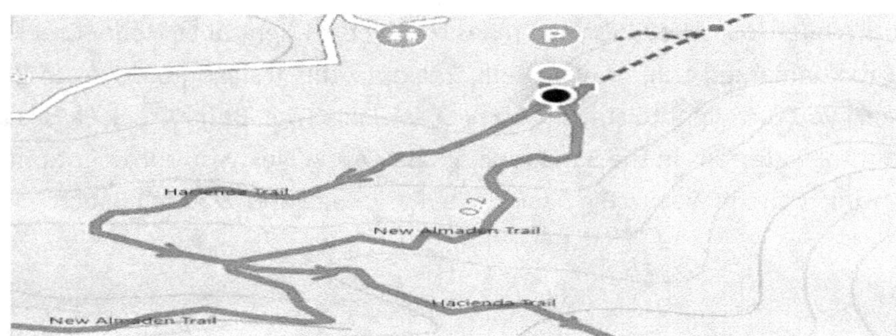

Next you turn right onto Capehorn Pass Trail for 0.2 miles. At the junction with Mine Hill Trail, take the right branch of Mine Hill Trail. Stay on Mine Hill Trail for 0.6 miles. Then turn left onto Castilero Trail. Stay on Castilero Trail until it meets with Wood Road.

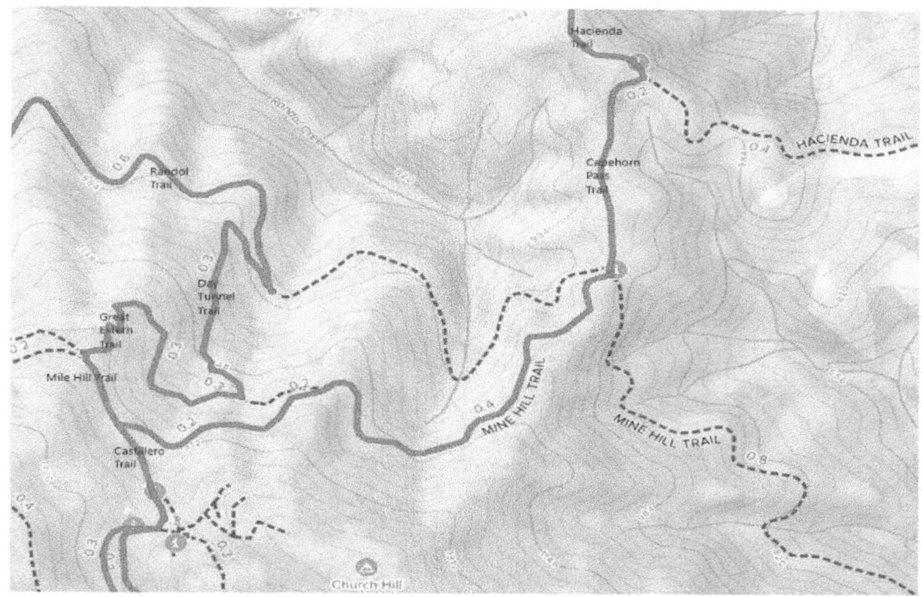

Now leave the Castilero Trail and get on Wood Road for about 1.4 miles. After crossing Hicks Road, get on Woods Trail for 2.8 miles. At the junction with Barlow Road, keep left at the junction to take on Barlow Road for 1.9 miles. Next you turn sharply right onto Mount Umunhum Trail. Follow this trail all the way to the peak and Mt Umunhum Radio Tower. When you are ready to go back, follow Mount Umunhum Trail to the junction with Barlow Road. Now you have the option to go Bald Mountain. To go Bald Mountain, you stay on Mount Umunhum Trail at the junction for another 0.3 miles. It ends at Mt. Umunhum Rd parking. From the parking, take Bald Mountain Trail for 0.7 miles to go the summit of Bald Mountain. Then retrace your steps back to the junction with Barlow Road. Follow Barlow Road and Woods Trail to Hicks Road. Cross Hicks Road to get on Wood Road to go back to Almaden Quicksilver County Pary. Turn right onto Yellow Kid Trail before Wood Road's end at Castilero Trail. You will see Mine Hill Rotary Furnace on your left. Continue on Yellow Kid Trail until its end at Castilero Trail. Turn toward the flag pole. Almost immediately turn left to stay on Castilero Trail. At the junction with Mine Hill Trail, turn left for only 0.1 miles. Next turn right onto Great Eastern Trail for 0.3 miles. Turn sharply left at the junction with Day Tunnel Trail for 0.3 miles. Next turn left onto Randol Trail for 0.9 miles(see map above). Then turn right onto Buena Vista Trail for 0.3 miles. Finally, turn right on New Almaden Trail and NAT ends at Mockingbird Hill Entrace parking lot.

Hike Overview

Distance=16.0 miles

Elevation gain= 2813 feet

Parking: Mockingbird Hill Entrance Parking Lot

Shaded: 20%

Trail Map:

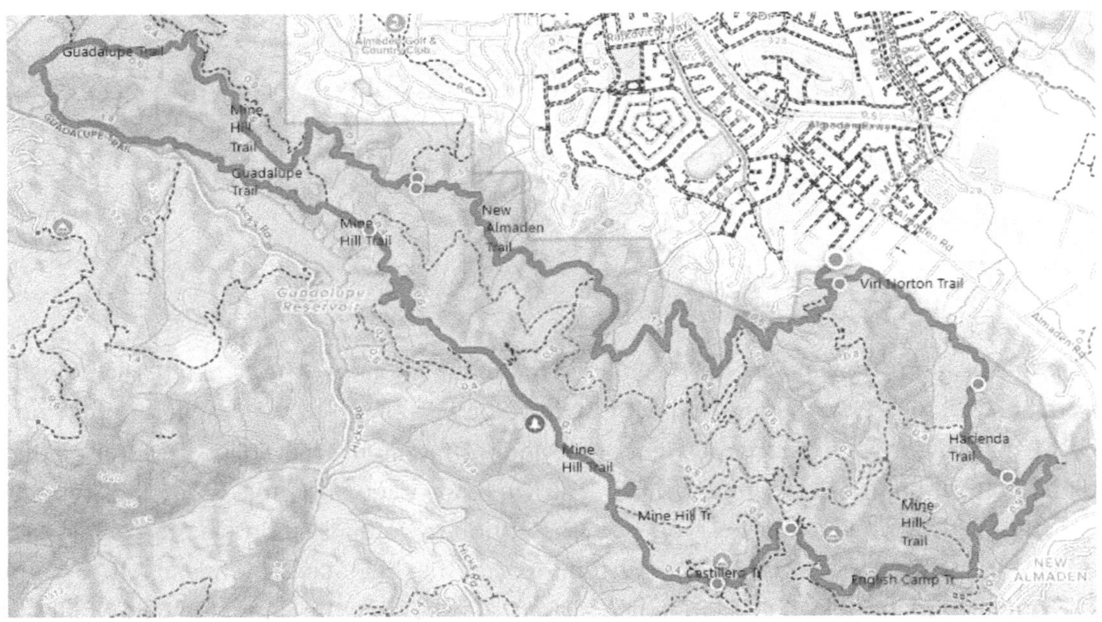

Detail Direction

Start your hike on Virl O. Norton Trail on your left if you are facing the hills. Stay on the trail until its end at Hacienda Trail. Turn left onto Hacienda Trail at the junction for 1.5 miles. Hacienda Trail ends at the junction with Mine Hill Trail and English Camp Trail. At the junction cross Mine Hill Trail and get onto English Camp Trail. Hike English Camp Trail till its end at Flag Pole. Cross Flag Pole area and get onto the right branch of Castillero Trail(Flag Pole should be on your right). Stay on Castillero Trail until its end at Mine Hill Trail. Stay left on the junction to hike on Mine Hill Trail. Stay on Mine Hill Trail until the junction with Guadalupe Trail. Keep left at the junction to get on board of Guadalupe Trail. Guadalupe Trail loops back to Mine Hill Trail. Get back on Mine Hill Trail by turn right at the junction. Next you turn left onto Cinnabar Trail before turn right onto New Alamaden Trail for 4.1 miles. New Alamaden Trail ends at the parking where your car is waiting.

Hike Overview

Distance=16.90 miles

Elevation gain=2913 feet

Parking: Grant Lake Parking Lot

Shaded: No

Trail Map:

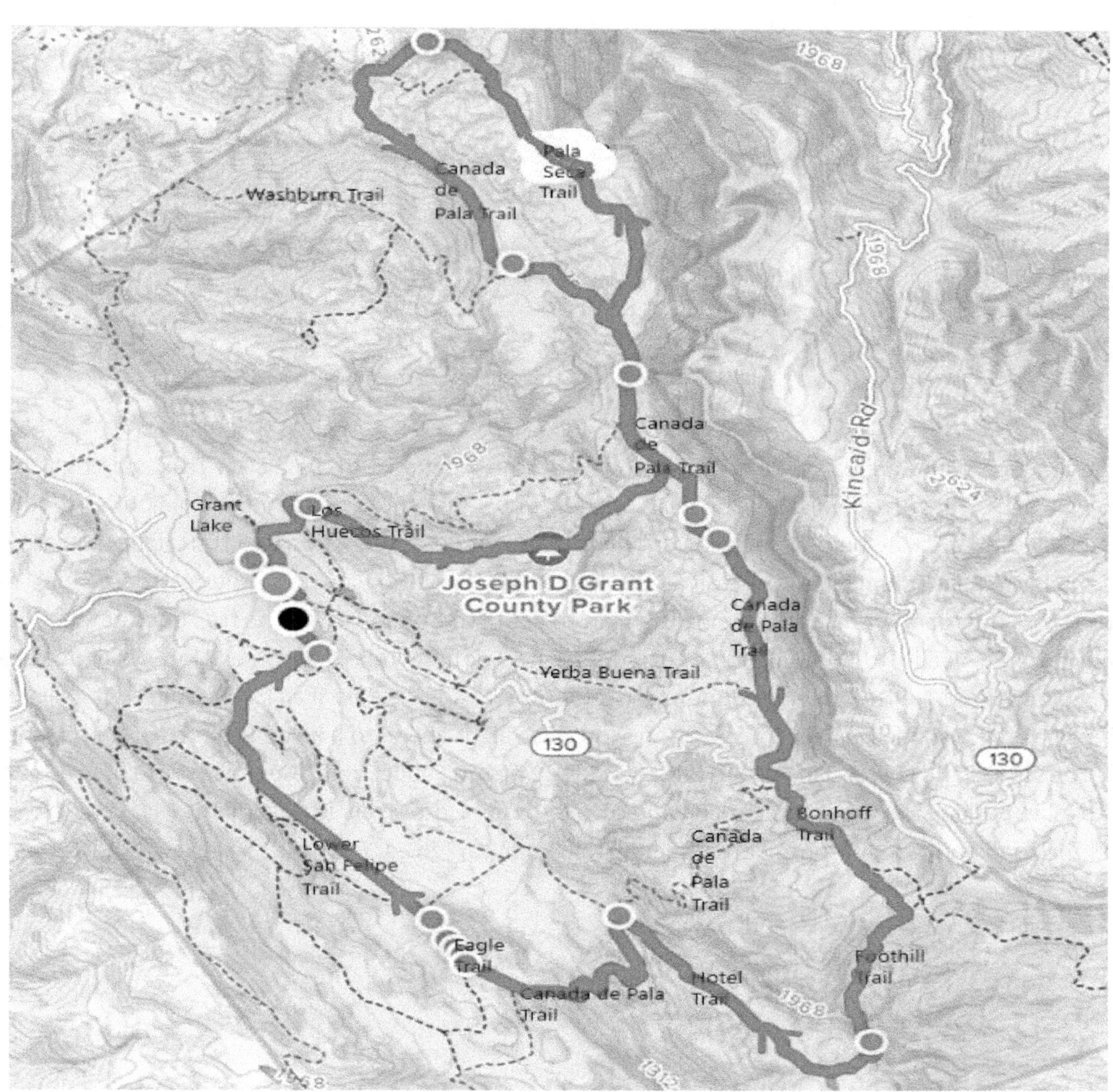

Detail Direction

After park your car at Grant Lake parking lot, walk toward Grant Lake. Turn right on lake shore and turn right again onto Halls Valley Trail for 0.2 miles. At the junction with Los Huecos Trail, turn right onto Los Huecos Trail for 2.8 miles.

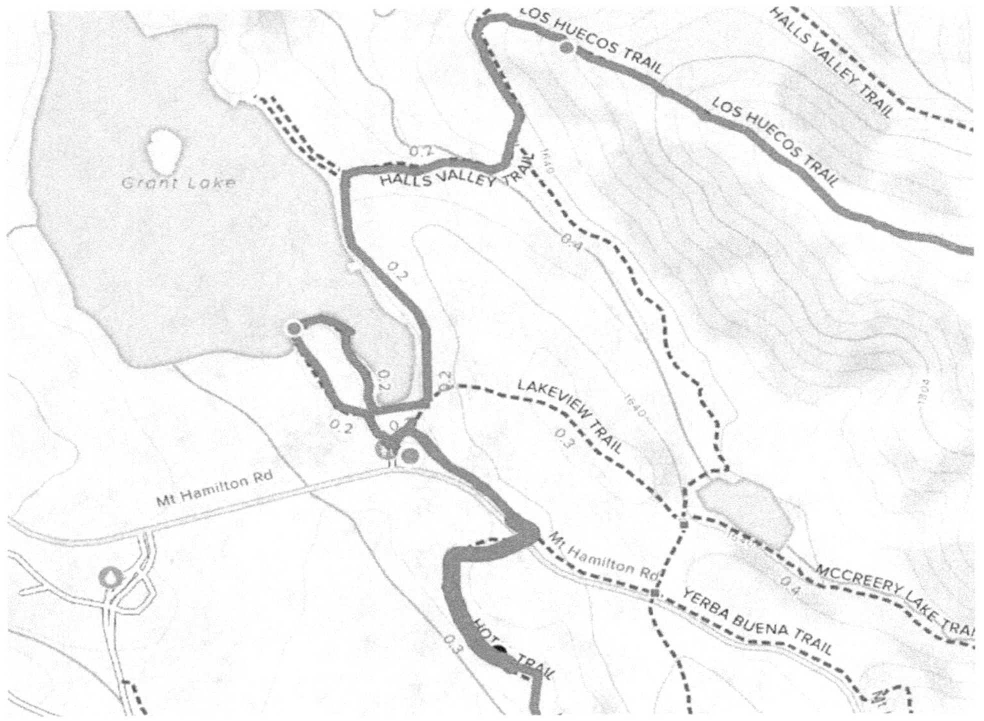

At the junction with Canada De Pala Trail, turn left. At the junction with Pala Seca Trail, stay right to get onto Pala Seca Trail for 1.3 miles. At the next junction, you stay right to go to Antler Point where you have a nice view of the valley below. Retrace your steps back to the last junction and turn right. You are now on Canada De Pala Trail. Follow the trail all the way to Mt Hamilton Road. Use the restroom if you need before cross the road. After road crossing, stay left to get onto Bonhoff Trail. The trail ends at the junction with Manzanita Trail and Foothill Trail. Turn right onto Foothill Trail. It becomes Hotel Trail near Eagle Lake. Follow Hotel Trail 1.2 miles and then turn left onto Canada De Pala Trail for 1.1 miles. At its junction with Eagle Trail, Canada De Pala Trail goes left. You go straight ahead to hike on Eagle Trail. At the junction with Corral Trail and Lower San Felipe Trail, choose Lower San Felipe Trail. The trail eventually ends at the park's main parking lot. Cross the parking and turn left onto Hotel Trail. Hotel ends at Mt Hamilton Road. Cross the road and turn left onto Yerba Buena Trail. Your parked car is just 0.1 miles away and is waiting for you.

Hike Overview

Distance=17.7 mile

Elevation gain=2802 feet

Parking: Berryessa Community Center parking lot

Shaded: 40%

Trail Map:

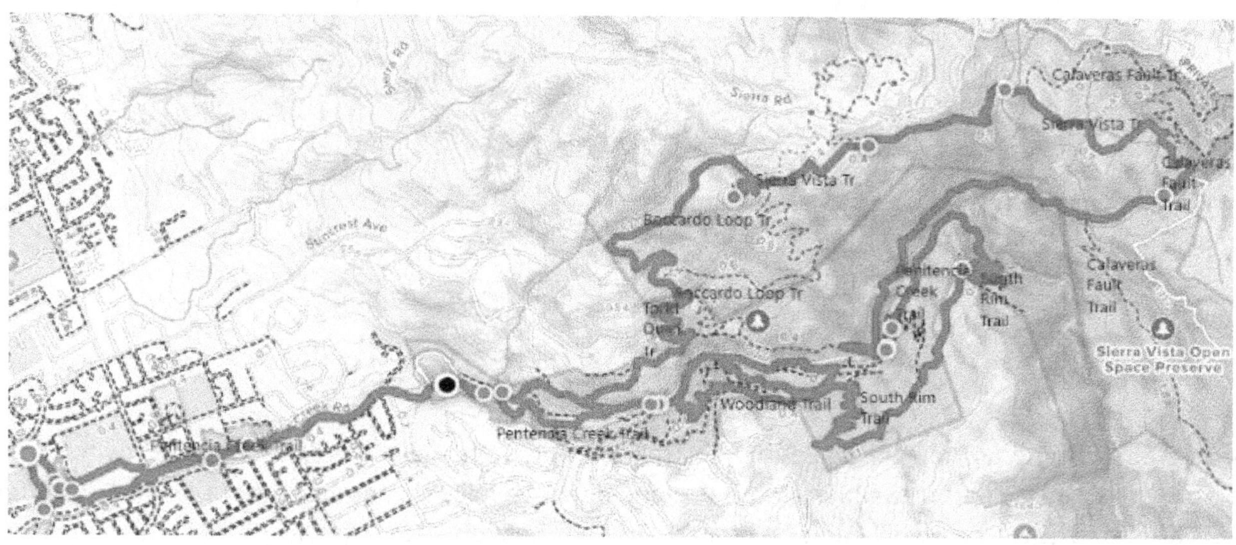

Detail Direction

You follow Penitencia Creek Trail into Alum Rock Park. Walk about 0.2 miles after enter the park, turn left to cross a bridge. Then walk another 0.1 miles before you across a drive way. Next you turn right onto an unmarked trail for 0.1 miles. At the junction with Lariat Trail, turn right. At the junction with North Rim Trail, turn left onto North Rim Trail for 0.2 miles. Next you turn right onto Eagle Rock Trail.

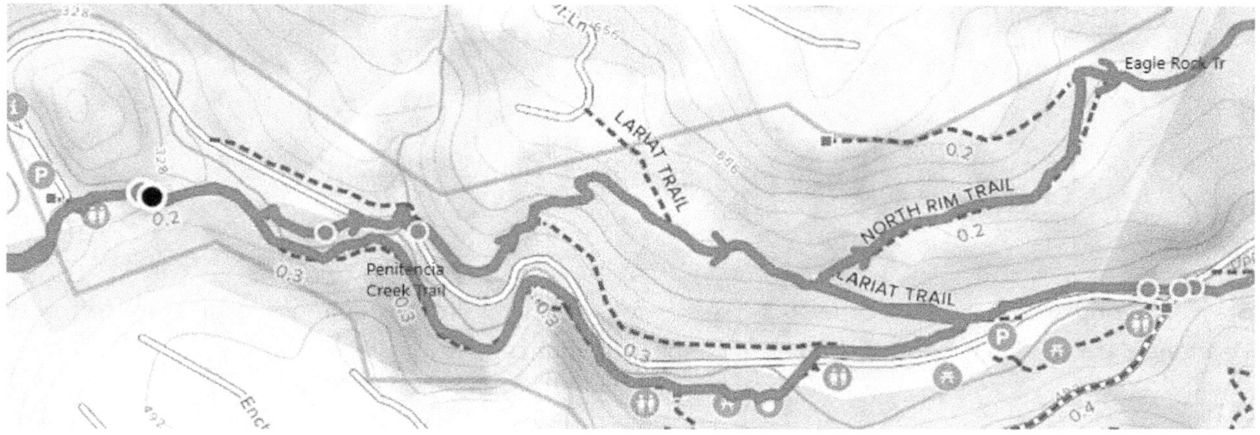

Next turn left onto Todd Quick Trail. After multiple switch backs, you arrive at the junction with Boccardo Loop Trail. Turn left onto Boccardo Loop Trail and stay left on next junction. At the top of the ridge, turn right on Boccardo Spur Trail to go to the vista where you have excellent view of Easter San Jose. Come down from the vista and continue on Boccardo Trail for a little longer. Next you stay left to get onto Sierra Vista Trail. Stay on Sierra Vista Trail until you meet with Calaveras Fault Trail for the second time. Then you turn right onto Calaveras Fault Trail for 0.3 miles. The trail ends at a closed driveway. Turn right onto the driveway and follow it out to the junction with Alum Rock Falls Road. Then turn left onto Alum Rock Falls Road. Take Mineral Springs Loop just for 0.1 miles. Then you turn left onto Penitencia Creek Trail.

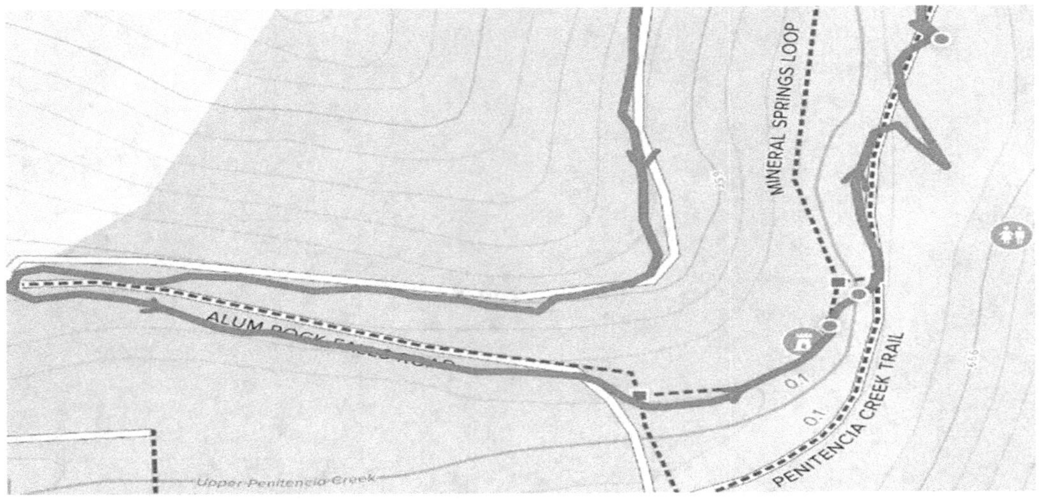

At the end of the trail, you get on South Rim Trail to climb up the hill. There are about 10 switchbacks before the trail stay flat for a while. Next you come down the hills via another set of switchbacks. After you are done with the switchbacks, you arrive at the junction with Woodland Trail. Turn left onto Woodland Trail for 0.4 miles. Then you come to junctions Peacock Gap Trail and a driveway.

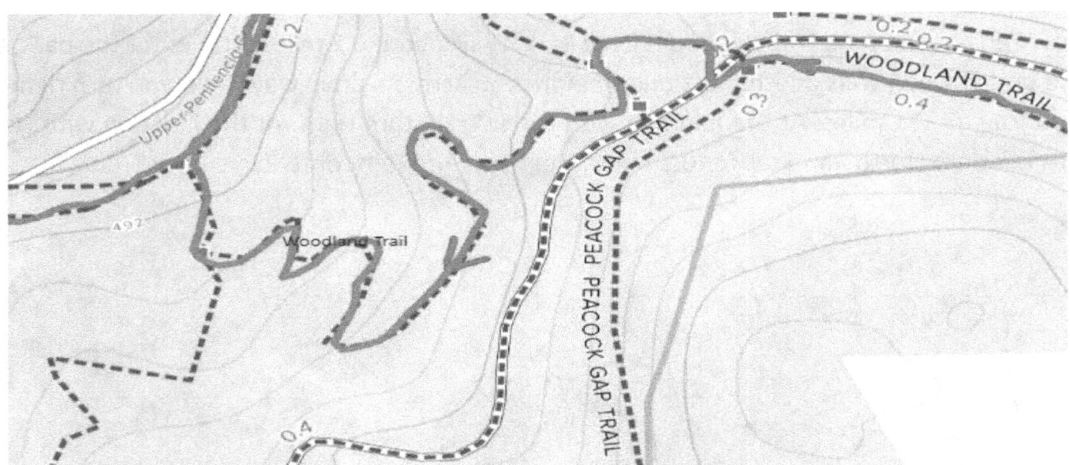

Stay on Woodland Trail for another 0.3 miles before you leave it for Penitencia Trail. Turn left onto Penitencia Trail and hike another 2 miles to get back to your car.